Security Awareness: Applying Practical Security in Your World

Fourth Edition

Mark Ciampa, Ph.D.

COURSE TECHNOLOGY
CENGAGE Learning®

Australia • Brazil • Japan • Korea • Mexico • Singapore • Spain • United Kingdom • United States

COURSE TECHNOLOGY
CENGAGE Learning

Security Awareness: Applying Practical Security in Your World, Fourth Edition

Mark Ciampa

Vice President, Careers and Computing: Dave Garza

Executive Editor: Stephen Helba

Director, Development-Careers and Computing: Marah Bellegarde

Product Development Manager: Juliet Steiner

Senior Product Manager: Michelle Ruelos Cannistraci

Developmental Editor: Deb Kaufmann

Editorial Assistant: Jennifer Wheaton

Brand Manager: Kristin McNary

Market Development Manager: Mark Linton

Senior Production Director: Wendy Troeger

Production Manager: Andrew Crouth

Content Project Manager: Brooke Greenhouse

Cover image(s): © www.Shutterstock.com

> For product information and technology assistance, contact us at
> **Cengage Learning Customer & Sales Support, 1-800-354-9706.**
>
> For permission to use material from this text or product,
> submit all requests online at **www.cengage.com/permissions.**
> Further permissions questions can be e-mailed to
> **permissionrequest@cengage.com.**

Library of Congress Control Number: 2012951457

ISBN-13: 978-1-111-64418-5   ISBN-10: 1-111-64418-7

Course Technology
20 Channel Center Street
Boston, MA 02210
USA

Cengage Learning is a leading provider of customized learning solutions with office locations around the globe, including Singapore, the United Kingdom, Australia, Mexico, Brazil, and Japan. Locate your local office at **international.cengage.com/region.**

Cengage Learning products are represented in Canada by Nelson Education, Ltd.

To learn more about Course Technology, visit **www.cengage.com/coursetechnology**

Purchase any of our products at your local college store or at our preferred online store **www.cengagebrain.com.**

Notice to the Reader
Publisher does not warrant or guarantee any of the products described herein or perform any independent analysis in connection with any of the product information contained herein. Publisher does not assume, and expressly disclaims, any obligation to obtain and include information other than that provided to it by the manufacturer. The reader is expressly warned to consider and adopt all safety precautions that might be indicated by the activities described herein and to avoid all potential hazards. By following the instructions contained herein, the reader willingly assumes all risks in connection with such instructions. The publisher makes no representations or warranties of any kind, including but not limited to, the warranties of fitness for particular purpose or merchantability, nor are any such representations implied with respect to the material set forth herein, and the publisher takes no responsibility with respect to such material. The publisher shall not be liable for any special, consequential, or exemplary damages resulting, in whole or part, from the readers' use of, or reliance upon, this material.

Printed in the United States of America
1 2 3 4 5 6 7 16 15 14 13 12

Brief Contents

Table of Contents

CHAPTER 3
Computer Security 75

CHAPTER 4
Internet Security 111

Introduction

Security continues to be a major concern of computer users today. Consider the evidence: Cybercrime has affected 431 million adults around the world in one year and cost $388 billion in time and money losses. That translates to 14 adults becoming victims of cybercrime *each second*, or over 1 million affected each day.[1] From January 2005 through July 2012, over 562 million electronic data records in the United States were breached, exposing to attackers a range of personal electronic data, such as addresses, Social Security numbers, health records, and credit card numbers.[2] A business that experiences a single data security breach that results in its customer names and credit card numbers being stolen will on average cost that business $7.2 million.[3] Over $41 billion have been lost by victims to the Nigerian General scam, which is the number one type of Internet fraud and is growing at a rate of 5 percent per year.[4] Due to the increased power of desktop computers to crack passwords, researchers now claim that any password of seven or fewer characters is "hopelessly inadequate."[5]

Yet knowing how to make a computer secure and keep it safe is still a mystery to most computer users. What type of attacks will antivirus software prevent? What does a firewall do? What is a botnet? How can I test my computer to be sure that it cannot be attacked through the Internet? How do I install software patches? Learning how to keep a computer secure can be a daunting task.

This book provides you with the knowledge and tools you need to make your computer and related technology equipment—tablets, laptops, smart phones, and wireless networks—secure. *Security Awareness: Applying Practical Security in Your World, Fourth Edition,* presents a basic introduction to practical computer security for all users, from students to home users to business professionals.

Security topics are introduced through a series of real-life user experiences, showing why computer security is necessary and providing the essential elements for making and keeping computers secure. Going beyond the concepts of computer security, you will gain practical skills on how to protect your computers and devices from increasingly sophisticated attacks. You will also learn how to practice good security at work.

Each chapter in the book contains Hands-On Projects that cover making computers secure. In addition, projects that show how to use and configure security hardware and software are included. These projects are designed to make what you learn come alive through actually performing the tasks. Besides the Hands-On Projects, each chapter provides realistic security case projects that put you in the role of a security consultant who works to solve the security problems of a variety of clients. Every chapter also includes review questions to reinforce your knowledge while helping you to apply practical security in your world.

Intended Audience

This book is intended to meet the needs of students and professionals who want to be able to protect their computers and technology devices from attacks. A basic working knowledge of computers is all that is required to use this book. The book's pedagogical features are designed to provide a truly interactive learning experience to help prepare you for the challenges of securing your technology. In addition to the information presented in the text, each chapter includes Hands-On Projects that guide you through implementing practical hardware, software, and network security step by step. Each chapter also contains a running case study that places you in the role of problem solver, requiring you to apply concepts presented in the chapter to achieve a successful solution.

Chapter Descriptions

Here is a summary of the topics covered in each chapter of this book:

Chapter 1, "Introduction to Security," begins by explaining the challenge of information security and why it is important. This chapter also introduces information security terminology, defines who the attackers are, and gives an overview of attacks and defenses.

Chapter 2, "Personal Security," examines attacks on passwords and those that use social engineering. It also covers personal security defenses to protect users from attacks.

Chapter 3, "Computer Security," explores attacks that use different types of malware, such as viruses, worms, Trojans, and botnets. Chapter 3 also includes information on how to protect a computer by managing patches, installing anti-malware software, and configuring personal firewalls. It also gives guidance on how to recover from an attack.

Chapter 4, "Internet Security," gives an overview of how the Internet works and the security risks that go along with using it. The chapter closes by exploring how to use the Internet securely.

Chapter 5, "Mobile Security," examines attacks that come through wireless networks, such as Wi-Fi and Bluetooth, along with attacks on mobile devices such tablets, laptops, and smartphones. It also explores how networks and devices can be secured.

Chapter 6, "Workplace Security," explores what to expect in terms of security as an employee in an office environment at a business or organization. It covers security regarding restricting physical access to the facility and to computer systems, security provisions that restrict access to data, and crisis preparedness.

Features

To aid you in fully understanding computer and network security, this book includes many features designed to enhance your learning experience.

- **Chapter Objectives.** Each chapter begins with a detailed list of the concepts to be mastered within that chapter. This list provides you with both a quick reference to the chapter's contents and a useful study aid.

- **Security in Your World.** Each chapter opens with a security-related vignette that introduces the chapter content and helps the reader to understand why these topics are important. These stories are continued throughout the chapter, providing additional information about real-life computer security.

- **Illustrations and Tables.** Numerous illustrations of security vulnerabilities, attacks, and defenses help you visualize security elements, theories, and concepts. In addition, the many tables provide details and comparisons of practical and theoretical information.

- **Security Defense Icons.** The different defenses listed in each chapter are classified by a security defense icon, which indicates the type of defense it is.

- **Chapter Summaries.** Each chapter's text is followed by a summary of the concepts introduced in that chapter. These summaries provide a helpful way to review the ideas covered in each chapter.

- **Key Terms.** All of the terms in each chapter that were introduced with bold text are gathered in a Key Terms list with definitions at the end of the chapter, providing additional review and highlighting key concepts.

- **Review Questions.** The end-of-chapter assessment begins with a set of review questions that reinforce the ideas introduced in each chapter. These questions help you evaluate and apply the material you have learned. Answering these questions will ensure that you have mastered the important concepts.

- **Hands-On Projects.** Although it is important to understand the theory behind network security, nothing can improve upon real-world experience. To this end, each chapter provides several Hands-On Projects aimed at providing you with practical security software and hardware implementation experience. These projects use the Windows 7 operating system, as well as software downloaded from the Internet.

- **Case Projects.** Located at the end of each chapter are several Case Projects. In these extensive exercises, you implement the skills and knowledge gained in the chapter through real design and implementation scenarios.

New to this Edition

- Updated information on the latest security attacks and defenses

- Expanded in-depth coverage of topics such as virus infections, social engineering attacks, Wi-Fi security, and others

- New material on security for mobile devices (laptops, smartphones, and tablets), different categories of attackers, crisis preparedness, fraudulent digital certificates, and other topics

- Additional Hands-On Projects in each chapter covering some of the latest security software

- More Case Projects in each chapter

- Information Security Community Site activity in each chapter allows learners to interact with other learners and security professionals from around the world

Text and Graphic Conventions

Wherever appropriate, additional information and exercises have been added to this book to help you better understand the topic at hand. Icons throughout the text alert you to additional materials. The icons used in this textbook are described below.

The Note icon draws your attention to additional helpful material related to the subject being described.

Tips based on the authors' experience provide extra information about how to attack a problem or what to do in real-world situations.

The Caution icons warn you about potential mistakes or problems, and explain how to avoid them.

Each Hands-On activity in this book is preceded by the Hands-On icon and a description of the exercise that follows.

Case Project icons mark Case Projects, which are scenario-based assignments. In these extensive case examples, you are asked to implement independently what you have learned.

The Block Attacks icon identifies computer and network defenses that are designed to block attacks by creating a strong security perimeter much like a castle wall or moat.

This Update Defenses icon points out defenses that must be continually updated in order to remain effective.

The Minimize Losses icon illustrates action to be taken in advance of attacks in order to be ready to pour water on them when they come.

The Send Secure Information icon shows proactive steps to be taken to thwart attackers.

Information Security Community Site

Stay Secure with the Information Security Community Site! Connect with students, professors, and professional from around the world, and stay on top of this ever-changing field.

Visit *www.community.cengage.com/infosec* to:

- **Download** resources such as instructional videos and labs.
- **Ask** authors, professors, and students the questions that are on your mind in our Discussion Forums.
- See up-to-date news, videos, and articles.
- **Read** weekly blogs from author Mark Ciampa.
- **Listen** to podcasts on the latest information security topics.

Each chapter includes information on a current security topic and asks the learner to post their reactions and comments to the Information Security Community Site. This allows users from around the world to interact and learn from other users as well as with security professionals and researchers.

Instructor's Materials

A wide array of instructor's materials is provided with this book. The following supplemental materials are available for use in a classroom setting. All the supplements available with this book are provided to the instructor on a single Instructor Resources CD-ROM (ISBN: 9781111644192) and online at the textbook's Web site.

Instructor Resources CD (ISBN: 9781111644192):

The following supplements are available when this book is used in a classroom setting and is available on a single CD-ROM and online at the textbook's Web site.

Electronic Instructor's Manual. The Instructor's Manual that accompanies this textbook includes the following items: additional instructional material to assist in class preparation, including suggestions for lecture topics, tips on setting up a lab for the Hands-On Projects, and solutions to all end-of-chapter materials.

ExamView Test Bank. This Windows-based testing software helps instructors design and administer tests and pre-tests. In addition to generating tests that can be printed and administered, this full-featured program has an online testing component that allows students to take tests at the computer and have their exams automatically graded.

PowerPoint Presentations. This book comes with a set of Microsoft PowerPoint slides for each chapter. These slides are meant to be used as a teaching aid for classroom presentations, to be made available to students on the network for chapter review, or to be printed for classroom distribution. Instructors are also at liberty to add their own slides for other topics introduced.

Figure Files. All of the figures and tables in the book are reproduced on the Instructor Resources CD. Similar to PowerPoint presentations, these are included as a teaching aid for classroom presentation, to make available to students for review, or to be printed for classroom distribution.

Please visit *login.cengage.com* and log in to access instructor-specific resources.

CourseMate

To access additional course materials, such as CourseMate, please visit *www.cengagebrain.com*. At the *CengageBrain.com* home page, search for the ISBN of your title (from the back cover of your book) using the search box at the top of the page. This will take you to the product page where these resources can be found.

Security Awareness: Applying Practical Security in Your World, Fourth Edition, offers Course-Mate, a complement to your textbook. CourseMate includes the following:

- An interactive eBook with highlighting, note-taking, and search capabilities
- Interactive learning tools, including quizzes, flash cards, PowerPoint slides, glossary, and more!
- Engagement Tracker, a first-of-its-kind tool that monitors student engagement in the course

PAC CourseMate w/eBook for *Security Awareness: Applying Practical Security in Your World* (ISBN: 9781111644215)

IAC CourseMate w/eBook for *Security Awareness: Applying Practical Security in Your World* (ISBN: 9781111644222)

Additional materials designed especially for you might be available for your course online. Go to *www.cengagebrain.com* and search for this book title periodically for more details.

About the Author

Mark Ciampa, Ph.D., Security+, is Assistant Professor of Computer Information Systems at Western Kentucky University in Bowling Green, Kentucky. Previously, he served as Associate Professor and Director of Academic Computing for 20 years at Volunteer State Community College in Gallatin, Tennessee. Dr. Ciampa has worked in the IT industry as a computer consultant for the U.S. Postal Service, the Tennessee Municipal Technical Advisory Service, and the University of Tennessee. He is also the author of many Cengage/Course Technology textbooks, including *CWNA Guide to Wireless LANs, Third Edition; Guide to Wireless Communications; Security+ Guide to Network Security Fundamentals, Fourth Edition;* and *Networking BASICS.* He holds a Ph.D. in digital communications systems from Indiana State University.

Acknowledgments

A large team of dedicated professionals all contributed to the creation of this book. I am honored to be part of such an outstanding group of professionals, and to everyone on the team I extend my sincere thanks. Thanks to Executive Editor Stephen Helba for giving me the opportunity to work on this project and for providing his continual support. Also thanks to Senior Product Manager Michelle Cannistraci, who helped keep this project on track, and to Nicole Ashton Spoto for carefully reviewing the book and identifying many corrections. And a big Thank-You to the team of peer reviewers who evaluated each chapter and provided very helpful suggestions and contributions:

Cynthia Burrus—Central Texas College, Killeen, TX

Angela Herring—Wilson Community College, Wilson, North Carolina

James Hicks—Los Angeles Southwest College, Los Angeles, California

Donna M. Lohn—Lakeland Community College, Kirtland, Ohio

Nina Milbauer—Madison Area Technical College, Madison, Wisconsin

David Rawlinson—Central Washington University, Ellensburg, Washington

Thomas Robbins—Clover Park Technical College, Lakewood, Washington

Once again special recognition goes to Developmental Editor Deb Kaufmann. What else could an author ask for? She found all of my errors, made many helpful suggestions, and kept track of every small detail—as she always does. It is a delight to work with Deb. Without question, Deb is simply the very best there is.

Finally, I want to thank my wonderful wife, Susan. Once again she was patient and supportive of me throughout this project. I could not have written this book without her love and support.

To the User

This book should be read in sequence, from beginning to end. However, each chapter is a self-contained unit, so after completing Chapter 1 the reader may elect to move to any subsequent chapter.

Hardware and Software Requirements

Following are the hardware and software requirements needed to perform the end-of-chapter Hands-On Projects.

- Microsoft Windows 7
- An Internet connection and Web browser
- Microsoft Office 2010 or 2007

Specialized Requirements

Whenever possible, the needs for specialized requirements were kept to a minimum. The following chapter features specialized hardware:

- Chapter 5: A laptop computer with a wireless network interface card adapter; a computer that either has built-in Bluetooth technology or a Bluetooth USB adapter and a Bluetooth device, such as a Bluetooth mouse, keyboard, or smartphone that supports Bluetooth
- Chapter 6: A USB flash drive

Free Downloadable Software Requirements

Free, downloadable software is required for the Hands-On Projects in the following chapters. Appendix B lists the Web sites where these can be downloaded.

Chapter 1:

- Microsoft Safety Scanner

Chapter 2:

- KeePass Password Safe
- LastPass
- SuperGenPass
- Google Hacking Diggity Attack Tools

Chapter 3:

- EICAR AntiVirus Test File
- Kaspersky TDSSKiller
- Macrium Reflect

Chapter 5:

- Xirrus Wi-Fi Monitor gadget
- Vistumbler
- Blueauditor

Chapter 6:

- Irongeek Thumbscrew
- Secunia Personal Software Inspector

References

1. "Norton Cybercrime Report." *Norton Enterprise.* Accessed Nov. 10, 2011, http://www.symantec.com/content/en/us/home_homeoffice/html/cybercrimereport.

2. "Chronology of Data Breaches: Security Breaches 2005–Present." *Privacy Rights Clearinghouse.* Updated Jul. 18, 2012, Accessed Feb. 28, 2011, <http://www.privacyrights.org/data-breach.

3. "Ponemon Cost of a Data Breach 2011." *Symantec.* Accessed Mar. 21, 2012. http://www.symantec.com/about/news/resources/press_kits/detail.jsp?pkid=ponemon-cost-of-a-data-breach-2011.

4. "419 Advance Fee Fraud Statistics 2009," Jan. 2010, accessed Feb. 28, 2011, http://www.ultrascan-agi.com/public_html/html/public_research_reports.html.

5. "Case Study: Teraflop Troubles: The Power of Graphics Processing Units May Threaten the World's Password Security System," *Georgia Tech Research Institute,* accessed Feb. 28, 2011, http://www.gtri.gatech.edu/casestudy/Teraflop-Troubles-Power-Graphics-Processing-Units-GPUs-Password-Security-System.

DEDICATION

To Braden, Mia, Abby, and Gabe

Introduction to Security

After completing this chapter you should be able to do the following:

- Describe the challenges of securing information
- Define information security and explain why it is important
- Identify the types of attackers that are common today
- Describe how to build a security strategy

"There you are!" said Megan. Amanda looked up from her textbook. "Is it noon already? I'm sorry; I must have let the time slip away from me again." Megan and Amanda both attended the same college and had become good friends. "That's OK," said Megan. "But can you tear yourself away from that book long enough to get some lunch now?" Amanda smiled and replied, "Oh, if you twist my arm I just might!" As Amanda closed her book Megan looked over her shoulder and asked, "What have you been doing?" "I'm studying for my first test in Introduction to Computer Security," Amanda replied. Amanda was majoring in Computer Information Systems and wanted to go into the field of information security.

"Oh, security," Megan said. "I've heard that is really overblown. I saw an online article last week that said, 'Hundreds of Thousands of Internet Users at Risk' but I never heard of anyone who had a problem. And I've never been attacked, and you know how much time I spend on Facebook!" Amanda grinned. "Oh, did you expect those hundreds of thousands of users to send you an e-mail about it? Actually, you've already had some attacks targeted at you just today." Megan looked puzzled. "Like what?"

Amanda handed her tablet computer to Megan and said, "Sign in to your school e-mail account." As Megan finished entering her password Amanda said, "Did you get a strange e-mail from Stephanos this morning?" Megan paused and pointed to that e-mail message. "Yes, here it is. It was addressed to me and a few of his friends, but all the e-mail had in it was a link to a Web site about discount drugs. Why did he send that to me? And how did you know about it?" Amanda said, "I received one, but it had a link about cheap car insurance. Stephanos' computer has probably been infected and it's sending out these spam e-mails to everyone in his address book, including you and me." "But doesn't he have antivirus software on his computer? Won't that stop these attacks?" asked Megan.

Amanda took the tablet computer from Megan. "No, antivirus software doesn't stop everything, and look at this next e-mail message: 'Due to so many spam/junk mails, all e-mail accounts need to be revalidated by clicking on the link below.' Of course, if you click on either of these links, you're bound to get infected, probably just like Stephanos. And did you see the e-mail this morning from the college that a database of personal records of over 100,000 students and alumni going back 10 years was stolen by attackers? They may already have your name, address, Social Security number, and even the financial data you used for that student loan. No antivirus software on your computer is going to stop that."

Megan pushed the chair in frustration. "Why can't they just stop these attacks? And how am I supposed to know what to do?"

Perhaps at no other time in history have the world's citizens been forced to continually protect themselves and their property from attacks by invisible foes. Random shootings, car bombings, hijackings, and other physical violence occur around the world with increasing frequency. To counteract this violence, new types of security defenses have been implemented. Passengers using public transportation are routinely searched. Fences are erected across borders. Telephone calls are monitored. These attacks and defenses have dramatically changed our everyday lives.

The attacks are not just physical. Our computers and technology devices are an especially frequent target of attacks. A seemingly endless array of attacks is directed at individuals, schools, businesses, and governments through desktop computers, laptops, smartphones, and tablet computers. Internet Web servers must resist thousands of attacks every day. Identity theft using stolen electronic data has skyrocketed. An unprotected computer connected to the Internet can be infected in fewer than 60 seconds. Phishing, rootkits, worms, back doors, zombies, and botnets—virtually unheard of just a few years ago—are now part of our everyday technology vocabulary.

Although all computer users have heard about attacks that can threaten their computers—and many have already been victims of attacks—the overwhelming majority of users remain unsure about how to actually make their computers secure. Ask yourself this question: If you were warned that a particularly nasty Internet attack was to be released tonight, what would you do to protect your computer and the information on it? Install antivirus software? Download a patch? Turn on a firewall? Unplug your Internet connection? Or do nothing and hope for the best?

It is important for all computer users today to be knowledgeable about computer security and to know what steps to take to defend against attacks. Applying practical security in your world has never been more important than it is right now.

This chapter introduces you to computer security. It begins by examining the current challenges in computer security and why it is so difficult to achieve. It then describes information security in more detail and explores why it is important. Finally, the chapter looks at who is responsible for these attacks and what the steps are in building a comprehensive security strategy.

Challenges of Securing Information

Although to a casual observer it may seem that there should be a straightforward and easy solution to securing computers, in reality there is no single simple solution. This can be seen through the different types of attacks that computer users face today as well as the difficulties in defending against these attacks.

Today's Attacks

Despite the fact that information security continues to rank as the number one concern and tens of billions of dollars are spent annually on computer security, the number of successful attacks continues to increase. Information regarding recent attacks includes the following:

- A business that experiences a data breach—such as customer names and credit card numbers being stolen—will have a significant financial loss because of expenses such as forensic and investigative activities, incident response, customer notification, and legal issues. In addition, the business has to be prepared for the loss of customers who are upset and move to a competitor (called the "churn rate"). A report by the Ponemon Institute and Symantec Research says that the average cost to a business of a single data breach is $7.2 million.[1]

- According to the Norton Cybercrime Report, cybercrime has affected 431 million adults around the world in one year and cost $388 billion in time and money losses. That translates to 14 adults becoming victims of cybercrime *each second*, or over 1 million affected each day. The cost of cybercrime is now approaching the value of all global drug trafficking (about $411 billion). On average it takes 10 days for a victim to recover from an attack. Almost four out of every five Internet users who spend over 49 hours each week on the Internet have been victims of attacks, making their odds of becoming a victim to attacks 1 in 2.27.[2]

- Many users of Apple computers feel they don't need antivirus or malware protection. However, in the last year, over 600,000 Apple Macs were infected with malicious software called Flashback, and a new version of Flashback has infected an additional 100,000 Macs. It is estimated that more than half of these infected computers are in the United States. The vulnerability that allowed this malicious software to infect the Mac computers was fixed by another vendor but the fix was not distributed by Apple to its users for almost 60 days. (Apple was criticized for its slow response to security vulnerabilities and also for not providing security updates to older versions of its software.) In another instance, a scan of over 100,000 Mac computers found that almost 20 percent of the computers contained at least one instance of Windows malware. Although this Windows malware cannot function on the Mac, it can be transferred to another Windows computer through USB flash drives and other removable media, or through network file sharing. At least eight different vendors now sell antivirus tools for Mac computers because as far back as 2008 Apple has recommended that Mac users install antivirus software for protection.

- Many security researchers are warning that personal medical devices could be the next target for attackers. A security researcher, who was himself a diabetic, demonstrated at a security conference a wireless attack on an insulin pump that could change the delivery of insulin to the patient. Another security vendor found that they could scan a public space from up to 300 feet (91 meters) away, find vulnerable pumps made by a specific medical device manufacturer, and then force these devices to dispense fatal insulin doses. In addition, a researcher "hacked" into a defibrillator (used to stabilize a heartbeat) and reprogrammed it, and also disabled its power-save mode so the battery ran down in hours instead of years. And 48 computer viruses were found on the Web site of a vendor who manufactures medical ventilators, from which software updates to the ventilators can be downloaded and installed. The U.S. Department of Homeland Security (DHS) issued a report entitled *Attack Surface: Healthcare and Public Health Sector* that says these attacks are "now becoming a major concern ... In a world in which communication networks and medical devices can dictate life or death, these systems, if compromised, pose a significant threat to the public and private sector."[3]

- Elantis, a credit provider located in Belgium, was the apparent victim of an attack in which employee login credentials and confidential loan application information—including name, job description, contact information, annual income, and ID card number—on 3,700 customers was stolen. The attackers contacted Elantis and threatened to publicly publish the information if the bank did not pay 150,000 euros (about $197,000). Elantis took their servers offline, contacted the Belgian Federal High Tech Crime Unit, and said "We are not prepared to pay. We don't like blackmail." The attackers then said, "While this could be called 'blackmail,' we prefer to think of it as an 'idiot tax' for leaving confidential data unprotected on a Web server."[4]

- An Austrian student aged 15 was, by his own admission, bored and wanted to prove himself. Craving recognition and affirmation for his limited technology knowledge and skills, he discovered an online forum in which the 2,000 registered members were given points for achieving successful attacks. That launched him into action. Over the next 90 days, this student, using attack software that searched for unpatched servers and software to hide his tracks, successfully breached the servers belonging to 259 different companies around the world. After defacing Web sites and stealing data, he boasted about it on his Twitter account, where he also posted links to the stolen data. In a few weeks he was ranked in the top 50 attackers on the online forum.

- A woman tried to log in to her Gmail account but could not. At the same time, her spouse began to receive e-mail messages from friends asking if everything was OK. An attacker had broken into the woman's Gmail account and starting sending out a message to everyone in her address book saying she had been "mugged in Madrid" and had no money. The message went on to ask her friends to wire money to her immediately. Even though the message was crudely written, several of the woman's friends were about to wire the funds when they received an e-mail from the husband telling them it was all a scam. The attacker also deleted all of her e-mails, dating back six years. Many of these messages had professional, as well as personal, value. According to Google, these account hijackings occur in the "low thousands" each day.[5]

- A family moved into a new neighborhood in Minnesota, but their neighbor Barry wasn't very neighborly. Barry downloaded wireless attack software and soon cracked the couple's wireless network. Barry then acted like a "depraved criminal," according to the prosecutors, and started a "calculated campaign to terrorize his neighbors, doing whatever he could to destroy the careers and professional reputations of [the couple], to damage [their] marriage, and to generally wreak havoc on their lives." Using the couple's wireless network, Barry created a fictitious social networking page with the husband's name on it and posted pictures of child pornography. He also posted a brash note that pretended to be from the husband stating he was a lawyer and could get away with "doing anything." Barry e-mailed the same pornography to the husband's coworkers and sent flirtatious e-mail to women in the husband's office. Barry even sent threatening e-mails to the vice president of the United States from the husband's e-mail account, saying he was a terrorist and would kill the VP (this prompted a visit from the U.S. Secret Service). Barry also instigated many other attacks on the couple and their relatives. Barry was ultimately caught, and evidence was discovered that Barry had attacked a previous neighbor in a similar manner.[6]

- At a hearing in the U.S. Congress, an official with the DHS acknowledged that there is a persistent threat of preexisting malware on computers and other electronic devices imported and sold in the United States. The problem is that the supply chain for electronic equipment has many stops (product development, manufacturing, assembly, and so on) with numerous people touching the equipment in locations around the globe. Protecting the security of a device as it moves through the supply chain is extremely difficult. And the problem is not limited to computer disk drives with preinstalled malware; it can also include network equipment that can have a hidden back door to allow attackers to enter or electronic photo frames that infect USB flash drives used to transfer photos to the device.

- "Car hacking" involves breaking into a car's electronic system. Recent work by researchers has revealed that a car's electronics can be infected to change a car's settings or bypass the standard car defenses like power door locks. This can now be done remotely through wireless connections. In one test researchers were able to take control of the car's electronics through this system by making calls to the car's Bluetooth-enabled cell phone and then upload malware to the car. Another type of car hacking stores malware on a USB flash drive, which is then inserted into the car's stereo system. Through this malware researchers were able to turn off the engine, lock the doors, turn off the brakes, and change the odometer readings on the car. With this level of control it is possible that an attacker could remotely direct a car to transmit its vehicle identification number and current location via the car's Global Positioning System (GPS) to a Web site. Car thieves could then check to see if a particular make and model car they wanted to steal was in their area. After paying the car hacker a fee, a command would be sent to unlock the car's doors.

- An immigrant pretending to be "Prince Nana Kamokai of Sierra Leone" or "an airport director from Ghana" sent thousands of e-mails, asking for help in moving money from Nigeria to the United States. By using fake documentation to convince his victims that he was legitimate, he persuaded his victims to wire him money to cover "courier services" or "PIN code fees." After five years he had made more than $1.3 million from 67 known victims. Yet this was only a drop in the bucket for this scam, known as the Nigerian 419 Advance Fee Fraud ("419" is the Nigerian criminal code that addresses fraud). To date it is estimated that over $41 billion dollars have been lost by victims in this scam, with $9.3 billion lost in one year alone. According to the U.S. Federal Bureau of Investigation (FBI), this scam is the number one type of Internet fraud, growing at a rate of 5 percent annually.[7]

- The number of security breaches that expose users' digital data to attackers continues to rise. From January 2005 through July 2012, over 562 million electronic data records in the United States were breached, exposing to attackers a range of personal electronic data, such as address, Social Security numbers, health records, and credit card numbers.[8] Table 1-1 lists some of the security breaches that occurred during only a one-month period, according to the Privacy Rights Clearinghouse.[9]

Difficulties in Defending against Attacks

The challenge of keeping computers secure has never been greater, not only because of the number of attacks but also because of the difficulties faced in defending against these attacks. These difficulties include the following:

- *Universally connected devices.* It is virtually unheard of today for a computing device (desktop computer, tablet, laptop, etc.) not to be connected to the Internet. Although this provides significant benefits, it also makes it easy for an attacker halfway around world to silently launch an attack against a connected device.

Organization	Description of Security Breach	Number of Identities Exposed
Safe Ride Services, Phoenix	Employee personal information as well as patient demographic and insurance information was exposed.	42,000
American Express Travel	Credit and debit card numbers from American Express, Visa, MasterCard, and Discover were in a man's possession and came from breaking into the computer systems of a restaurant and a restaurant supply business in the Seattle area.	27,257
Yahoo! Voices	Attackers accessed passwords of over 450,000 Yahoo! Voices users and the information was posted online.	453,492
Formspring, San Francisco	Attackers accessed Formspring's development server and posted the passwords of its users online.	28,000,000
University of Texas M.D. Anderson Cancer Center, Houston	A laptop with sensitive patient information was stolen from the home of a faculty member. It contained unencrypted patient names, medical record numbers, treatment and/or research information, and in some instances Social Security numbers.	30,000
The Public Employees Retirement Association (PERA) of New Mexico Albuquerque	A computer containing PERA information was stolen from a consulting agency.	100,000
Bethpage Federal Credit Union, Bethpage, NY	An employee accidentally posted data onto a file transfer protocol site that was not secure. The data contained customer Visa debit card names, addresses, dates of birth, card expiration dates, and checking and savings account numbers.	86,000
University of North Florida (UNF), Jacksonville	Multiple servers exposed Social Security numbers and other sensitive information. Students who submitted housing contracts since 1997 were affected.	23,246

Table 1-1 Selected security breaches involving personal information in a one-month period
© Cengage Learning 2014

- *Increased speed of attacks.* With modern tools at their disposal, attackers can quickly scan hundreds of thousands of systems to find weaknesses and launch attacks with unprecedented speed. Many attack tools initiate new attacks without any human participation, thus increasing the speed at which systems are attacked.

- *Greater sophistication of attacks.* Attacks are becoming more complex, making it more difficult to detect and defend against them. Attackers today use common Internet protocols and applications to perform attacks, making it more difficult to distinguish an attack from legitimate traffic. Other attack tools vary their behavior so the same attack appears differently each time, further complicating detection.

- *Availability and simplicity of attack tools.* Whereas in the past an attacker needed to have an extensive technical knowledge of networks and computers, as well as the ability to write a program to generate the attack, that is no longer the case. Today's attack tools do not require any sophisticated knowledge. In fact, many of the tools have a graphical user interface (GUI) that allows the user to easily select options from a menu, as seen in Figure 1-1. These tools are freely available or can be purchased from other attackers at a low cost.

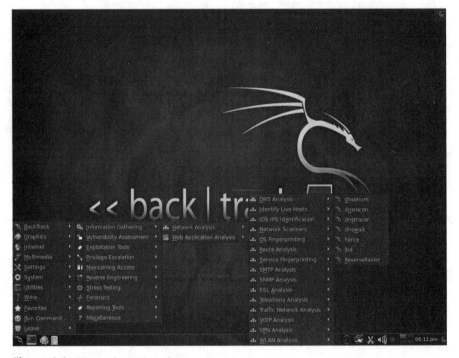

Figure 1-1 Menu of attack tools
Source: www.backtrack-linux.org

- *Faster detection of vulnerabilities.* Weakness in hardware and software can be more quickly uncovered and exploited with new software tools and techniques.
- *Delays in security updating.* Hardware and software vendors are overwhelmed trying to keep pace with updating their products against attacks. One antivirus software vendor receives over 200,000 submissions of potential malware each month.[10] At this rate the antivirus vendors would have to create and distribute updates *every 10 minutes* to keep users protected. This delay in distributing security updates adds to the difficulties in defending against attacks.
- *Weak security update distribution.* While manufacturers of mainstream products, such as Microsoft Windows and Apple Mac OS, have a system for notifying users of security updates and distributing them on a regular basis, few other software vendors have invested in these costly distribution systems. Users are generally unaware that a security update even exists for a product because there is no reliable means for the vendor to alert the user. Also, vendors often do not create small security updates that "patch" the existing software, but instead they fix the problem in an entirely new

version of the software and may even require the user to pay for the updated version that contains the patch. Attackers today are focusing more on uncovering and exploiting vulnerabilities in these products.

- *Distributed attacks.* Attackers can use hundreds of thousands of computers under their control in an attack against a single server or network. This "many against one" approach makes it virtually impossible to stop an attack by identifying and blocking a single source.

- *User confusion.* Increasingly, users are called upon to make difficult security decisions regarding their computer systems, sometimes with little or no information to guide them. It is not uncommon for a user to be asked security questions such as *Do you want to view only the content that was delivered securely?* or *Is it safe to quarantine this attachment?* or *Do you want to install this add-on?* With little or no direction, users are inclined to provide answers to questions without understanding the security risks.

Table 1-2 summarizes the reasons why it is difficult to defend against today's attacks.

Reason	Description
Universally connected devices	Attackers from anywhere in the world can send attacks.
Increased speed of attacks	Attackers can launch attacks against millions of computers within minutes.
Greater sophistication of attacks	Attack tools vary their behavior so the same attack appears differently each time.
Availability and simplicity of attack tools	Attacks no longer limited to highly skilled attackers.
Faster detection of vulnerabilities	Attackers can discover security holes and hardware or software more quickly.
Delays in security updating	Vendors are overwhelmed trying to keep pace by updating their products against attacks.
Weak security update distribution	Many software products lack a means to distribute security patches in a timely fashion.
Distributed attacks	Attackers use thousands of computers in an attack against a single computer or network.
User confusion	Users are required to make difficult security decisions with little or no instruction.

Table 1-2 Difficulties in defending against attacks
© Cengage Learning 2014

What Is Information Security?

Before it is possible to defend against attacks, it is necessary to understand what security is. In addition, knowing the common information security terminology that is used can be helpful when creating defenses for computers. Understanding the importance of information security is also important.

After lunch Megan went back to her dorm room and told her roommate Mia about the conversation she had with Amanda. Mia said, "You hear about this security stuff all the time, but I don't have a clue what they're talking about. It's like they're talking a foreign language about 'vulnerabilities' and 'threats.'" Megan nodded her head. "I know what you mean." Mia continued, "Besides, who would want to break into our computers? And so what if they did? What's the worst thing that can happen? They would read our e-mail? Let them! Really, what do we have that somebody would want?"

Megan said down on the couch. "Amanda told me that there are all sorts of bad things that can happen if you're attacked." "Like what?" asked Mia skeptically. "Remember yesterday when you went online and bought that birthday present for your brother and used your credit card number?" Megan asked. "Amanda said that an attacker online could steal your credit card number and then use it to charge things to your account." Mia paused. She remembered that her Uncle Greg had his credit card number stolen earlier this year, and it took several months to get everything straightened out. "And what if an attacker got into your computer and just erased everything? Think of all those photos you have stored on your computer. You wouldn't want to lose them." "Well, OK," said Mia.

"And," Megan continued, "Remember when my brother Jackson got a virus on his computer, and it wouldn't work right? He couldn't even use it. That was right before the end of the semester, and he had all of those papers he had written stored on the computer but he could not get to them. He had to stay up all night for a week to rewrite them. He barely passed his economics class because of that." Mia sat on the couch next to Megan. "I do remember you talking about that. What else did Amanda say these attackers could do?"

Understanding Security

In a general sense *security* can be defined as the necessary steps to protect a person or property from harm. This harm comes from one of two sources: from a direct action that is intended to inflict damage or from an indirect and unintentional action. Consider a typical house. It is necessary to provide security for the house and its inhabitants from these two different sources. For example, the house and its occupants must be secure from the direct attack of a criminal who wants to inflict bodily harm to someone inside or a burglar who wants to steal a television. This security may be provided by locked doors, a fence, or a strong police presence. In addition, the house must also be protected from indirect acts that are not exclusively directed against it. That is, the house needs to be protected from a hurricane (by being built with strong materials and installing hurricane shutters) or a flash flood (by being built off the ground).

Security usually includes both preventive measures and rapid response. An individual who wants to be secure would take the preventive measures of keeping the doors to the house locked and leaving outside lights turned on at night. An example of a rapid response could include the homeowner programming *911* into his cell phone so that if anything suspicious begins to occur around the house an emergency call can be made quickly to the police.

It is important to understand the relationship between *security* and *convenience*. As security is increased, convenience is decreased (security is "inversely proportional" to convenience). That is, the more secure something is, the less convenient it may become to use. This is illustrated in Figure 1-2. Consider again a typical house. A homeowner may install an automated alarm system that requires a code to be entered on a keypad within 30 seconds of entering the house. Although the alarm system makes the house more secure, it is less convenient to use than just entering the house and closing the door. Thus, security may be understood as *sacrificing convenience for safety*. Another way to think of security is *giving up short-term ease for long-term protection*. In any case, security usually requires sacrificing convenience to achieve a greater level of safety or protection.

Security

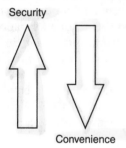

Convenience

Figure 1-2 Security vs. convenience
© Cengage Learning 2014

Defining Information Security

The term **information security** is frequently used to describe the tasks of securing information that is in a digital format. This digital information is typically processed by a microprocessor (for example, on a personal computer), stored on a storage device (such as a hard drive or USB flash drive), and transmitted over a network (such as a local area network or the Internet). Information security can be understood by examining its goals and how it is accomplished.

First, information security ensures that protective measures are properly implemented. But just as the security measures taken for a house can never guarantee complete safety, information security cannot completely prevent attacks or guarantee that a system is totally secure. Rather, information security creates a defense that attempts to repel attacks and prevent the collapse of the system when a successful attack occurs. Thus, information security is *protection*.

Second, information security should protect information that has a value to users and organizations. There are three protections that must be extended over information. These three protections are confidentiality, integrity, and availability:

1. *Confidentiality.* It is important that only approved individuals should be able to access important information. For example, the credit card number used to make an online purchase must be kept secure and not made available to other parties. **Confidentiality** ensures that only authorized parties can view the information and prevents the disclosure to others. Providing confidentiality can involve several different tools, ranging from software to "scramble" the credit card number stored on the Web server to door locks to prevent access to those servers.

2. *Integrity.* **Integrity** ensures that the information is correct and no unauthorized person or malicious software has altered that data. In the example of the online purchase, an attacker who could change the amount of her purchase from $1,000.00 to $1.00 would violate the integrity of the information.

3. *Availability.* Information cannot be "locked up" so tight that no one can access it; otherwise, the information would not be useful. **Availability** ensures that data is accessible when needed to authorized users. The total number of items ordered as the result an online purchase must be made available to an employee in a warehouse so that the correct items can be shipped to the customer.

Protecting information is accomplished by protecting the devices on which the information is found. Because this information is stored, processed, and transmitted by devices, each of these three areas must be protected on those devices. The third objective of information security is to protect the integrity, confidentiality, and availability of information *on the devices that store, process, and transmit information.*

 The devices that store, process, and transmit information use both hardware and software. Thus, the hardware as well as software on these devices can be attack points; therefore, both elements on the devices must be protected.

Information security is achieved through a combination of three entities. As shown in Figure 1-3 and Table 1-3, information (contained on the devices) is protected by three layers: products, people, and policies and procedures. These three layers interact with each other. For example, policies and procedures tell people how to use products to protect information. Thus, a more comprehensive definition of information security is *that which protects the integrity, confidentiality, and availability of information on the devices that store, process, and transmit information and is achieved through products, people, and policies and procedures.*

Information Security Terminology

As with many advanced subjects, information security has its own set of terminology. The following scenario helps to illustrate information security terms and how they are used.

Suppose that Gabe wants to purchase a new set of rims for his car. However, because several cars have had their rims stolen near his condo, he is concerned about someone stealing his rims. Although he parks the car in the gated parking lot, a hole in the fence surrounding his

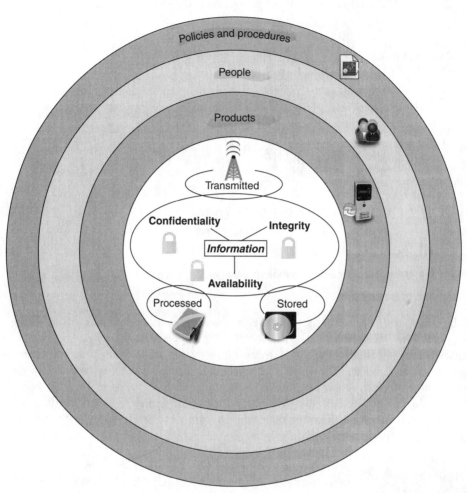

Figure 1-3 Information security components
© Cengage Learning 2014

Layer	Description
Products	Form the physical security around the data; may be as basic as door locks or as complicated as network security equipment
People	Those who implement and properly use security products to protect data
Policies and procedures	Plans and policies established by an organization to ensure that people correctly use the products

Table 1-3 Information security layers
© Cengage Learning 2014

condo makes it possible for someone to access the parking lot without restriction. Gabe's car and the threats to the rims are illustrated in Figure 1-4, along with their corresponding information security component.

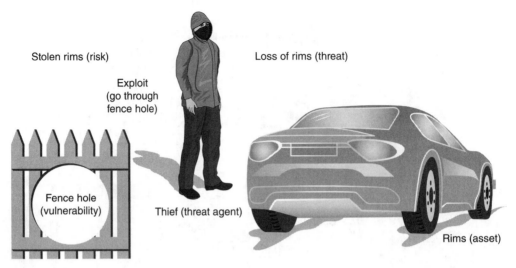

Figure 1-4 Information security components analogy
© Cengage Learning 2014

Gabe's new rims are an **asset,** which is defined as an item that has value. Gabe is trying to protect his rims from a **threat,** which is a type of action that has the potential to cause harm. Information security threats are events or actions that represent a danger to information assets. The mere existence of a threat does not mean that security has been compromised; it simply means that the potential for loss is real. For Gabe, the loss would be the theft of his rims. In information security, a loss could take the form of information theft, a delay in information being transmitted, or even the loss of good will or reputation.

 In an organization, assets have the following qualities: they provide value to the organization; they cannot easily be replaced without a significant investment in expense, time, worker skill, and/or resources; and they can form part of the organization's corporate identity.

A **threat agent** is a person or element that has the power to carry out a threat. For Gabe the threat agent is a thief. In information security a threat agent could be a person attempting to break into a secure computer network. It could also be a force of nature, such as a tornado or flood that could destroy computer equipment and thus destroy information, or it could be malicious software that attacks the computer network.

Gabe wants to protect his rims and is concerned about a hole in the fencing around his condo. The hole in the fencing is a **vulnerability,** which is a flaw or weakness that allows a threat agent to bypass security. An example of a vulnerability in the world of information security is a software defect in an operating system that allows an unauthorized user to gain control of a computer without the user's knowledge or permission.

If a thief can get to Gabe's car because of the hole in the fence, then that thief is taking advantage of the vulnerability. This is known as **exploiting** the security weakness. An attacker, knowing that an e-mail system does not scan attachments for a virus, is exploiting the vulnerability by sending infected e-mail messages to its users.

Gabe must decide if the risk of theft is too high for him to purchase the new rims. A **risk** is the likelihood that the threat agent will exploit the vulnerability; that is, that the rims will be stolen. Realistically, risk can never be entirely eliminated because this would cost too much and take too long. Rather, some degree of risk must always be assumed. There are three options for dealing with risks: accept the risk, diminish the risk, or transfer the risk. In Gabe's case, he could accept the risk and buy the new rims, knowing there is the chance of them being stolen, or he could diminish the risk by parking the car in a rented locked garage. A third option is for Gabe to transfer the risk to someone else. He can do this by purchasing additional car insurance; the insurance company then absorbs the loss and pays if the rims are stolen. In information security, most risks should be diminished if possible.

Table 1-4 summarizes information security terms.

Term	Example in Scenario	Example in Information Security
Asset	Rims	Employee database
Threat	Steal rims from car	Steal data
Threat agent	Thief	Attacker, virus, flood
Vulnerability	Hole in fence	Software defect
Exploit	Climb through hole in fence	Send virus to unprotected e-mail server
Risk	Rims will be stolen	Information will be stolen

Table 1-4 Information security terminology
© Cengage Learning 2014

Understanding the Importance of Information Security

Information security is important to individuals as well as to organizations. Although the goals of information security are many, they include preventing data theft, thwarting identity theft, avoiding the legal consequences of not securing information, maintaining productivity, and foiling cyberterrorism.

Preventing Data Theft Security is often associated with theft prevention: Gabe parks his car in a locked garage in order to prevent the rims from being stolen. The same is true with information security: preventing data from being stolen is often cited by organizations as a primary goal of information security. Business data theft involves stealing proprietary business information, such as research for a new drug or a list of customers that competitors would be eager to acquire.

 According to a recent survey of 800 chief information officers, the companies they represented estimated they lost a combined $4.6 billion worth of intellectual property in one year alone and spent **NOTE** approximately $600 million repairing damage from data breaches.[11]

Data theft is not limited to businesses. Individuals are often victims of data thievery. One type of personal data that is a prime target of attackers is credit card numbers. These can be used to purchase thousands of dollars of merchandise online—without having the actual card—before the victim is even aware the number has been stolen. Reported losses from the fraudulent use of stolen credit card information continue to soar, exceeding $5 billion annually.[12]

The extent to which stolen credit card numbers are available can be seen in the price that online thieves charge each other for stolen card numbers. Because credit card numbers are so readily available, a stolen number can be purchased for as little as $2 per card, although for a card that has a guaranteed balance of over $82,000 the cost of the stolen number is $700. If a buyer wants to use a stolen card number to purchase products online yet is afraid of being traced through the delivery address, a third-party online thief will make the purchase and forward the goods for a fee starting at only $30.[13]

Thwarting Identity Theft Identity theft involves stealing another person's personal information, such as a Social Security number, and then using the information to impersonate the victim, generally for financial gain. The thieves create new bank or credit card accounts under the victim's name. Large purchases are then charged to these accounts that are then left unpaid, leaving the victim potentially responsible for the debts and ruining his or her credit rating.

In some instances, thieves have bought cars and even houses by taking out loans in someone else's name.

The costs to individuals who have been victims of identity theft as a result of data breaches are significant. A study by Utica College's Center for Identity Management and Information Protection (CIMIP) revealed that the median actual dollar loss for identity theft victims was $31,356.[14]

Avoiding Legal Consequences Several federal and state laws have been enacted to protect the privacy of electronic data. Businesses that fail to protect data that they possess may face serious financial penalties. Some of these laws include the following:

- *The Health Insurance Portability and Accountability Act of 1996.* Under the **Health Insurance Portability and Accountability Act (HIPAA)**, healthcare enterprises must guard protected health information and implement policies and procedures to safeguard it, whether it be in paper or electronic format. Those who wrongfully disclose individually identifiable health information with the intent to sell it can be fined up to $250,000 and spend 10 years in prison.

- *The Sarbanes-Oxley Act of 2002.* As a reaction to a rash of corporate fraud, the **Sarbanes-Oxley Act (Sarbox)** is an attempt to fight corporate corruption. Sarbox covers the corporate officers, auditors, and attorneys of publicly traded companies. Stringent reporting requirements and internal controls on electronic financial reporting systems are required. Corporate officers who willfully and knowingly certify a false financial report can be fined up to $5 million and serve 20 years in prison.

- *The Gramm-Leach-Bliley Act.* Like HIPAA. The **Gramm-Leach-Bliley Act (GLBA)** passed in 1999 protects private data. GLBA requires banks and financial institutions to alert customers of their policies and practices in disclosing customer information. All electronic and paper containing personally identifiable financial information must be protected. The penalty for noncompliance for a class of individuals is up to $500,000.

- *The California Database Security Breach Act.* The **California Database Security Breach Act** was the first state law that covers any state agency, person, or company that does business in California. It requires businesses to inform California residents within 48 hours if a breach of personal information has or is believed to have occurred. It defines personal information as a name with a Social Security number, driver's license number, state ID card, account number, credit card number, or debit card number and required security access codes. Since this act was passed by California in 2003, all other states now have similar laws with the exception of Alabama, Kentucky, New Mexico, and South Dakota.

 Although these laws pertain to the United States, other nations are enacting their own legislation to protect electronic data.

The penalties for violating these laws can be sizeable. Businesses must make every effort to keep electronic data secure from hostile outside forces to ensure compliance with these laws and avoid serious legal consequences.

Maintaining Productivity Cleaning up after an attack diverts resources such as time and money away from normal activities. Employees cannot be productive and complete important tasks during an attack and its aftermath because computers and networks cannot function properly. Table 1-5 provides a sample estimate of the lost wages and productivity during an attack and the subsequent cleanup.

Number Total Employees	Average Hourly Salary	Number of Employees to Combat Attack	Hours Required to Stop Attack and Clean Up	Total Lost Salaries	Total Lost Hours of Productivity
100	$25	1	48	$4,066	81
250	$25	3	72	$17,050	300
500	$30	5	80	$28,333	483
1000	$30	10	96	$220,000	1,293

Table 1-5 Costs of attacks
© Cengage Learning 2014

 The single most expensive malicious attack was the Love Bug in 2000, which cost an estimated $8.7 billion.[15]

Foiling Cyberterrorism The FBI defines **cyberterrorism** as any "premeditated, politically motivated attack against information, computer systems, computer programs, and data which results in violence against non-combatant targets by sub-national groups or clandestine agents." Unlike an attack that is designed to steal information or erase a user's hard disk drive, cyberterrorism attacks are intended to cause panic, provoke violence, or cause a financial catastrophe.

The U.S. Commission of Critical Infrastructure Protection identifies possible cyberterrorist targets as the banking industry, military installations, power plants, air traffic control centers, and water systems. These are likely targets because they can significantly disrupt business and personal activities by destroying relatively few targets. For example, disabling an electrical power plant could cripple businesses, homes, transportation services, and communications over a wide area.

One of the challenges in combating cyberterrorism is that many of the prime targets are not owned and managed by the federal government. For example, almost 85 percent of the nation's most critical computer networks and infrastructures are owned by private companies.[16] Because these networks are not centrally controlled, it is difficult to coordinate and maintain security.

Who Are the Attackers?

There are several different categories of attackers. These categories include cybercriminals, script kiddies, spies, insiders, cyberterrorists, hactivists, and government agencies.

In the past the term *hacker* was commonly used to refer to a person who uses advanced computer skills to attack computers. *White hat hackers* were said to only expose security flaws and not steal or corrupt data, whereas *black hat hackers* were those who wanted to steal and destroy. Although "hacker" is often used by the mainstream media to refer to an attacker, this term is no longer commonly used by the security community.

Cybercriminals

Cybercriminals is used as a generic term used to describe individuals who launch attacks against other users and their computers (another generic word is simply *attackers*). However, strictly speaking cybercriminals are a loose network of attackers, identity thieves, and financial fraudsters who are more highly motivated, less risk-averse, better funded, and more tenacious than an "ordinary" attacker. Some security experts believe that many cybercriminals belong to organized gangs of young attackers, often clustered in Eastern European, Asian, and Third World regions. Reasons why these areas may harbor large number of cybercriminals are summarized in Table 1-6.

Security in Your World

Megan set her fork down and listened to her friends while they ate lunch in the cafeteria. The school had recently been the victim of another hoax in which students and faculty had received an e-mail from an attacker pretending to be from the school's IT department. The e-mail asked the users to enter their username and password for verification. Because so many users had submitted their passwords the school decided to prevent anyone from logging in until new security procedures were implemented. Megan's psychology class was canceled because they could not use the computers in the lab.

"Teenagers," said Giulio, one of Megan's friends. "They're the ones who do these things. They have nothing better to do than write these programs that mess up somebody else's computer.

Esteban said, "I read somewhere that it's international terrorists who are behind it. They want to bring our country down so they're after our computers."

"I don't know," said Li. "I wonder if it's the companies that sell security programs. They could write these attack programs so that people will have to buy their stuff."

Just then Professor Helba walked by their table. "Who do you think is behind these attacks?" Megan asked him. He smiled and said, "Teachers. They do it to cancel classes."

Characteristic	Explanation
Strong technical universities	Since the demise of the Soviet Union in the early 1990s a number of large universities have left teaching communist ideology and turned to teaching technology.
Low incomes	With the transition from communism to a free market system, individuals in several nations have suffered from the loss of an economy supported by the state, and incomes remain relatively low.
Unstable legal system	Many nations continue to struggle with making and enforcing new laws that combat computer crime.
Tense political relations	Some new nations do not yet have strong ties to other foreign countries, and this sometimes complicates efforts to obtain cooperation with local law enforcement.

Table 1-6 Characteristics of cybercriminals
© Cengage Learning 2014

Cybercriminals often meet in online "underground" forums that have names like *DarkMarket.org* and *theftservices.com*. The purpose of these meetings is to trade information and coordinate attacks around.

NOTE

Instead of attacking a computer to show off their technology skills (*fame*), cybercriminals have a more focused goal of financial gain (*fortune*). Cybercriminals exploit vulnerabilities to steal information or launch attacks that can generate income. This difference makes the new attackers more dangerous and their attacks more threatening. These targeted attacks against financial networks, unauthorized access to information, and the theft of personal information are sometimes known as **cybercrime**.

Financial cybercrime is often divided into two categories. The first category focuses on individuals and businesses. Cybercriminals steal and use stolen data, credit card numbers, online financial account information, or Social Security numbers to profit from its victims or send millions of spam e-mails to peddle counterfeit drugs, pirated software, fake watches, and pornography.

The second category focuses on businesses and governments. Cybercriminals attempt to steal research on a new product from a business so that they can sell these to an unscrupulous foreign supplier who will then build an imitation model of the product to sell worldwide. This deprives the legitimate business from profits after investing millions of dollars in product development, and because these foreign suppliers are in a different country they are beyond the reach of domestic courts and domestic enforcement agencies. Governments are also the targets of cybercriminals: if the latest information on a new missile defense system can be stolen it can be sold—at a high price—to that government's enemies.

 Some security experts maintain that European cybercriminals are mostly focused on activities to steal money from individuals and businesses, whereas cybercriminals from Asia are more interested in stealing data from governments or businesses.

Script Kiddies

Script kiddies are individuals who want to attack computers yet they lack the knowledge of computers and networks needed to do so. Instead, script kiddies do their work by downloading automated attack software (scripts) from Web sites and using it to perform malicious acts. Figure 1-5 lists the skills needed for creating attacks. Over 40 percent of attacks require low or no skills and are frequently conducted by script kiddies.

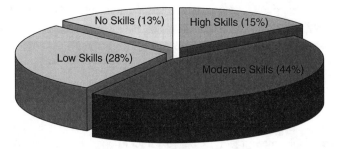

Figure 1-5 Skills needed for creating attacks
© Cengage Learning 2014

Today script kiddies can acquire entire "exploit kits" from other attackers to easily craft an attack. Script kiddies license the kit (for a fee) from its authors and then can specify various options to customize their attacks.

The Blackhole exploit kit is one of the most widely used kits. It is estimated that 28 percent of all Web threats are based on this single kit.[17]

Spies

A computer **spy** is a person who has been hired to break into a computer and steal information. Spies do not randomly search for unsecured computers to attack as script kiddies and other attackers do; rather, spies are hired to attack a specific computer or system that contains sensitive information. Their goal is to break into that computer and take the information without drawing any attention to their actions. Spies generally possess excellent computer skills to attack and then cover their tracks.

Insiders

Another serious threat to an organization actually comes from an unlikely source: its employees, contractors, and business partners, often called *insiders*. In one study of 900 cases of business "data leakage," over 48 percent of the breaches were attributed to insiders who abused their right to access corporate information.[18]

In most instances insider attacks are more costly than an attack from the outside.

Examples of several recent high-profile insider attacks include:

- A California healthcare worker, disgruntled over an upcoming job termination, illegally gathered health records on celebrities and sold them to the media.

- A French securities trader lost over $7 billion on bad stock bets and then used his knowledge of the bank's computer security system to conceal the losses through fake transactions.

- A U.S. Army private in Iraq accessed secret U.S. diplomatic cables and other sensitive documents, which were then given to an international whistleblower, who posted them on the Internet.

Most insider attacks consist of the sabotage or theft of intellectual property. One study revealed that most cases of sabotage come from employees who have announced their resignation or have been formally reprimanded, demoted, or fired. When theft is involved, the offenders are usually salespeople, engineers, computer programmers, or scientists who actually believe that the accumulated data is owned by them and not the organization (most of these thefts occur within 30 days of the employee resigning). In some instances the employees are moving to a new job and want to take "their work" with them, while in other cases the employees have been bribed or pressured into stealing the data. In about

8 percent of the incidences of theft, employees have been pressured into stealing from their employer through blackmail or the threat of violence.[19]

Although it generally is not intentional, in many instances carelessness by employees has resulted in serious security breaches. For example, almost 10,000 laptop computers *each week* are lost in airports, and over half contain confidential or sensitive information. Only one out of every three lost laptops are returned to their owner.[20]

Cyberterrorists

Many security experts fear that terrorists will turn their attacks to a nation's network and computer infrastructure to cause panic among citizens. Known as **cyberterrorists**, their motivation may be ideology, or attacking for the sake of their principles or beliefs. A report distributed by the Institute for Security Technology Studies at Dartmouth College lists three goals of a cyberattack:

- To deface electronic information (such as Web sites) and spread misinformation and propaganda

- To deny service to legitimate computer users

- To commit unauthorized intrusions into systems and networks that result in critical infrastructure outages and corruption of vital data

Cyberterrorists may be the attackers that are most feared, for it is almost impossible to predict when or where an attack may occur. Unlike cybercriminals who continuously probe systems or create attacks, cyberterrorists can be inactive for several years and then suddenly strike in a new way. Their targets may include a small group of computers or networks that can affect the largest number of users, such as the computers that control the electrical power grid of a state or region.

Hactivists

Hactivists are also motivated by ideology. Unlike cyberterrorists, who launch attacks against nations, hactivists (a combination of the words *hack* and *activism*) direct their attacks at specific Web sites. Generally these attacks are intended to promote a political agenda and are in retaliation for a prior event. For example, hactivists might attempt to disable a bank's Web site because that bank stopped accepting online payments that were deposited into accounts belonging to the hactivists.

Government Agencies

In recent years government agencies appear to have been behind attacks on foreign governments and even their own citizens whom they consider hostile or threatening. Instead of using an army to march across the battlefield to strike an adversary, government agencies are launching computer attacks against their foes. The following are several examples of these attacks:

- The malware known as Flame was discovered in mid-2012 and appears to be targeted against computers in Middle Eastern countries. One of Flame's most ingenious tricks, which had many security researchers in awe, created a fake Microsoft electronic document so that Flame appeared to be an update from Microsoft and was easily distributed to any Windows computer.

- Perhaps the most infamous government-backed malware to date was called Stuxnet. Stuxnet's primary target was a nuclear power plant near the Persian Gulf, which was a source of tension between nations because of fear that spent fuel from the reactor could be reprocessed elsewhere in the country to produce weapons-grade plutonium for use in nuclear warheads. At first it was thought that Stuxnet took advantage of a single previously unknown software vulnerability. Upon closer inspection, it was found that Stuxnet exploited four unknown vulnerabilities, something never seen before.

- It is estimated that over 300,000 Iranian citizens were having their e-mail messages read without their knowledge by the Iranian government seeking to locate and crack down on dissidents. It appears that the government used stolen electronic documents to permit its spies to log in directly to the e-mail mailboxes of the victims and read any stored e-mails. In addition, another program could pinpoint the exact location of the victim.

Building a Comprehensive Security Strategy

What would a practical, comprehensive security strategy look like? There are four key elements to creating a practical security strategy: block attacks, update defenses, minimize losses, and send secure information. These elements are by no means new; these tactics go back to the days of medieval castles in Europe and probably much earlier. Understanding these key elements as they were used during the Middle Ages helps bring them into focus for developing practical security today.

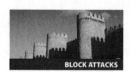

Block Attacks

The word *castle* comes from a Latin word meaning *fortress*, and most ancient castles served in this capacity. One of a castle's primary functions was to protect the king's family and citizens of the countryside in the event of an attack from an enemy. A castle was designed to block enemy attacks in two distinct ways. First, a castle was surrounded by a deep moat that was filled with water, which prevented the enemy from getting close to the castle. In addition, many castles had a high protective stone wall between the moat and the outer walls of the castle. The purpose of the moat and protective wall was to create a *security perimeter* around the castle: any attacker would have to get through the strong perimeter to get inside.

Effective information security follows this same model of blocking attacks by having a strong security perimeter. Usually, this security perimeter is part of the computer network to which a personal computer is attached. If attacks are blocked by the network security perimeter, the attacker will be unable to reach the personal computer on which the data is stored. Security devices can be added to a computer network that will continually analyze traffic coming into the network from the outside (such as e-mail or Web pages) and block unauthorized or malicious traffic.

In addition to perimeter security, most castles provided *local security*. If an arrow shot by an attacker traveled over the moat and outer wall, those inside the castle would be vulnerable to these attacks, even if there was a strong security perimeter. The solution is to provide each defender with a personal shield to deflect the arrows. This analogy also applies to information security. As important as a strong network security perimeter is to blocking attacks, some attacks will slip through the defenses. It is vital to also have local security on all of the personal computers to defend against any attack that breaches the perimeter.

One security technique is for the network to automatically check the security settings of each personal computer on the network. Computers that lack the proper local security hardware or software are immediately disconnected from the network until their configurations have been corrected.

Update Defenses

Imagine a castle in which each defender has been given a personal leather shield to protect him- or herself against arrows shot over the wall. The defenders may feel that they have adequate protection against the attacker's arrows. Yet what if suddenly the arrows came over the wall with their tips on fire? If the defenders have never seen flaming arrows before, they would be at a loss regarding how to prevent their leather shields from catching on fire when struck with one of these arrows. This "new technology" of flaming arrows could prove to be disastrous if the defenders have no means to change their type of shields.

Today's information security attackers are equally, if not more, inventive than attackers of 1,000 years ago. New types of attacks appear on a daily basis. It is essential that users today continually update their defenses to protect their information. This involves updating defensive hardware and software as well as applying operating system security updates on a regular basis.

Minimize Losses

As a flaming arrow sails over the castle wall, it might strike a bale of hay and set it ablaze. If the defenders were not prepared with a bucket of water to douse the flames, then the entire castle could burn up. Being prepared to minimize losses was essential in defending a castle.

Likewise, in information security, it is important to realize that some attacks will get through security perimeters and local defenses. It is important that action be taken in advance in order to minimize losses. This may involve keeping backup copies of important data stored in a safe place, or, for an organization, it may mean having an entire business recovery policy that details what to do in the event of a successful attack.

Send Secure Information

A castle that is under siege for an extended period of time may require outside help from an ally. So how can these friendly distant forces receive the cry for help? In some instances a messenger might be sent out from the castle on horseback to break through the enemy lines to reach the supporters. To have any chance of delivering the message, the messenger would need a swift horse and layers of protective body armor.

A parallel can be drawn in today's world of information security. As users send e-mail and other information from their local computer out over the Internet, it is important that it be protected and kept secure. This might involve "scrambling" the data so that unauthorized eyes cannot read it. In other instances it might require establishing a secure electronic link between the sender and receiver that would prevent an attacker from being able to read the information. In any case, information security is more than just being on the defensive; it often involves taking proactive steps to thwart attackers.

Chapter Summary

- Attacks against information security have grown exponentially in recent years, despite the fact that billions of dollars are spent annually on security. No computer system is immune to attacks or can be considered as entirely secure.

- There are several reasons why it is difficult to defend against today's attacks. These include the fact that virtually all devices are connected to the Internet, the speed of the attacks, greater sophistication of attacks, the availability and simplicity of attack tools, faster detection of vulnerabilities by attackers, delays in security updating, weak security update distribution, distributed attacks coming from multiple sources, and user confusion.

- Information security may be defined as that which protects the integrity, confidentiality, and availability of information on the devices that store, process, and transmit information and is achieved through products, people, and policies and procedures. As with many advanced subjects, information security has its own terminology. A threat is an event or action that represents a danger to information assets, which is something that has value. A threat agent is a person or element that has the power to carry out a threat, usually by exploiting a vulnerability, which is a flaw or weakness. A risk is the likelihood that a threat agent will exploit the vulnerability.

- The main goals of information security are to prevent data theft, thwart identify theft, avoid the legal consequences of not securing information, maintain productivity, and foil cyberterrorism.

- The types of people behind computer attacks fall into several categories. The term "cyber-criminals" generally refers to someone who attacks computers, yet strictly speaking cyber-criminals are a loose network of attackers, identity thieves, and financial fraudsters who are more highly motivated, less risk averse, better funded, and more tenacious than an "ordinary" attacker. Script kiddies do their work by downloading automated attack software from Web sites and then using it to break into computers. A computer spy is a person who has been hired to break into a computer and steal information. One of the largest information security threats to a business actually comes from its employees. Cyberterrorists are motivated by their principles and beliefs, and turn their attacks to the network and computer infrastructure to cause panic among citizens. In recent years government agencies appear to have been behind attacks on foreign governments and even their own citizens whom they consider hostile or threatening.

- A practical, comprehensive security strategy involves four key elements. The first is to block attacks by having a strong security perimeter, both on the network and on the personal computer as well. Another strategy is to regularly update defenses to protect against the latest attacks. Also, it is important to minimize losses for any attacks that may be successful. Finally, sending secure information to prevent attackers from accessing it is another key element.

Key Terms

asset   An item that that has value.

availability   Security actions that ensures that data is accessible to authorized users.

California Database Security Breach Act   The first state law that covers any state agency, person, or company that does business in California.

confidentiality   Security actions that ensure that only authorized parties can view the information and prevents the disclosure to others.

cybercrime   Targeted attacks against financial networks, unauthorized access to information, and the theft of personal information.

cybercriminals   A generic term used to describe individuals who launch attacks against other users and their computers; also describes a loose-knit network of attackers, identity thieves, and financial fraudsters.

cyberterrorism   A premeditated and politically motivated attack that results in violence.

cyberterrorists   Attackers who attack other nations and whose motivation is ideology, or attacking for the sake of their principles or beliefs.

exploiting   The act of taking advantage of a vulnerability.

Gramm-Leach-Bliley Act (GLBA)   A law that requires banks and financial institutions to alert customers of their policies and practices in disclosing customer information.

hactivists   Attackers who attack Web sites as a form of protest, usually in retaliation for a prior event.

Health Insurance Portability and Accountability Act (HIPAA)   A law designed to guard protected health information and implement policies and procedures to safeguard it.

identity theft   Stealing another person's personal information, such as a Social Security number, and then using the information to impersonate the victim, generally for financial gain.

information security   The tasks of securing information that is in a digital format.

integrity   Security actions that ensure that the information is correct and no unauthorized person or malicious software has altered that data.

risk   The likelihood that a threat agent will exploit the vulnerability.

Sarbanes-Oxley Act (Sarbox)   A law designed to enforce internal controls on electronic financial reporting systems.

script kiddies   Individuals who want to break into computers to create damage yet lack the advanced knowledge of computers and networks needed to do so.

spy   A person who has been hired to break into a computer and steal information.

threat   A type of action that has the potential to cause harm.

threat agent   A person or element that has the power to carry out a threat.

vulnerability   A flaw or weakness that allows a threat agent to bypass security.

Review Questions

1. Each of the following is a reason why it is difficult to defend against today's attackers except _____.

   a. complexity of attack tools

   b. faster detection of vulnerabilities

   c. greater sophistication of attacks

   d. user confusion

2. In a general sense "security" is _____.

   a. protection from only direct actions

   b. the steps necessary to protect a person or property from harm

   c. only available on specialized computers

   d. impossible to achieve

3. _____ ensures that only authorized parties can view the information.

   a. Integrity

   b. Confidentiality

   c. Availability

   d. Authorization

4. Each of the following is a successive layer in which information security is achieved except _____.

   a. products

   b. purposes

   c. policies and procedures

   d. people

5. By definition a(n) _____ is a person or thing that has the power to carry out a threat.

   a. vulnerability

   b. threat agent

   c. exploit

   d. risk

6. In information security terminology a(n) _____ is a flaw or weakness that allows an attacker to bypass security protections.

   a. access

   b. worm hole

   c. access control

   d. vulnerability

7. Each of the following is a goal of information security except _____.

   a. decrease user productivity

   b. foil cyberterrorism

   c. avoid legal consequences

   d. prevent data theft

8. The _____ requires that enterprises must guard protected health information and implement policies and procedures to safeguard it.

   a. Hospital Protection and Insurance Association Agreement (HPIAA)

   b. Sarbanes-Oxley Act (Sarbox)

   c. Gramm-Leach-Bliley Act (GLBA)

   d. Health Insurance Portability and Accountability Act (HIPAA)

9. The motivation of _____ is attacking for the sake of their principles or beliefs.

   a. insiders

   b. script kiddies

   c. cyberterrorists

   d. computer spies

10. Each of the following is an element to creating a practical security strategy except _____.

    a. send secure information

    b. update defenses

    c. maximize losses

    d. block attacks

11. Keeping backup copies of important data stored in a safe place is an example of:

    a. sending secure information

    b. blocking attacks

    c. minimizing losses

    d. layering

12. Each of the following could be classified as an "insider" except _____.

    a. business partners

    b. contractors

    c. cybercriminals

    d. employees

13. _____ are a network of attackers, identity thieves, and financial fraudsters.
   a. Script kiddies
   b. Hackers
   c. Cybercriminals
   d. Spies

14. Each of the following is a characteristic of cybercriminals except _____.
   a. better funded
   b. less risk averse
   c. low motivation
   d. more tenacious

15. Each of the following is a characteristic of cybercrime except_____.
   a. targeted attacks against financial networks
   b. exclusive use of worms and viruses
   c. unauthorized attempts to access to information
   d. theft of personal information

16. An example of a(n) _____ is a software defect in an operating system that allows an unauthorized user to gain access to a computer without a password.
   a. asset exploit (AE)
   b. threat agent
   c. vulnerability
   d. threat
   e. vulnerability

17. _____ requires banks and financial institutions to alert customers of their policies and practices in disclosing customer information and to protect all electronic and paper containing personally identifiable financial information.
   a. California Savings and Loan Security Act (CS&LSA)
   b. Sarbanes-Oxley Act (Sarbox)
   c. Gramm-Leach-Bliley Act (GLBA)
   d. USA Patriot Act

18. The term _____ is sometimes used to identify anyone who illegally breaks into a computer system.
   a. cyberrogue
   b. cybercriminal
   c. Internet Exploiter
   d. cyberterrorist

19. _____ ensures that the information is correct and no unauthorized person or malicious software has altered that data.

    a. obscurity

    b. integrity

    c. confidentiality

    d. layering

20. Protecting information is accomplished by:

    a. protecting the devices on which the information is found

    b. securing only local servers

    c. hiring an Information Security Officer (CISO)

    d. reducing risk factors

Hands-On Projects

Project 1-1: Examine Data Breaches

The Privacy Rights Clearinghouse (PRC) is a nonprofit organization whose goals are to raise consumers' awareness of how technology affects personal privacy and empower consumers to take action to control their own personal information. The PRC maintains a searchable database of security breaches that impact consumer's privacy. In this project you will gather information from the PRC Web site.

1. Open your Web browser and enter the URL **www.privacyrights.org/data-breach**.

The location of content on the Internet may change without warning. If you are no longer able to access the site through the above Web address, use a search engine to search for "Privacy Rights Clearinghouse data breach."

2. First spend time reading about the PRC. Click **About Us** in the toolbar.

3. Scroll down to the content under Mission and Goals and also under Services. Spend a few minutes reading about the PRC.

4. Click your browser's Back button to return to the previous page.

5. On the **Chronology of Data Breaches** scroll down and observe the different breaches listed in chronological order.

6. Now create a customized list of the data that will only list data breaches of educational institutions. Scroll back to the top of the page.

7. Under Select organization type(s), uncheck all organizations except EDU-Educational Institutions.

8. Click **GO**.

9. Scroll down to Breach Subtotal if necessary. How many breaches that were made public pertain to educational institutions?

10. Scroll down and observe the breaches for educational institutions.

11. Click **New Search,** located beneath the GO button.

12. Now search for breaches that were a result of lost, discarded, or stolen equipment that belonged to the government and military. Under Choose the type of breaches to display, uncheck all types except Portable device (PORT) - Lost, discarded or stolen laptop, PDA, smartphone, portable memory device, CD, hard drive, data tape, etc.

13. Under Select organization type(s), uncheck all organizations except GOV – Government and Military.

14. Click **GO.**

15. Scroll down to Breach Subtotal, if necessary. How many breaches that were made public pertain to this type?

16. Scroll down and observe the breaches for governmental institutions.

17. Scroll back to the top of the page.

18. Now create a search based on criteria that you are interested in, such as the Payment Card Fraud against Retail/Merchants during the current year.

19. Close all windows.

Project 1-2: Scan for Malware Using the Microsoft Safety Scanner

In this project you will download and run the Microsoft Safety Scanner to determine if there is any malware on your computer. Note that this scanner only functions under Windows 7, Vista, and XP.

1. Determine which system type of Windows you are running. Click **Start, Control Panel,, System and Security,** and then **System.** Look under System type for the description.

2. Open your Web browser and enter the URL **www.microsoft.com/security/ scanner/en-us/default.asp.**

 The location of content on the Internet may change without warning. If you are no longer able to access the site through the above Web address, then use a search engine to search for "Microsoft Safety Scanner."

3. Click **Download Now.**

4. Select either **32-bit** or **64-bit,** depending upon which system type of Windows you are running.

5. When the program finishes downloading, right-click on **Start** and click **Open Windows Explorer.**

6. Click the **Downloads** icon in the left pane.

7. Double-click the **msert.exe** file.

8. Click **Run.** If the **User Account Control** dialog box appears, click **Yes.**

9. Click the check box to accept the license terms for this software. Click **Next.**

10. Click **Next**.

11. Select **Quick scan** if necessary.

12. Click **Next**.

13. Depending on your computer this scan may take several minutes. Analyze the results of the scan to determine if there is any malicious software found in your computer.

14. If there are problems you can click **View detailed results of the scan**. After reviewing the results, click **OK**. If there are no problems found, click **Finish**.

15. If any malicious software was found on your computer run the scan again and select **Full scan**. After the scan is complete, click **Finish** to close the dialog box.

16. Close all windows.

Project 1-3: Automatically Receive the Latest Security Information

With the face of security changing daily, it is important to keep current with the latest security threats and defenses. One way to keep current is to use RSS (Really Simple Syndication), which automatically distributes Web content from a variety of different sources (blogs, news headlines, audio, video, etc.) in a standardized format and aggregates the content. Users subscribe to a Web site, and then the content is "pushed" to their computer to be viewed using an RSS reader or Web browser. This eliminates the need to visit multiple sites. In this project you will use the Google Reader aggregator.

1. Open a Web browser and enter the Web address **www.google.com/reader**.

The location of content on the Internet may change without warning. If you are no longer able to access the site through the preceding Web address, use a search engine to search for "Google Reader."

2. If you already have a Google account, log in. If you do not have an account, click on **Create an account** and create a Google account.

3. Open a new window in your Web browser (for example, in Internet Explorer press **Ctrl+t**).

4. Enter the URL **googleonlinesecurity.blogspot.com**, which is a blog about security information from Google.

The location of content on the Internet may change without warning. If you are no longer able to access the site through the above Web address, use a search engine to search for "Google Online Security Blog."

5. Click the **+Google** icon.

6. Click **Subscribe to this feed**.

7. Click **Add to Google Reader**.

8. You are now subscribed to this RSS feed.

9. Click **Sign out** and exit Google.

10. Log back in to Google. You will see your security blog RSS feeds, which you can read.

11. Log out of Google.

12. Close all windows.

Project 1-4: Use an EULA Analyzer

Although malicious attackers are often considered to be the only enemies that view user's data without their permission, there are several examples of commercial software that can also invade a user's privacy by tracking or monitoring their activities. Software companies often "bury" the approval of these actions in their end-user license agreements, or EULA. In this project you will use tools to analyze EULA agreements.

1. Open your Web browser and enter the URL **www.microsoft.com/About/ Legal/EN/US/IntellectualProperty/UseTerms/Default.aspx**.

2. Under How is the software acquired? select **Pre-Installed on your computer from the computer manufacturer?** from the pull-down menu.

3. Under **Product Name**, select **Windows 7** from the pull-down menu.

4. Under **Version**, select **Professional** from the pull-down menu.

5. Under **Language**, select **English** from the pull-down menu.

6. Click **Go**.

7. Under **Search Results** click on the PDF file.

8. When the File download dialog box appears, click **Save** to download the file to your local computer.

9. When the download is complete, click **Open**.

10. Select the contents of the entire document by clicking **CTRL + a**.

11. Copy the contents of the selected text to the clipboard by clicking **CTRL + c**.

12. Go to the Web site **www.spywareguide.com/analyze/analyzer.php**.

The location of content on the Internet may change without warning. If you are no longer able to access the site through the preceding Web address, use a search engine to search for "Spyware Guide License Analyzer."

13. Under **Title** enter **Windows 7**.

14. Under **Paste license here**, click in the box and then paste the contents of the clipboard by clicking **CTRL + v**.

15. Under Display Results as … be sure that **Detailed analysis** is selected.

16. Click **Start Analyzer**.

17. After the analysis is completed, scroll down through the document and note the references to tracking or monitoring. Read the accompanying sections. Were you aware of these agreements when you installed this software or a

similar Windows operating system on your computer? Do you agree with these conditions?

18. Search the Internet for the EULA of another program that you commonly use, and analyze it. Are there similar tracking or monitoring features? Do you agree with them?

19. Close all windows.

Case Projects

Case Project 1-1: Security Podcasts

A number of different security vendors and security researchers now post weekly podcasts on security topics. Using a search engine, locate three different podcasts about computer security. Download them to your media player or computer and listen to them. Then, write a summary of what was discussed and a critique of the podcasts. Were they beneficial to you? Were they accurate? Would you recommend them to someone else? Write a one-page paper on your research.

Case Project 1-2: Information Security Terminology in Your World

The scenario of Gabe protecting his rims was used in this chapter to introduce the six key terms used in information security: asset, threat, threat agent, vulnerability, exploit, and risk. Create your own one-paragraph scenario with those six key terms using a situation with which you are familiar. Also, create a table similar to Table 1-4 that lists these terms and how they are used in your scenario.

Case Project 1-3: Attack Experiences

Based on your own personal experiences or those of someone you know (you may have to interview other students or a friend), write a paragraph regarding a computer attack that occurred. When did it happen? What was the attack? What type of damage did it inflict? How was the computer "fixed" after the attack? What could have prevented it? Write a one-page paper about these experiences.

Case Project 1-4: Helping Others with Security

Although Amanda explained to Megan about security in the Security in Your World boxes in this chapter, what could Megan have done to learn about security if she did not have a friend like Amanda who studied computer security? Make a list of the different options available that would help your friends learn more information about security. Are there short classes at a local college in your area that cover security from a user's perspective? Do computer stores have workshops on making computers more secure? Are there any magazines that explore home security that are easy to read and understand? What about Web sites that contain important information? Create a list of several different options for the area in which you live or go to school.

Case Project 1-5: Information Security Community Site Activity

The Information Security Community Web site is an online companion to this textbook. It contains a wide variety of tools, information, discussion boards, and other features to assist learners. In order to gain the most benefit from the site, you will need to set up a free account.

Go to **http://community.cengage.com/Infosec**. Click JOIN at the top of the page. On the Register and Join our Community page, enter the requested information. For your sign-in name use the first letter of your first name followed by an underscore (_) and then your last name. For example, John Smith would create his sign-in name as J_Smith.

Note that your instructor may have a different naming convention that you should use, such as the name of your course followed by your initials. Check with your instructor before creating your Sign-in name.

Explore the various features of the Information Security Community Web site, and become familiar with it. Visit the blog section and read the blog postings to learn about some of the latest events in IT security.

Case Project 1-6: North Ridge Computer Consultants

North Ridge Computer Consultants (NRCC) is a local information technology company that specializes in security. In order to encourage students to enter the field of information security, NRCC often hires student interns to assist with projects. Collier Electronics, a local chain of technology stores, was recently the victim of a security attack that caused their computers and network to be unavailable for several days. Collier Electronics has contacted NRCC for help.

NRCC has hired you to create a presentation about computer security. The presentation should cover what computer security is, why it is important, and the basic steps in an attack and defense. Create a PowerPoint presentation of at least eight slides that covers this information. Because the audience does not have a strong technical background, your presentation should be general in its tone.

References

1. "Ponemon Cost of a Data Breach 2011." *Symantec*. Accessed Mar. 21, 2012. <http://www.symantec.com/about/news/resources/press_kits/detail.jsp?pkid=ponemon-cost-of-a-data-breach-2011>.

2. "Norton Cybercrime Report." *Norton Enterprise*. Accessed Nov. 10, 2011. <http://www.symantec.com/content/en/us/home_homeoffice/html/cybercrimereport/>.

3. "DHS Wireless Medical Devices/Healthcare Cyberattacks Report." *Public Intelligence*. May 4, 2012. Accessed May 22 2012. <http://publicintelligence.net/nccic-medical-device-cyberattacks/>.

4. "Hackers hold bank to ransom over stolen data." *ZDNet*. Accessed Aug. 13, 2012. <http://www.zdnet.com/hackers-hold-bank-to-ransom-over-stolen-data-3040155167/>.

5. "Hacked!" *The Atlantic*. Nov. 2011. Accessed Aug. 13, 2012. <http://www.theatlantic.com/magazine/archive/2011/11/hacked/8673/1/?single_page=true>.

6. "This lawyer had the worst neighbor ever." *Above the Law*. Jul. 14, 2011. Accessed Aug. 13, 2012. <http://abovethelaw.com/2011/07/this-lawyer-had-the-worst-neighbor-ever/>.

7. "419 Advance Fee Fraud Statistics 2009." Jan 2010. Accessed Feb. 28, 2011. <http://www.ultrascan-agi.com/public_html/html/public_research_reports.html>.

8. "Chronology of Data Breaches: Security Breaches 2005–Present." *Privacy Rights Clearinghouse*. Updated Jul. 18, 2012. Accessed Feb. 28, 2011. <http://www.privacyrights.org/data-breach>.

9. *Privacy Rights Clearinghouse*. Accessed Aug, 13, 2012. <https://www.privacyrights.org/data-breach>.

10. Larkin, Erik, "Services Are Tapping PeoplePower to Spot Malware." PCWorld. Feb. 20, 2008. Accessed Feb. 20, 2011. <http://www.pcworld.com/article/142653/services_are_tapping_people_power_to_spot_malware.html>.

11. Thorpe, Simon, "ROI for IRM? Businesses risk $1 trillion losses from data theft." Oracle IRM Blog, Data Loss Archives. Feb. 3, 2009. Accessed Feb. 28, 2011. <http://blogs.oracle.com/irm/data_loss/>.

12. National Fraud Center, Inc., "The Growing Global Threat of Economic and Cyber Crime." *Economic Crime Investigation Institute, Utica College*. Dec. 2000. Accessed Feb. 28, 2011. <http://www.utica.edu/academic/institutes/ecii/publications/media/global_threat_crime.pdf>.

13. Bazzell, Michael. "Buy a stolen debit card for $2.00." *Computer Crime Info Blog*. Jan. 22, 2011. Accessed Feb. 28, 2011. <http://blog.computercrimeinfo.com/>.

14. Gordon, Gary R, et al., "Identity Fraud Trends and Patterns." *Center for Identity Management and Information Protection, Utica College*. 2007. Accessed Feb. 28, 2011. <http://www.utica.edu/academic/institutes/ecii/publications/media/cimip_id_theft_study_oct_22_noon.pdf>.

15. "The cost of 'Code Red': $1.2 billion." *USA Today*. Aug. 1, 2001. Accessed Feb. 28, 2011. <http://www.usatoday.com/tech/news/2001-08-01-code-red-costs.htm>.

16. "Cybersecurity: Next Steps to Protect Our Critical Infrastructure." *Hearing before the U.S. Senate Committee on Commerce, Science, and Transportation*. Feb. 23, 2010. Accessed Feb. 28, 2011. <http://www.fas.org/irp/congress/2010_hr/cybersec.pdf>.

17. "Blackhole Exploit." *Zomobo*. Accessed Jul. 20, 2012. <http://zomobo.net/blackhole-exploit.

18. Cappelli, Dawn, "Internal review: The insider threat risk." *SC Magazine*. Feb. 2, 2011. Accessed Feb. 28, 2011. <http://inform.com/government-and-politics/internal-review-insider-threat-risk-4737197a>.

19. *Ibid*.

20. "Airport Insecurity: The Case of Lost Laptops." *Ponemon Institute*. Jun. 30, 2008. Accessed Feb. 28, 2011. <http://www.nymity.com/Free_Privacy_Resources/Previews/ReferencePreview.aspx?guid=fe5b4c2c-d07f-4d3e-a1ba-76594de5a4db>.

© Shutterstock.com

chapter 2

Personal Security

After completing this chapter you should be able to do the following:

- Define what makes a weak password
- Describe the attacks against passwords
- Identify the different types of social engineering attacks
- Describe identity theft and the risks of using social networking
- Describe personal security defenses

Security in Your World

"Wow, I didn't know that!" said Sergei, as he put his backpack in the empty chair next to Tatiana. Sergei and Tatiana attended the same college and often met at the local coffee shop between classes. Tatiana looked up from her tablet computer and asked, "Didn't know what?"

"I just came from my Introduction to Computers class, where we were talking about Facebook," he said. "Well, you'd better tell me," said Tatiana. "I'm on it right now." She was an avid Facebook user and spent all of her free time on Facebook, Twitter, and other social networking sites.

"Did you know," said Sergei, "That if you apply for a job in this state that they can demand that you give them your password to your Facebook and Twitter accounts?" "They can't do that!" said Tatiana. Sergei replied, "Oh, yes they can. And if you don't give it to them then they can refuse to hire you." Tatiana put her coffee cup on the table. "How can they do that?"

Sergei sat down. "I was shocked, too. But our instructor showed us some job listings where it actually said that candidates must provide these passwords to be considered for employment. Can you imagine what they could find on my Facebook page? They'd probably never hire me if they saw what I've posted!" Tatiana looked down at her tablet. She remembered a video she had recently posted about her vacation and some nasty comments she had made online. "If they read my Facebook page, they wouldn't hire me, either," she said.

"And that's not all", Sergei said. "Remember those new features that Facebook added? That potential employer who's got your password can now see an entire digital history of your life without needing to dig around. Someone who didn't know you could easily get the wrong idea about the sort of person you are," Sergei said. Tatiana nodded.

"Plus," said Sergei, "There's a new attack going around Facebook now. The attackers are pretending to be Facebook employees and are tricking users into sending them their passwords. Since so many people reuse the same password on different accounts, once they have that password they can easily break into your other accounts."

Tatiana set her tablet on the table. All of her accounts used the same password. "I think I've got some work to do," she said.

Many early computer attacks were malicious in nature: they were intended to erase a user's data on the computer or corrupt the hard disk drive so that the computer could not properly function. These types of attacks are similar to vandalism, where the goal is to deface or destroy.

Today, however, most attacks are not designed to *destroy* data on the computer; instead, these attacks attempt to *steal* that data and then use it for financial gain. For example, some attacks trick users into revealing personal information such as a credit card number or password in response to a fictitious e-mail that pretends to come from a reputable bank. In fact, so many credit card numbers have been stolen in this way that a criminal can now purchase a stolen credit card number online for as little as $2.00.[1] Other attacks take advantage of the fact that many users reuse the same password on multiple accounts or create short passwords that are relatively easy to break. Some attacks take advantage of the trusting relationships that often exist in social networking sites: an attacker pretends to be an "old high school friend" and convinces the victim to open a file that secretly installs software on the computer that monitors keystrokes, in order to steal passwords or credit card numbers.

These types of attacks are not strictly targeted at specific types of devices or certain kinds of software. Instead, these attacks are directed at all users of desktop computers as well as tablets, notebooks, and smartphones using the Microsoft Windows, Apple Mac OS and iOS, and Android operating systems. Because these attacks are directly aimed at the user's personal security no matter what type of device they may be using, the defenses against these attacks can apply to all devices and all users.

In this chapter, you'll examine attacks directed at users and their personal security. First, you'll explore personal security attacks that target passwords and also that take advantage of social engineering. Then, you'll look at identity theft and risks associated with using social networking. Finally, you will examine the defenses you can use to protect yourself from attacks on your personal security.

Passwords

Consider this scenario: Joshua stops at the health club in the afternoon to exercise. After he locks his car, he walks into the club and chats with Li, the clerk at the desk. Li recognizes Joshua and allows him to pass on to the locker room. Once inside, Joshua opens his locker's combination padlock with a series of numbers that he has memorized.

It is necessary to protect the contents of Joshua's car, entrance into the health club, and what is stored in his locker from a criminal. This protection can be accomplished by one of three different elements that are unique to Joshua. First, by locking the doors of his car, its contents are protected by something only Joshua *has*, namely the wireless key fob (the car will not open its doors to an "imposter" but only for the "real" Joshua who has the key fob). Next, access to the locker room is protected by what Joshua *is*. Li has to recognize Joshua's unique characteristics (his hair color, his face, his body type, his voice, etc.) before he would be allowed to enter the locker room. Finally, the contents of Joshua's locker are protected by what only Joshua *knows*, namely the lock combination (the lock will not open to an imposter but only for the real Joshua who knows the combination). Because only the real or "authentic" Joshua possesses these elements— what he has, what he is, and what he knows—they can be considered as types of *authentication*. These three types of authentication are illustrated in Figure 2-1. This authentication confirms Joshua's identity and thus protects his belongings by preventing access by an imposter.

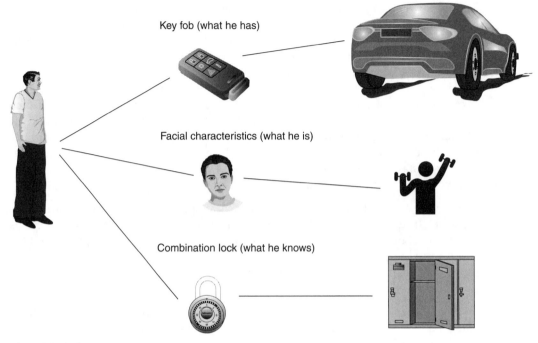

Key fob (what he has)

Facial characteristics (what he is)

Combination lock (what he knows)

Figure 2-1 Three types of authentication
© Cengage Learning 2014

When accessing a computer or a secure Web site, users are typically required to provide information that both identifies them and provides proof that they actually are that person. Each user is assigned a **username**, which is a unique name used for identification, such as *BGeller* or *Administrator*. Yet virtually anyone could type in a person's username and pretend to be that person. How can the computer or Web site be certain that the person entering that username is authentic and not an imposter?

Computers have typically relied upon authenticating users by what they—and no one else—would know. This is done by using a password. A **password** is a secret combination of letters, numbers, and/or symbols that serves to authenticate a user by what he knows. Just as Joshua is the only one who knows the padlock combination at the health club, the password that a computer user knows can authenticate him; because (ideally) nobody else knows that password, the computer can be certain that the user is authentic.

Despite the fact that passwords are the primary—and usually exclusive—means of authenticating a user for access to a computer or a Web site, passwords are no longer considered a strong defense against attackers. This is because passwords can be weak and subject to different types of attacks.

Password Weaknesses

The weakness of passwords centers on human memory. Human beings can only memorize a limited number of items. Passwords place heavy loads on human memory in two ways. First, long and complex passwords—known as **strong passwords**, which are the most effective type—can be difficult to memorize and can strain the ability to accurately recall them. Second, users today must remember multiple passwords for many different accounts. Most users have accounts for different computers at work, school, and home, as well as for accounts such as e-mail, school, social media, and online banking to name only a few. In one study, 28 percent of a group of users had over 13 passwords each,[2] while in another study, a group of 144 users had an average of 16 passwords per user.[3] Each account should have its own unique password.

This problem is often made even worse for users by security policy settings on computers that require all passwords to expire after a set period of time, such as every 60 days, when a new one must be created. And some security policies prevent a previously used password from being recycled and used again, forcing users to repeatedly memorize new passwords.

All of these factors cause many users to take "shortcuts" and create **weak passwords**, or those that compromise security. Characteristics of weak passwords include:

- *A common word used as a password (such as* tigers*)*. Attackers can use an electronic dictionary of common words to easily discover the password.

- *Short passwords (such as 12345)*. Short passwords are easier to break than long passwords.

- *Personal information in a password (such as the name of a child or pet)*. These passwords can be easy to guess or the information can be found on the user's social networking site.

- *A static password*. If a user does not change a password, an attacker who gains access to a device or account will have unlimited access for the foreseeable future.

The alarming use of weak passwords can be easily illustrated. Several attacks have stolen passwords for all users of a Web site, then posted them on the Internet for anyone to view. In one case over 32 million user passwords were stolen and posted by attackers. These passwords were later analyzed by security researchers. The analysis showed that 30 percent of users had created passwords of only five characters (the minimum length for that Web site) or six characters, while just 12 percent of the user passwords were a stronger nine characters in length. About one in every five users created a password that was one of the 5,000 most common passwords, including names, slang words, dictionary words, or trivial passwords (consecutive digits, adjacent keyboard keys, etc.). The 10 most common passwords found and their number of occurrences is listed in Table 2-1.

One security expert said, "The problem is that the average user can't and won't even try to remember complex enough passwords to prevent attacks. As bad as passwords are, users will go out of the way to make it worse. If you ask them to choose a password, they'll choose a lousy one. If you force them to choose a good one, they'll write it [down] and change it back to the password they changed it from the last month. And they'll choose the same password for multiple applications."[4]

Rank	Password	Number of Users with Password
1	123456	290,731
2	12345	79,078
3	123456789	76,790
4	Password	61,958
5	iloveyou	51,622
6	princess	35,231
7	rockyou	22,588
8	1234567	21,726
9	12345678	20,553
10	abc123	17,542

Table 2-1 Ten most common passwords
© Cengage Learning 2014

Attacks on Passwords

There are a variety of attacks that can be used to uncover a password. One attack technique that is *not* used is online guessing. Although it is possible for an attacker to enter different passwords at the login prompt in order to attempt to guess a password, this is not practical. An eight-character password that can use any of 76 characters of uppercase and lowercase letters, digits, and common symbols (known as its *character set*) would result in 1.11×10^{15} possible passwords. At two or three tries per second, it could take 5,878,324 years to guess the right password. In addition, most accounts can be set to disable all logins after a limited number of incorrect attempts (such as five), thus locking out the attacker.

Because of the limitations of online guessing, most password attacks today use offline cracking. When a password is created usually a digital representation of the password is stored on a computer or Web site (technically speaking, the process for creating this digital representation is based on a *hash algorithm,* which creates a *digest*). For example, the password *jurghbtref* could be represented and stored as *38e6b7cb3b7e66777c625 fade02736e9*. When a user enters her password to log on, the same hash algorithm is applied to what she entered and then compared with the stored version; if it matches, the user is approved. Attackers try to steal the file of the password digests and then compare them with the digests of known passwords. If a match occurs, then the password has been broken.

There are two primary offline cracking techniques. The first is a **dictionary attack**. A dictionary attack begins with the attacker creating digests of common dictionary words, and then comparing them against those in the stolen password file. This type of attack is successful because users often create passwords that are simple dictionary words. A dictionary attack is illustrated in Figure 2-2.

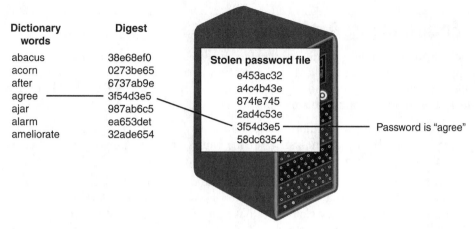

Figure 2-2 Dictionary attack
© Cengage Learning 2014

A variation of the dictionary attack slightly alters dictionary words by adding numbers to the end of the password, spelling words backward, slightly misspelling words, or including special characters such as @, $, !, or %. This is done because most passwords consist of a root (not necessarily a dictionary word but generally "pronounceable") along with an attachment, either an ending suffix (about 90 percent of the time) or a prefix (10 percent of the time). This attack first tests the password against 1,000 common passwords (such as *123456, password1*, and *letmein*). If this is not successful, it then combines these common passwords with 100 common suffixes (such as *1, 4u,* and *abc*). This results in almost 100,000 different combinations that can crack 25 percent of all passwords. Next, the program (in order) uses 5,000 common dictionary words, 10,000 names, 100,000 comprehensive dictionary words, and combinations from a phonetic pattern dictionary, varying the dictionary words between lowercase (the most common), initial uppercase (the second most common), all uppercase, and then final character as uppercase. The program also makes common substitutions with letters in the dictionary words, such as $ for *s,* @ for *a, 3* for *E,* etc. Finally it uses a variation of attachments, such as two-digit combinations, dates from 1900 to the present, three-digit combinations, single symbols *(#, $, %),* single digit plus single symbol, and two-symbol combinations.

NOTE Many users think that adding a prefix or suffix (such as *123* or *abc*) to a password makes it significantly stronger. As the preceding variation of the dictionary attack illustrates, this provides little additional security.

The second type is an automated **brute force attack,** in which every possible combination of letters, numbers, and characters is used to create "candidate" passwords that are matched with those in the stolen password file. Although slower than a dictionary attack, a brute force attack is more thorough because it tests for all possible passwords.

NOTE Given the fast speed of today's computers that use multiple processors and graphics processors, a standard desktop computer can create over *one billion* candidate passwords each second. Online computing resources can also be rented to crack passwords that can create billions of candidate passwords per second.

Social Engineering Attacks

One morning a small group of strangers walked into the corporate offices of a large shipping firm and soon walked out with access to the firm's entire computer network, which contained valuable and highly sensitive information. They were able to accomplish this feat with no technical tools or skills:

1. Before entering the building, one person of the group called the company's human resources (HR) office and asked for the names of key employees. The office willingly gave out the information without asking any questions.

2. As the group walked up to the building one of them pretended to have lost their key code to the door, so a friendly employee let them in. When they entered a secured area on the third floor, they claimed to have misplaced their identity badges, so another smiling employee opened the door for them.

3. Because these strangers knew that the chief financial officer (CFO) was out of town because of his voicemail greeting message, they walked unchallenged into his office and gathered information from his unprotected computer. They also dug through trash receptacles and retrieved useful documents. A janitor was stopped and asked for a garbage pail in which to place these documents, so they could be carried out of the building.

4. One of the group's members then called the company's help desk from the CFO's office and pretended to be the CFO (they had listened to his voice from his voicemail greeting message and knew how he spoke). The imposter CFO claimed that he desperately needed his password because he had forgotten it and was on his way to an important meeting. The help desk gave out the password, and the group left the building with complete access to the network.

This true story illustrates that technology is not always needed for attacks.[5] **Social engineering** is a means of gathering information for an attack by relying on the weaknesses of individuals. Social engineering attacks can involve psychological approaches as well as physical procedures.

Psychological Approaches

Many social engineering attacks rely on psychology, which is a mental and emotional approach rather than a physical one. At its core, social engineering relies on an attacker's clever manipulation of human nature in order to persuade the victim to provide information or take actions. These basic methods of persuasion include ingratiation (flattery or insincerity), conformity (everyone else is doing it), and friendliness. The attacker attempts to convince the victim that the attacker can be trusted.

Conformity is a group-based behavior, yet it can be used on an individual by convincing the victim that everyone else has been giving the attacker the requested information. This type of attack is successful because it is used as a way to diffuse the responsibility of the employee cooperating and alleviates the stress on the employee.

Because many of the psychological approaches involve person-to-person contact, attacks use a variety of techniques to gain trust without moving so quickly as to arouse suspicion. For example:

- An attacker will not ask for too much information at one time, but instead will gather small amounts—even from several different victims—in order to maintain the appearance of credibility.

- The request from the attacker needs to be believable. Asking a victim to go into the CFO's office to retrieve a document may raise suspicion, yet asking if the CFO is on vacation would not.

- Slight flattery or flirtation can be helpful to "soften up" the victim to gain cooperation.

- An attacker works to "push the envelope" just far enough when probing for information before the victim suspects anything unusual.

- A smile and a simple question such as "I'm confused, can you please help me?" or a "Thanks" can usually clinch the deal.

Psychological social engineering approaches often involve impersonation, phishing, and hoaxes.

Social media sites such as Facebook are popular with attackers, who create a trust relationship with a user and then gather information.

Impersonation Social engineering **impersonation** means to create a fictitious character and then play out the role of that person on a victim. For example, an attacker could impersonate a help desk technician who calls the victim, pretends that there is a problem with the network, and asks her for her user name and password to reset the account.

Common roles that are often impersonated include a repairperson, IT support, a manager, a trusted third party, or a fellow employee. Often attackers will impersonate individuals whose roles are authoritative because victims generally resist saying "no" to anyone in power.

A twist on impersonation occurs when an attacker impersonates someone in authority so that the victims asks *him* for information instead of the other way around. This is an excellent way for an attacker to gain information because a deep level of trust has already been established. However, it requires a large amount of advance preparation and research by the attacker.

Phishing One of the most common forms of social engineering is phishing. **Phishing** is sending an e-mail or displaying a Web announcement that falsely claims to be from a legitimate enterprise, in an attempt to trick the user into surrendering private information. Users are asked to respond to an e-mail or are directed to a Web site, where they are requested to update personal information, such as passwords, credit card numbers, Social Security numbers, bank account numbers, or other information. However, the Web site is actually an imposter site and is set up to steal the information the user enters. It is estimated that between 15,000 and 20,000 new phishing attacks are launched each month.[6]

The word *phishing* is a variation on the word "fishing," with the idea being that bait is thrown out knowing that, while most will ignore it, some will "bite."

Figure 2-3 illustrates an actual phishing e-mail. These messages contain the logos, color schemes, and wording used by the legitimate site so that it is difficult to determine that they are fraudulent.

PayPal

You sent a payment   Transaction ID:
                                                    5Y544235VM010428T

Dear PayPal User,
You sent a payment for $1297.20 USD to Morris Cope.
Please note that it may take a little while for this payment to appear in the Recent Activity list on your Account Overview.
View the details of this transaction online

This payment was sent using your bank account.

By using your bank account to send money, you just:

- Paid easily and securely

- Sent money faster than writing and mailing paper checks

- Paid instantly -- your purchase won't show up on bills at the end of the month.

Thanks for using your bank account!

Your monthly account statement is available anytime; just log in to your account at https://www.paypal.com/us/cgi-bin/webscr?cmd=_history. To correct any errors, please contact us through our Help Center at https://www.paypal.com/us/cgi-bin/webscr?cmd=_contact_us.

Amount: $1297.20 USD

Sent on: August 22, 2012

Payment method: Bank account

Sincerely,
PayPal

Figure 2-3 Phishing message
Source: Dr. Mark Reveals

The average phishing site only exists for 3.8 days to prevent law enforcement agencies from tracking the attackers. In that short period, a phishing attack can net over $50,000.[7]

Following are several variations on phishing attacks:

- *Pharming*. Instead of asking the user to visit a fraudulent Web site, **pharming** automatically redirects the user to the fake site. This is accomplished by attackers penetrating the servers on the Internet that direct traffic.

- *Spear phishing*. Whereas phishing involves sending millions of generic e-mail messages to users, **spear phishing** targets only specific users. The e-mails used in spear phishing are customized to the recipients, including their names and personal information, in order to make the message appear legitimate. Because the volume of the e-mail in a spear phishing attack is much lower than in a regular phishing attack, spear phishing scams may be more difficult to detect.

- *Whaling*. One type of spear phishing is **whaling**. Instead of going after the "smaller fish," whaling targets the "big fish"; namely, wealthy individuals who typically have larger sums of money in a bank account that an attacker could access. By focusing upon this smaller group, the attacker can invest more time in the attack and finely tune the message to achieve the highest likelihood of success.

- *Vishing*. Instead of using e-mail to contact the potential victim, a telephone call can be used. Known as **vishing** (*voice phishing*) an attacker calls a victim who, upon answering, hears a recorded message that pretends to be from the user's bank, stating that their credit card has experienced fraudulent activity or that their bank account has had unusual activity. The victim is instructed to call a specific phone number immediately (which has been set up by the attacker). When the victim calls, it is answered by automated instructions telling them to enter their credit card number, bank account number, Social Security number, or other information on the telephone's key pad.

NOTE Phishing is often used to validate e-mail addresses to ensure that the account exists. A phishing e-mail can display an image that has been retrieved from a Web site. When that image is requested, a unique code is used to link the image to the recipient's e-mail address, and the phisher then knows that the e-mail address is valid. That is the reason why most e-mail clients today do not automatically display images that are received in e-mails.

Hoaxes Attackers can use hoaxes as a first step in an attack. A **hoax** is a false warning, often contained in an e-mail message claiming to come from the IT department. The hoax purports that there is a "really bad virus" circulating through the Internet and that the recipient should erase specific files or change security configurations (as well as forward the message to others). However, changing configurations could allow an attacker to compromise the system. Erasing files may make the computer unstable and the victim would then call the telephone number in the hoax e-mail message for help, which is actually the phone of the attacker.

Physical Procedures

Just as some social engineering attacks rely on psychological manipulation, other attacks rely on physical acts. These attacks take advantage of user actions that can result in weak security. Two of the most common are dumpster diving and shoulder surfing.

Dumpster Diving Dumpster diving involves digging through trash receptacles to find information that can be useful in an attack. Table 2-2 lists the different items in an organization that can be retrieved—many of which appeared to be useless when disposed—and how they can be used.

Item Retrieved	Why Useful
Calendars	A calendar can reveal which employees are out of town at a particular time.
Inexpensive computer hardware, such as USB flash drives or portal hard drives	These devices are often improperly disposed of and may contain valuable information.
Memos	Seemingly unimportant memos can often provide small bits of useful information for an attacker who is building an impersonation.
Organizational charts	These identify individuals within the organization who are in positions of authority.
Phone directories	A phone directory can provide the names and telephone numbers of individuals in the organization to target or impersonate.
Policy manuals	These may reveal the true level of security within the organization.
System manuals	A system manual can tell an attacker the type of computer system that is being used so that other research can be conducted to pinpoint vulnerabilities.

Table 2-2 Dumpster diving items and their usefulness
© Cengage Learning 2014

Although dumpster diving is commonly found in attacks against organizations, individuals can likewise be victims of attacks that were made possible or facilitated by items that were improperly disposed of.

Shoulder Surfing Consider this scenario: A man walks up to a bank's automated teller machine (ATM) located on a busy downtown street to make a deposit. After inserting his ATM card the machine asks him to enter his personal identification code (PIN) number on the keypad. As he types in the four-digit number, he notices that a young woman has walked up behind him and is waiting to use the ATM. As the man navigates through the menus, the woman begins to mutter, "Come on, come on, come on. I've got to get going!" Flustered by the woman's impatience the man clicks on an incorrect menu option and then has to backtrack through several additional options. The woman sighs loudly and then says, "Are you almost finished?" The man hurriedly completes his deposit, takes his receipt and card, and quickly walks away. That evening, when he returns home, he checks his online bank account and discovers that five cash withdrawals from his account occurred at the same ATM for $200, $100, $200, $100, and $200, all within one minute of his original transaction.

This man was the victim of **shoulder surfing,** in which information entered is observed by another person. In this incident after the man completed his transaction on the ATM the message "Do you want to perform another transaction?" appeared on the screen. Because he already had his card and receipt the man just walked away. However, the question remained on the screen long enough for the woman behind him to tap the "YES" key and reenter his PIN, which she had watched him enter. This gave her the opportunity to make the withdrawals from his account.

Shoulder surfing can be performed in virtually any public location where an individual is asked to enter personal identification. This includes:

- Entering a PIN at an ATM
- Completing a purchase in a store by entering a debit card PIN at the register
- Writing down a Social Security number on a paper form
- Entering a password on a computer keyboard in a coffee shop or airport

Casually observing what is entered can be done from a distance of up to 15 feet (4.5 meters). More sophisticated techniques include using binoculars (such as in a large train or airport terminal) or using small closed-circuit television cameras that are concealed in a book or backpack.

A technique similar to shoulder surfing is often used in areas of restricted access. Organizations can invest tens of thousands of dollars to install specialized doors that only permit access to authorized users who possess a special card or who can enter a specific code. These automated access control systems are designed to restrict entry into an area. However, a weakness of these systems is that they cannot control *how many* people enter the building when access is allowed; once an authorized person opens the door then virtually any number of individuals can follow behind and also enter the building or area. This is known as **tailgating.** A tailgater waits at the end of the sidewalk until an authorized user opens the door. She then calls out to him to "Please hold the door!" as she hurries up to the door. In most cases, good etiquette usually wins out over good security practices, and the door is held open for the tailgater.

Identity Theft

Identity theft involves using someone's personal information, such as their name, Social Security number, or credit card number, to commit financial fraud. Using this information to obtain a credit card, set up a cellular telephone account, or even rent an apartment, thieves can make excessive charges in the victim's name. The victim is charged for the purchases and suffers a damaged credit history that can be the cause for being turned down for a new job or denied for loans for school, cars, and homes.

The following are some of the actions that can be undertaken by identity thieves:

- Produce counterfeit checks or debit cards and then remove all money from the bank account
- Establish phone or wireless service in the victim's name
- File for bankruptcy under the person's name to avoid eviction
- Go on spending sprees using fraudulently obtained credit and debit card account numbers to buy expensive items such as large-screen televisions that can easily be resold

- Open a bank account in the person's name and write bad checks on that account
- Open a new credit card account, using the name, date of birth, and Social Security number of the identity-theft victim. When the thief does not pay the bills, the delinquent account is reported on the victim's credit report.
- Obtain loans for expensive items such as cars and motorcycles

Table 2-3 illustrates some of the ways in which attackers can steal personal information.

Technique	Explanation
Dumpster diving	Discarded credit card statements, charge receipts, and bank statements can be retrieved for personal information.
Phishing	Attackers convince victims to enter their personal information at an imposter Web site after receiving a fictitious e-mail from a bank.
Change of address form	Using a standard change-of-address form the attackers divert all mail to their post office box so that the victim never sees any charges made.
Pretexting	An attacker who pretends to be from a legitimate research firm asks for personal information.
Stealing	Stolen wallets and purses contain personal information that can be used in identity theft.

Table 2-3 **How attackers steal personal information**
© Cengage Learning 2014

One of the areas of identity theft that is growing most rapidly involves identity thieves filing fictitious income tax returns with the U.S. Internal Revenue Service (IRS). According to the IRS, it delivered over $5 billion in refund checks to identity thieves who filed fraudulent tax returns for 2011. Although the IRS detected and stopped about 940,000 fraudulent returns for that year, claiming $6.5 billion in refunds, 1.5 million undetected false returns were processed. These were filed by thieves seeking refunds after assuming the identity of a dead person, child, or someone else who normally would not file a tax return. It is estimated that identity theft based on tax returns could increase by another $21 billion through 2017.

IRS investigators found that a single address in Lansing, Michigan, was used to file 2,137 separate tax returns, and the IRS issued over $3.3 million in refunds to that address. In another instance the IRS deposited 590 refunds totaling more than $900,000 into a single bank account.[8]

Social Networking Risks

Grouping individuals and organizations into clusters based on their likes and interests is called **social networking**. The popularity of online social networking has skyrocketed. Social networking Web sites facilitate linking individuals with common interests and function as an online community of users. A user on a social networking site can read information posted by others and share documents, photos, and videos.

It is estimated that one out of every seven human beings belongs to the popular social networking site Facebook. If Facebook were a county, it would be the third most populous country in the world. The United States has the most Facebook users, followed by Brazil, India, Indonesia, and Mexico.

Although using any Web site has risks associated with it, social networking sites can carry additional risks. These risks include:

- *Personal data can be used maliciously.* Users post personal information on their pages for others to read, such as birthdays, where they live, their plans for the upcoming weekend, and the like. However, attackers can use this information for a variety of malicious purposes. For example, knowing that a person is on vacation could allow a burglar to break into an empty home, the name of a pet could be a weak password that a user has created, or too much personal information could result in identity theft.

- *Users may be too trusting.* Attackers often join a social networking site and pretend to be part of the network of users. After several days or weeks, users begin to feel they know the attackers and may start to provide personal information or click on embedded links provided by the attacker that loads malware onto the user's computer.

- *Social networking security is lax or confusing.* Because social networking sites by design are intended to share information, these sites have often made it too easy for unauthorized users to view other people's information. To combat this many sites change their security options on a haphazard basis, making it difficult for users to keep up with the changes.

- *Accepting friends may have unforeseen consequences.* Some social networking users readily accept any "friend" request they receive, even if they are not familiar with that person. This can result in problem, since whomever is accepted as a friend may then be able to see not only all of that user's personal information but also the personal information of their friends'.

Facebook is now targeting mobile users in emerging markets, which may also create additional security concerns.

Personal Security Defenses

Despite the growing number of attacks on users' personal security, there are defenses that can be used to ward off these attacks. These defenses include using strong passwords, recognizing phishing attacks, taking steps to avoid identity theft, and securing social networking sites.

Password Defenses

The best approach to establishing strong security with passwords is to use a password management tool. If these tools are not used then techniques for creating and memorizing strong passwords must instead be implemented.

"This is impossible!" Tatiana said as she put down her pencil. At Sergei's suggestion she decided to write down the names of all of her different computer and Web accounts and then try to create a unique strong password for each one. "I have come up with a new password for my Facebook account. It's *nittfagm*." Sergei smiled. "Hey, that's really good." Tatiana said, "It's the first letter of each word of the title of a story that I wrote. Now I can memorize that one, but I can't remember passwords like that for all of my accounts. I can't even add a *1* after it to make a new password for my Twitter account and a *2* for my e-mail account, because I'll get confused if Twitter gets a *1* or a *2*. It's useless."

Sergei sat down next to her. "I know what you mean. But my instructor showed the class something that works just great, and you don't have to try to remember a lot of different passwords. You only have to know one really strong password and that's it." Tatiana frowned. "I thought you said you shouldn't reuse passwords, and now you're telling me that it's OK?" "No," said Sergei. "This is using technology instead of our memory for storing passwords." Tatiana picked up her tablet computer and said, "Show it to me."

Using Password Management Tools In addition to the characteristics listed previously regarding weak passwords (such as using a common dictionary word, creating a short password, or using personal information in a password), there are two additional characteristics of weak passwords that may be alarming to most users:

- Any password that can be *memorized* is a weak password.
- Any password that is *repeated* on multiple accounts is a weak password.

Because of the limitations of human memory and the fast processing speed of today's computers, it is not possible for the average user to memorize multiple long passwords that can resist today's attacks.

Instead of relying on human memory for passwords, security experts today recommend that technology be used to store and manage passwords. A **password management application** is a program that lets a user create and store multiple strong passwords in a single user database file that is protected by one strong master password. Users can retrieve individual passwords as needed, thus freeing them from the need to memorize multiple passwords. Yet most password management applications are much more than a password-protected list of passwords. Many of these applications also include the following features:

- *In-memory protection.* Passwords are encrypted while the application is running, so even when the operating system performs functions (like caching to disk), it will not reveal any passwords.

- *Key files.* A **key file** is a separate unique file that can be carried on a USB flash drive or other similar device. In order to open the password database, not only must the password be entered, but the key file must also be present. This prevents an attacker who obtains the database password from using it.

- *Lock to user account.* The database can be locked so that it can only be opened by the same person who created it.

- *Import and export.* The password list can be exported to various formats and new passwords can be imported.

- *Password groupings.* User passwords can be arranged as a tree, so that a group can have subgroups.

- *Random password generator.* A built-in random password generator can create strong random passwords based on different settings like the KeePass generator shown in Figure 2-4.

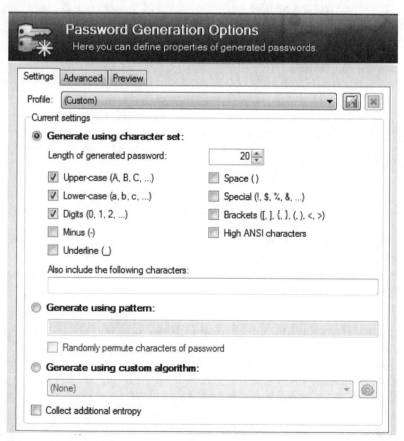

Figure 2-4 KeePass random password generator
Source: KeePass 2.19 (keepass.info)

The value of using a password management program is that unique strong passwords such as *WUuAxB2aWBndTf7MfEtm* can be easily created and used for all accounts.

Table 2-4 lists the advantages and disadvantages of different types of password management applications.

Type	Description	Advantages	Disadvantages
Installed application	Installed as a program on the local computer	Allows the user to access passwords without having to memorize them	It must be installed on each computer used and the database file must also be updated on every computer used.
Portable application	Stand-alone application carried on a USB flash drive	The user is not limited to computers that have the application preinstalled with the vault file.	User must always have flash drive present to use the application
Internet storage	Application and/or vault is stored online	Can access program and/or database from any computer	Storing passwords online may expose them to attacks.

Table 2-4 **Password management applications**
© Cengage Learning 2014

The obvious limitation to password management tools is that, if the password database file is erased, then all of the passwords are lost. It is recommended that backups of this file be made and stored in secure locations.

Another password management tool is a feature common on Web browsers that allows a user to save a password that has been entered while using the browser. However, this feature has several disadvantages. Users can only retrieve passwords on the computer on which they are stored (unless the browser information is synched with other computers). Also, the passwords may be vulnerable if another user is allowed access to their computer. In addition, applications are freely available that allow all of the passwords to be displayed without entering a master password.

Creating Strong Passwords If a password management application is not used, then strong passwords should be created for each separate account. When creating passwords the most important principle is that *length is more important than complexity*. That is, the password *thisisalongerpassword* is considered stronger than *u$^#16*. Although it is composed of several dictionary words, the length of the password makes it stronger than the shorter and more complex password.

In technical terms, increasing the length of a password increases the strength *exponentially*, while increasing the complexity will only increase it *linearly*.

The following are general recommendations regarding creating strong passwords:

- Do not use passwords that consist of dictionary words or phonetic words.
- Do not use birthdays, family member names, pet names, addresses, or any personal information.
- Do not repeat characters (*xxx*) or use sequences (*abc, 123, qwerty*).
- The password should be a minimum of 12 characters in length. For online accounts that require higher security, such as an online banking account, a minimum of 18 characters is recommended.
- Because attack programs cannot parse passwords as humans can (and see individual words), consider using a longer passphrase (*theraininspainfallsmainlyontheplain*).

One way to make passwords stronger is to use nonkeyboard characters, or special characters that do not appear on the keyboard. Although not all applications can accept these nonkeyboard characters, an increasing number can, including Microsoft operating systems and applications. These characters are created by holding down the Alt key while simultaneously typing a number on the numeric keypad (but not the numbers across the top of the keyboard). For example, Alt+0163 produces the £ symbol. A list of all the available nonkeyboard characters can be seen by clicking Start, entering charmap.exe in the search box, and then clicking on a character. The code ALT+0*xxx* will appear in the lower-right corner of the screen (if that character can be reproduced in Windows). Figure 2-5 shows a Windows character map.

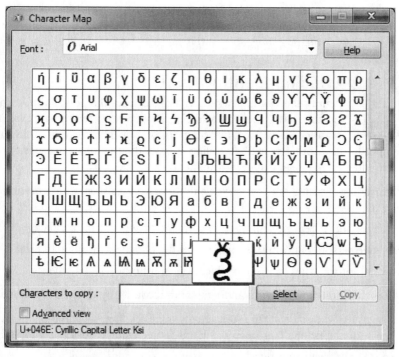

Figure 2-5 Windows character map
Source: Microsoft Windows 7

Because of the difficulty in creating and memorizing multiple strong passwords, using a password management application is highly recommended.

Recognizing Phishing Attacks

Although phishing attacks vary, they generally start with the receipt of an e-mail message that claims to come from a reputable source, such as a bank or Web site with which the user has an account. The e-mail message may contain the following:

- *Official logos*. Phishers often include the logo of the vendor and otherwise try to make the e-mail look like the vendor's Web site as a way to convince the recipient that the message is genuine. Yet the presence of logos does not mean that the e-mail is legitimate.

- *Web links*. Phishing e-mails almost always contain a link that the user is asked to click on. Often these addresses are close variations of a legitimate address, such as *www.ebay_secure.com, www.e–bay.com, or www.e-baynet.com*.

- *Urgent request*. Most phishing e-mails encourage the recipient to act immediately or else their account will be deactivated or a similar threatening action will occur shortly.

Even if you carefully scrutinize your e-mail messages, it can be difficult to recognize phishing attacks. The best approach is to consider any unexpected e-mail that claims to come from a reputable source as a phishing message.

You should never click a Web link contained in e-mail message. This is because the link that is displayed (such as *www.ebay.com) may mask the true link hidden in the message (such as www.evil.com)*.

Avoiding Identity Theft

Identity theft occurs when an attacker uses the personal information of someone else, such as a Social Security number, credit card number, or other identifying information, to impersonate that individual with the intent to commit fraud or other crimes. Avoiding identity theft involves two basic steps. The first step is to deter thieves by safeguarding information. This includes:

- Shred financial documents and paperwork that contains personal information before discarding it.
- Do not carry a Social Security number in a wallet or write it on a check.
- Do not provide personal information either over the phone or through an e-mail message.
- Keep personal information in a secure location in a home or apartment.

The second step is to monitor financial statements and accounts by doing the following:

- Be alert to signs that may indicate unusual activity in an account, such as a bill that did not arrive at the normal time or a large increase in unsolicited credit cards or account statements.
- Follow up on calls regarding purchases that were not made.
- Review financial and billing statements each month carefully as soon as they arrive.

Legislation has been passed that is designed to help U.S. users monitor their financial information. The **Fair and Accurate Credit Transactions Act (FACTA) of 2003** contains rules regarding consumer privacy. FACTA grants consumers the right to request one free credit report from each of the three national credit-reporting firms every 12 months. Because a credit report can only be ordered once per year from each of the credit agencies, security experts recommend that one report be ordered every 4 months from one of the three credit agencies. This allows the user to view a credit report each quarter without being charged for it.

To access your credit report, go to *www.AnnualCreditReport.com.*

If a consumer finds a problem on her credit report, she must first send a letter to the credit-reporting agency. Under federal law, the agency has 30 days to investigate and respond to the alleged inaccuracy and issue a corrected report. If the claim is upheld, all three credit-reporting agencies must be notified of the inaccuracies, so they can correct their files. If the investigation does not resolve the problem, a statement from the consumer can be placed in the file and in any future credit reports.

Although the credit reports are free, the law does not grant consumers free access to their credit score, which is a numerical measurement used by lenders to assess a consumer's creditworthiness. Those reports cost about $10.

Setting Social Networking Defenses

There are several defenses that can be used for social networking sites. First and foremost, users should be cautious about what information is posted on social networking sites. Posting *I'm going to Florida on Friday for two weeks* could indicate that a home or apartment will be vacant for that time, a tempting invitation for a burglar. Other information posted could later prove embarrassing. Asking questions such as *Would my boss approve?* Or *What would my mother think of this?* before posting may provide an incentive to rethink the material one more time before posting.

In several court cases individuals have been ordered by judges to turn over their social networking passwords. For example, a woman who claimed she was seriously injured in an automobile accident was told to turn over her Facebook password to the defense attorneys, who found posts and photographs that indicated she was not seriously injured, including status updates about exercising at a gym.

Second, users should be cautious regarding who can view their information. Certain types of information could prove to be embarrassing if read by certain parties, such as a prospective employer. Other information should be kept confidential. Users are urged to consider carefully who is accepted as a friend on a social network. Once a person has been accepted as a friend, that person will be able to access any personal information or photographs. Instead, it may be preferable to show "limited friends" a reduced version of a profile. This can be useful for casual acquaintances or business associates.

Finally, the available security settings in social networking sites are often updated frequently by the site with little warning. Users should pay close attention to information about new or updated security settings. Also, it is a good idea to disable options and then enable them only as necessary. Users should disable options until it becomes apparent that the options are needed, instead of making everything accessible and restricting access after it is too late.

Table 2-5 lists several Facebook features along with the associated risks.

Feature	Description	Risks
Games and applications	When your Facebook friends use games and applications, these can request information about friends like you, even if you do not use the application.	Information such as your biography, photos, and places where you check in can be exposed.
Social advertisements	A "social ad" pairs an advertisement with an action that a friend has taken, such as "liking" it.	Your Facebook actions could be associated with an ad.
Places	If you use Places, you could be included in a "People Here Now" list once you check in to a location.	Your name and Facebook profile picture appear in the list, which is visible to anyone who checks in to the same location, even if they are not a friend.
Web Search	Entering your name in a search engine like Google can display you Facebook profile, profile picture, and information you have designated as public.	Any Web user can freely access this information about you.
Photo Albums	Photos can be set to be private but that may not include photo albums.	The albums Profile Pictures, Mobile Uploads, and Wall Photos are usually visible to anyone.

Table 2-5 Facebook features and risks
© Cengage Learning 2014

Table 2-6 contains recommendations for contact information settings at Facebook.

Option	Recommended Setting	Explanation
Profile	Only my friends	Facebook networks can contain hundreds or thousands of users, and there is no control over who else joins the network to see the information.
Photos or photos tagged of you	Only my friends	Photos and videos have often proven to be embarrassing. Only post material that would be appropriate to appear with a resume or job application.
Status updates	Only my friends	Because changes to status such as "Going to Florida on January 28" can be useful information for thieves, only approved friends should have access to it.
Online status	No one	Any benefits derived by knowing who is online are outweighed by the risks.
Friends	Only my friends (minimum setting)	Giving unknown members of the community access to a list of friends may provide attackers with opportunities to uncover personal information through friends.

Table 2-6 Recommended Facebook profile settings
© Cengage Learning 2014

Facebook configuration settings change frequently and without advance warning. The settings listed here may change at any time.

Chapter Summary

- When accessing a computer or a secure Web site, users are typically required to provide information that both identifies them and provides proof that they actually are that person. Computers have typically relied upon authenticating users by what they—and no one else—would know. This is done by using a password. A password is a secret combination of letters, numbers, and/or symbols that serves to authenticate a user by what he knows. Despite the fact that passwords are the primary—and usually exclusive—means of authenticating a user for access to a computer or a Web site, passwords are no longer considered to be a strong defense against attackers.

- The weakness of passwords centers on human memory. Human beings can only memorize a limited number of items. Long and complex passwords can be difficult to memorize and can strain our ability to accurately recall them. Also, users must remember multiple passwords for many different accounts. Users often take shortcuts and create weak passwords, which compromise security. There are a variety of attacks that can be used to uncover a password. A dictionary attack begins with the attacker creating digests of common dictionary words and then comparing them to those in a stolen password file. This type of attack is successful because users often create passwords that are simple dictionary words. An automated brute force attack uses every possible combination of letters, numbers, and characters to create candidate passwords that are matched to those in the stolen password hash file. Although slower than a dictionary attack, a brute force attack is more thorough because it tests for all possible passwords.

- Social engineering is a means of gathering information for an attack by relying on the weaknesses of individuals. Social engineering impersonation means to create a fictitious character and then play out the role of that person to influence a victim. Phishing is sending an e-mail or displaying a Web announcement that falsely claims to be from a legitimate enterprise in an attempt to trick the user into surrendering private information. One of the reasons that phishing succeeds is that the e-mails and the fake Web sites appear to be legitimate. A hoax is a false warning, often contained in an e-mail message claiming to come from an IT department or other authority. Attackers can use hoaxes as a first step in an attack.

- Some social engineering attacks rely on psychological manipulation, other attacks rely on physical acts. These attacks take advantage of user actions that can result in weak security. Two of the most common are dumpster diving and shoulder surfing. Dumpster diving involves digging through trash receptacles to find information that can be useful in an attack. Shoulder surfing involves gathering information by observing another person enter the information.

- Identity theft involves using someone's personal information, such as their name, Social Security number, or credit card number to commit financial fraud. Identity theft results in the victim's being charged for the purchases as well as a damaged credit history that can be the cause for being turned down for a new job or denied for loans for school, cars, and homes.

- The popularity of online social networking has skyrocketed. Social networking Web sites link individuals with common interests and function as an online community. While using any Web site has associated risks, social networking sites carry additional risks. Personal data posted can be used maliciously. Because social networking sites by design are intended to share information, these sites have often made it too easy for unauthorized users to view other people's information. To combat this, many sites change their security options on a haphazard basis, making it difficult for users to keep up with the changes.

- The best approach to establishing strong security with passwords is to use a password management tool. A password management application is a program that lets a user create and store multiple strong passwords in a single user database file that is protected by one strong master password. Users can retrieve individual passwords as needed, thus freeing them from the need to memorize multiple passwords. Many password management applications include other tools as well. If a password management application is not used, then strong passwords should be created for each separate account. When creating passwords the most important principle is that length is more important than complexity.

- Although phishing attacks vary, they generally start with the receipt of an e-mail message that claims to come from a reputable source, such as a bank or Web site with which the user has an account. Despite scrutinizing e-mail messages, it still can be difficult to recognize phishing attacks. The best approach is to consider any unexpected e-mail that claims to come from a reputable source to be a phishing message.

- Identity theft occurs when an attacker uses the personal information of someone else, such as a Social Security number, credit card number, or other identifying information, to impersonate that individual with the intent to commit fraud or other crimes. Avoiding identity theft involves two basic steps. The first step is to deter thieves by safeguarding information. The second step is to monitor financial statements and accounts.

- There are several defenses that can be used for social networking sites. Users should be cautious about what information is posted on social networking sites. Users must also be cautious regarding who can view their information. Users should pay close attention to information about new or updated security settings. It is a good idea to disable options and then enable them only as necessary.

Key Terms

brute force attack   A password attack in which every possible combination of letters, numbers, and characters is used to match passwords in a stolen password file.

dictionary attack   A password attack that compares common dictionary words against those in a stolen password file.

dumpster diving   Digging through trash receptacles to find information that can be useful in an attack.

Fair and Accurate Credit Transactions Act (FACTA) of 2003   A U.S. law that contains rules regarding consumer privacy.

hoax   A false warning.

impersonation   Creating a fictitious character and then playing out the role of that person to influence a victim.

key file   A separate unique file used in password management applications that can be carried on a USB flash drive or other similar device.

password   A secret combination of letters, numbers, and/or symbols that serves to authenticate a user by what he or she knows.

password management application   A program that lets a user create and store multiple strong passwords in a single user database file that is protected by one strong master password.

pharming   Automatically redirecting a user to a fake Web site.

phishing   Sending an e-mail or displaying a Web announcement that falsely claims to be from a legitimate enterprise in an attempt to trick the user into surrendering private information.

shoulder surfing   Viewing information that is entered by another person.

social engineering   A means of gathering information for an attack by relying on the weaknesses of individuals.

social networking   Grouping individuals and organizations into clusters based on an affiliation.

spear phishing   A phishing attack that targets only specific users.

strong password   A long and complex password.

tailgating   Following an authorized person into a restricted area.

username   A unique name used for identification.

vishing   A phishing attack in which the attacker calls the victim on the telephone.

weak passwords   A password that can easily be broken and compromises security.

whaling   A phishing attack that targets wealthy individuals, who typically would have larger sums of money in a bank account that an attacker could access.

Review Questions

1. The process of providing proof that the user is "genuine" or authentic is known as_____.

    a. authentication

    b. registration

    c. genuinization

    d. identification

2. Each of the following is a characteristic of a weak password except:

    a. a password with fewer than two characters

    b. it is complicated

    c. personal information in a password

    d. a common dictionary word

3. Relying on deceiving someone to obtain secure information is known as_____.

    a. social engineering

    b. magic attack

    c. brute force attack

    d. sleight attack

4. The goal of a phishing attack is_____.

    a. to send a fraudulent e-mail to a user

    b. to trick a user into surrendering personal information

    c. to duplicate a legitimate service

    d. to capture keystrokes

5. Each of the following may be performed by an identity thief except:

    a. produce counterfeit checks or debit cards and then remove all money from the bank account

    b. file for bankruptcy under the person's name to avoid paying debts they have incurred or to avoid eviction

    c. open a bank account in the person's name and write bad checks on that account

    d. send malware into a bank's online accounting system

6. Each of the following is a step to deter identity theft except:

    a. carry a copy of a Social Security card in a wallet instead of the original

    b. keep personal information in a secure location

    c. shred financial documents and paperwork that contains personal information

    d. do not provide personal information either over the phone or through an e-mail message

7. Each of the following is a means of authentication except:

    a. what you have

    b. what you do

    c. What you know

    d. What you are

8. A(n) _____ is a unique name for identification.

    a. password

    b. value

    c. authentication

    d. username

9. Each of the following is a characteristic of a strong password except:

   a. it must be lengthy

   b. it must be easy to memorize

   c. it must be complex

   d. it must not be repeated on multiple accounts

10. When a user creates a password the _____ of that password is stored on the computer.

    a. symbol

    b. digest

    c. hash code

    d. co-mark

11. Which of these password attacks is the most thorough?

    a. dictionary attack

    b. brute force attack

    c. online guessing attack

    d. offline grill attack

12. Observing someone entering a keypad code from a distance is known as _____.

    a. shoulder surfing

    b. piggybacking

    c. spoofing

    d. watching

13. _____ is following an authorized person through a secure door.

    a. Tagging

    b. Tailgating

    c. Social Engineering Following (SEF)

    d. Backpacking

14. Which of the following is not an item that could be retrieved through dumpster diving that would provide useful information?

    a. calendars

    b. memos

    c. USB flash drive

    d. dictionary

15. How can an attacker use a hoax?

    a. A hoax could convince a user that malware is circulating and that he should change his security settings.

    b. By sending out a hoax, an attacker can convince a user to read his e-mail more often.

    c. A user who receives multiple hoaxes could contact his supervisor for help.

    d. Hoaxes are not used by attackers today.

16. Erin pretends to be a manager from another city and calls Nick to trick him into giving her his password. What social engineering attack has Erin performed?

    a. aliasing

    b. luring

    c. impersonation

    d. duplicity

17. _____ sends phishing messages only to wealthy individuals.

    a. Spear phishing

    b. Target phishing

    c. Microing

    d. Whaling

18. Which of the following is a social engineering technique that uses flattery on a victim?

    a. conformity

    b. friendliness

    c. fear

    d. ingratiation

19. Each of the following may be used by an attacker when performing a social engineering attack except:

    a. ask for all the information available

    b. make the request believable

    c. smile and ask simple questions

    d. flirtation

20. Each of the following could be performed in a shoulder surfing attack except:

    a. watching the victim insert her plastic card into an ATM

    b. viewing a person writing down his Social Security number on a paper form

    c. observing a person entering a password on a computer keyboard

    d. watching a person enter a PIN at a register in a store

Hands-On Projects

Project 2-1: Download and Install a Password Management Program

The drawback to using strong passwords is that they can be very difficult to remember, particularly when a unique password is used for each account that a user has. As an option there are password management programs that allow the user to store account information such as a user-name and password. These elements are then protected by a single strong password. One example of a password storage program is KeePass Password Safe, which is an open source product. In this project, you will download and install KeePass.

1. Use your Web browser to go to **keepass.info**, and then click **Downloads**.

It is not unusual for Web sites to change the location of where files are stored. If the URL above no longer functions, then open a search engine and search for "KeePass".

2. Under Professional Edition, locate the most recent portable version of KeePass, and click it to download the application. Save this file on your desktop, in a folder designated by your instructor, or on your portable USB flash drive. When the file finishes downloading, install the program. Accept the installation defaults.

Because this is the portable version of KeePass, it does not install automatically under Windows. In order to use it, you must double-click the filename **KeePass.exe**.

3. Launch KeePass to display the opening screen, as shown in Figure 2-6.
4. Click **File** and **New** to start a password database. Enter a strong master password for the database to protect all of the passwords in it. When prompted, enter the password again to confirm it.
5. Click **Edit** and **Add Entry**. You will enter information about an online account that has a password that you already use.
6. Under **Group**, select an appropriate group for this account.
7. Enter a title for this account under **Title**.
8. Under **User Name** enter the username that you use to log in to this account.
9. Erase the entries under Password and Repeat, enter the password that you use for this account and confirm it.
10. Enter the URL for this account under URL.
11. Click **OK**.

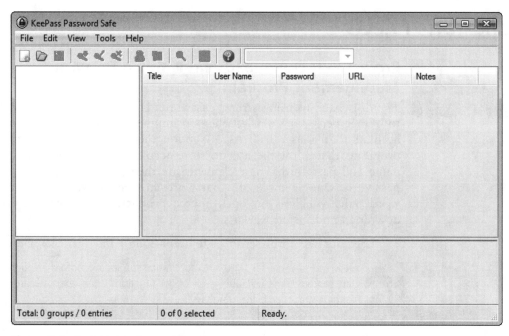

Figure 2-6 KeePass opening screen
Source: KeePass 2.19 (keepass.info)

12. Click **File** and **Save**. Enter your last name as the filename, and then click **Save**.

13. Exit KeePass.

14. If necessary, navigate to the location of KeePass, and double-click the file **KeePass.exe** to launch the application.

15. Enter your master password to open your password file.

16. If necessary, click the group to locate the account you just entered; it will be displayed in the right pane.

17. Double-click under URL to go to that Web site.

18. Click KeePass in the taskbar so that the window is now on top of your browser window.

19. Drag and drop your username from KeePass into the log in user name box for this account in your Web browser.

20. Drag and drop your password from KeePass for this account.

21. Click the button on your browser to log in to this account.

22. Because you can drag and drop your account information from KeePass, you do not have to memorize any account passwords and can instead create strong passwords for each account. Is this an application that would help users create and use strong passwords? What are the strengths of these password programs? What are the weaknesses? Would you use KeePass?

23. Close all windows.

Project 2-2: Download and Install a Browser-Based Password Management Program

One of the drawbacks to using a password management program like KeePass is that it must be launched whenever a password must be retrieved or the program must be left open, which could be a security risk. An option is to use a browser-based password management program that retrieves the passwords automatically. One example of a browser-based password storage program is LastPass, which enables you to access your passwords from any computer. In this project, you will download and install LastPass.

1. Use your Web browser to go to *lastpass.com* and click **Free – Download LastPass** (be sure *not* to select "Get LastPass Premium").

It is not unusual for Web sites to change the location of where files are stored. If the URL above no longer functions, then open a search engine and search for "LastPass".

2. Click **Watch screencast tutorials to learn the basics**.

3. Click **Basic Instructions** to open the tutorial screen, and then click the **Play** button in the middle of the screen.

4. When the Basic Instructions tutorial has completed, click your browser's **Back** button.

5. Click **Watch screencast tutorials to learn the basics** again.

6. Click **How to Automatically Fill Webpage Forms With 1 Click** to open the tutorial screen, and then click the **Play** button in the middle of the screen.

7. When the tutorial has completed, click your browser's **Back** button.

8. Click the **Download *xx*bit** button (where *xx* is either 32 or 64 bit, depending upon your computer) to download LastPass.

9. Click **Save** to save the downloaded program.

10. After the program has downloaded, click **Run** and follow the instructions for the default installation.

11. Under Step 2, be sure that **I do not have a LastPass account, create one for me** is selected. Click **Next**.

12. Enter your e-mail address and create a password. Be sure to remember this information. Enter a **Password Reminder**.

13. Be sure the three check boxes are selected, and then click **Next**.

14. Enter your password again and click **Save**.

15. Be sure that **Yes, let me choose which items I want imported into LastPass** is selected. Click **Next**.

16. If LastPass finds any passwords stored in your Web browser, you can import them. Click **Next** when finished.

17. In Step 4, click **No, do not remove any insecure items**. Click **Next**.

18. Click **Done**.

19. When asked **Would you like to view a short video tutorial on how to use LastPass?** click **No**.

20. Click **OK**.

21. Close all windows.

Project 2-3: Using a Browser-Based Password Management Program

In this project, you will use the LastPass program installed in the previous project.

1. Launch your Web browser.

2. Notice that you now have a LastPass button at the top of the screen. Click **LastPass**.

3. Enter your Master Password and then click **Login**.

4. Point your Web browser to a Web site you frequently use that requires you to enter your username and password.

5. Enter your user name and password. Notice that LastPass now asks **Should LastPass remember this password?** Click **Save Site**.

6. When the Add LastPass Site window opens, enter **Test** for the group and click **Save Site**.

7. Log out of the Web site.

8. Point your Web browser again to that site. Notice that this time your username and password are already entered for you. Log on to this site.

9. Log out of the Web site.

10. Now log in to two other Web sites and record their passwords in LastPass.

11. Close the Web browser.

12. Reopen the Web browser and click the **LastPass** icon on the toolbar. Notice that you are still logged in.

13. Revisit the two Web sites in Step 10 for which you recorded your LastPass information. What happens when you go to these sites?

 Your LastPass passwords can be retrieved from any other computer's Web browser that has LastPass installed; you are not restricted to only this computer.

14. Because your login information automatically appears in LastPass, you do not have to memorize any account passwords and can instead create strong passwords for each account. Is this an application that would help users create and use strong passwords? What are the strengths of browser-based password program? What are the weaknesses? How does LastPass compare to KeePass? Would you use LastPass?

15. Close all windows.

Project 2-4: Download and Install a Password Management Browser Extension

Another option to password management is browser extensions that generate passwords. Instead of storing user-created passwords, these extensions transparently combine multiple elements (such as the username, master password, and site's domain name) into a single site-specific password. The user begins by entering their username and master password, and then the extension generates their site-specific password. The remote site only sees a domain-specific hash instead of the master password itself.

One example is SuperGenPass. SuperGenPass does not store passwords or require users to memorize multiple unique passwords. Instead, the user enters a single master password to begin the process. SuperGenPass then takes the master password along with the domain name of the Web site that asks for the password as the "seed" values and creates a unique password. The user does not need to remember this site-specific password; instead, whenever the Web site requests the password, the user only enters the master password and the site-specific password is automatically generated. In this project you install and use SuperGenPass.

1. Launch the Web browser Microsoft Internet Explorer (IE).

SuperGenPass also supports other browsers. The instructions in this project illustrate how to use it for IE.

2. Use your Web browser to go to *supergenpass.com*.

It is not unusual for Web sites to change the location of where files are stored. If the URL above no longer functions, then open a search engine and search for "supergenpass".

3. Scroll down to Start Using SuperGenPass v2.01.

4. Locate the version of SuperGenPass for Microsoft's Internet Explorer.

5. Right-click on the link and click **Add to favorites.**

6. Click **Add.**

7. Think of a 12-character master password and memorize it.

8. Now create an account that requires a password. Go to **gmx.com.**

9. Click **Sign Up Now.**

10. Enter the requested information under the **Personal Information** section.

11. Enter the e-mail address that you want to have under the **Check Availability** section. Click **Check Availability** to be sure that this address is available. Select the e-mail address that you want to have.

12. Do not enter a user-created password at this point. Instead, click on the favorites "star" in the upper-right corner.

13. If necessary, click on the **Favorites** tab. Scroll down to the SuperGenPass bookmark and click on it.

14. The SuperGenPass dialog box opens. Enter your 12-character master password created in Step 7.

15. Click **Submit**. Note that the password is automatically entered into the password fields.

16. Because GMX requires a special character in passwords, enter @ at the end of each password.

17. Enter the remaining personal information on the form.

18. Click **I Accept. Create My Account.**

19. Go to your GMX e-mail account.

20. If necessary, click the **Close** button. Click **Logout** to exit your GMX e-mail account.

21. Now access your GMX account with SuperGenPass entering your password. Go to *gmx.com*.

22. Enter your e-mail address in the Email Address box.

23. Click on the favorites "star" in the upper-right corner.

24. Scroll down to the SuperGenPass bookmark, and click on it.

25. The SuperGenPass dialog box opens. Enter your 12-character master password created in Step 7.

26. Click **Submit**.

27. Enter your SuperGenPass master password in the Password field, and then click the SuperGenPass bookmark.

28. Click **Login**.

29. Note that you have entered the Web site without the need to memorize a unique password for each site.

30. Click **Logout** to exit your GMX e-mail account.

31. How would you rate SuperGenPass compared to KeePass? How does it compare to LastPass? Which of these do you consider the most convenient to use?

32. Close all windows.

Project 2-5: Search the Web for Personal Information

Where is personal information about you stored on the Internet? Most users are surprised to discover the large amount of information about themselves that is available on the Web. This information is available to virtually anyone. In this project you will download an application to search the Web for personal information.

1. Open your Web browser and enter the URL **www.stachliu.com/resources/tools/google-hacking-diggity-project/attack-tools/**

The location of content on the Internet such as this program may change without warning. If you are no longer able to access the program through the above URL, then use a search engine to search for "Google Hacking Diggity Attack Tools".

2. Scroll down to **Downloads**.

3. Click the latest version of **SearchDiggity** to start the download.

4. Double-click to open the downloaded file.

5. Double-click **Setup**.

6. Accept all of the default settings to install the program.

It may take several minutes to download and install all of the program components. If necessary, reboot the computer when prompted.

7. Launch the SearchDiggity program.

8. Click the **NotInMyBackyard** tab.

9. Click the **Targets** button.

10. Under **Methods** check the **Quotes** box.

11. In the left pane under **Locations** select one location to scan.

Multiple locations can be selected but it will increase the search time.

12. Under **Extensions** check the box **Database**.

13. Under **Keywords** select **Places of Birth**.

14. In the text box next to the **Add** button in the upper right pane, enter your name.

SearchDiggity can also accept other types of information to search for, including e-mail address, domain name, and Social Security number.

15. Click **Add**.

16. Click **SCAN** to start searching for the information.

17. The results of the scan will appear in the **Output** box at the bottom of the screen, and the entire scan may take several minutes to complete.

18. Were you surprised at the information it found about you?

19. Change the settings and create a different SearchDiggity scan.

20. Close all windows.

Case Projects

CASE PROJECTS

Case Project 2-1: Phishing Test

Detecting phishing e-mails can often be difficult. Point your Web browser to *survey.mailfrontier.com/survey/quiztest.cgi*, and then click on *The MailFrontier Phishing IQ Test v2.0.* Click on each hyperlink to display an e-mail message or Web site, and then decide whether or not it is phishing. When you are finished your score will be displayed along with an explanation regarding why the example is or is not phishing. Then, click on *The MailFrontier Phishing IQ Test* and take another phishing test. Did what you learn on the first test help? Did your score on this test improve? Write a one-paragraph summary on what you learned about phishing in this test.

Case Project 2-2: Testing Password Strength

How strong are your passwords? There are various online tools that can provide information on password strength, but not all feedback is the same. First, assign the numbers 1 through 3 to three of the passwords you are currently using, and write down the number (not the password) on a piece of paper. Then, enter those passwords into these three online password testing services:

- How Secure Is My Password (*howsecureismypassword.net/*)
- Check Your Password (*www.microsoft.com/security/pc-security/ password-checker.aspx)*
- The Password Meter (*www.passwordmeter.com/*)

Record next to each number the strength of that password as indicated by these three online tools. Then, use each online password tester to modify the password by adding more random numbers or letters to increase its strength. How secure are your passwords? Would any of these tools encourage someone to create a stronger password? Which provided the best information? Create a one-paragraph summary of your work

Case Project 2-3: Password Management Applications

Research at least four password management applications, one of which is a stand-alone application and another of which is a browser-based application. Create a table that lists and compares their features. Which would you recommend? Why? Create a report on your findings.

Case Project 2-4: Facebook Security Manual

Use the Internet to research security settings for Facebook. Then, create a one-page paper that lists your recommendations for different Facebook security settings. Share this with at least two other Facebook users. What was their response? Would they use these security settings? Why or why not?

Case Project 2-5: Information Security Community Site Activity

The Information Security Community Site is a Course Technology/Cengage Learning information security course enrichment site. It contains a wide variety of tools, information, discussion boards, and other features to assist learners. Go to *community.cengage.com/infosec.* Click **Login** at the top of the page and enter the sign-in name and password credentials that you created in Chapter 1. Visit the Discussions page by going to the Students tab and selecting the **Discussion Boards** link from the drop-down menu, where you can read the following case study.

Take the challenge to convince three of your friends that they must strengthen their passwords. Create a script of what you will say to them and how you will attempt to convince them of the seriousness of this problem, the dangers of weak passwords, and what the practical solutions are. Then, approach each of them individually and see if you can be successful. Make a record of their responses and reactions to stronger passwords.

Record what occurred on the Community Site discussion board. What did you learn from this? How hard or easy is it to challenge users to create strong passwords? What arguments did you hear against it? What helped convince your friends to create stronger passwords?

Case Project 2-6: North Ridge Computer Consultants

North Ridge Computer Consultants (NRCC) is a local information technology company that specializes in security. In order to encourage students to enter the field of information security, NRCC often hires student interns to assist them with projects.

Street and Gore is a regional home center retailer. After several recent successful attacks it was determined that attackers were able to breach security because users provided their passwords in response to phishing attacks. Working with Street and Gore, NRCC has determined that their users are confused regarding phishing attacks.

NRCC has hired you to create a presentation about phishing. The presentation should cover what phishing is, how it used, and what users should do to protect themselves and the company. Create a PowerPoint presentation of at least eight slides that covers this information. Because the audience does not have a strong technical background, your presentation should be general in its tone.

References

1. "Underground Activity Index." *Cloudeyez.* Accessed Aug. 2, 2012. *<https://www.cloudeyez.com/intel>.*

2. Vu, K.-P., Proctor, R., Bhargav-Spantzel, A., Tai, B.-L., Cook, J., and Schultz, E., "Improving password security and memorability to protect personal and organizational information," *International Journal of Human-Computer Studies* (65), 744–757.

3. Sasse, M., and Brostoff, S. W., "Transforming the 'weakest link': A human/computer interaction approach to usable and effective security," *BT Technology Journal*, 19 (3), 122–131.

4. Schneier, Bruce, *Secrets and lies: Digital security in a networked world*, New York: Wiley Computer Publishing, 2004.

5. Granger, Sarah, "Social Engineering Fundamentals, Part 1: Hacker Tactics," *Symantec*, Dec. 18, 2001, accessed Mar. 3, 2011. *<http://www.symantec.com/connect/articles/social-engineering-fundamentals-part-i-hacker-tactics>*.

6. "RSA Online Fraud Report," Jul. 2010, accessed Mar. 3, 2011, *<http://www.rsa.com/solutions/consumer_authentication/intelreport/11047_Online_Fraud_report_0710.pdf>*.

7. Danchev, Dancho, "Average Online Time for Phishing Sites," *Dancho Danchev's Blog - Mind Streams of Information Security Knowledge,* Jul. 31, 2007, accessed Mar. 3, 2011. *<http://ddanchev.blogspot.com/2007/07/average-online-time-for-phishing-sites.html>*.

8. "IRS missing billions in ID theft." *Chron.com.* Accessed Aug. 4, 2012. *<http://www.chron.com/business/article/IRS-missing-billions-in-ID-theft-3757389.php>*.

Computer Security

After completing this chapter you should be able to do the following:

- List and describe the different types of attacks on computers
- Explain how to manage patches
- Describe how to install and use antivirus software
- Explain User Account Control
- Describe how to recover from an attack

"Hi Uncle Greg. Look at what I got for a graduation present! A new computer!" Greg smiled at as niece as he said, "Yes, your parents told me they were buying it. That's great."

Abby sat down on the couch. "We're having a big argument here about it. But I knew that you'd have the right answer since you're a computer genius." Greg worked as a security administrator in information technology (IT) for a large corporation. "I'm certainly no genius, but I'll try to help. What's the argument about?"

"It's all about antivirus software." Abby went on to explain that her new computer came with the software already installed. However, her older brother and mother said she did not need to run antivirus software, while her father said that she should. "What's the reason they're giving for not running it?" Greg asked.

"Mom says that it slows the computer down too much," Abby replied. Greg set his coffee cup on the table. "I would say that 10 to 15 years ago that may have been the case, but it's not really true today." "Why not?" asked Abby. Greg replied, "Today computers run much faster than they used to. Your computer has a processor that runs multiple 'cores' so it's very unlikely that antivirus software would slow the computer down so much that you'd notice it at all." Abby grinned. "OK. Well, my brother says that there are so many viruses out there that that antivirus software can't catch all of them, so why waste your time." Greg smiled as he said, "Brian is telling you that? Tell him his uncle says he should know better! It's true that with so many new viruses it's hard for antivirus software to keep up. But that doesn't mean you shouldn't have it. That would be like saying I'm not going to wear my seat belt while driving just because somebody had their seat belt on but still got hurt in an accident. You want to have the best protection that you can, even if it's not completely perfect."

"Thank you," said Abby. "I can't wait to tell my brother he's wrong—again! So this antivirus software is all that I need, right?"

Greg leaned forward as he said, "No, it's not. Antivirus software can help defend against some types of attacks. But it's not the silver bullet." Abby looked puzzled. "What do you mean?" "Well," said Greg, "There are other types of attacks out there that antivirus software won't stop."

Abby picked up her pen. "What are they?"

Protecting your personal computer—be it a desktop, laptop, or tablet—is a challenge, even for the most advanced computer users. This is because many different types of attacks can be launched against a personal computer today, and attackers are constantly modifying these attacks as well as creating new ones on a regular basis.

Although virtually every computer user wishes for a single defensive program or one configuration setting that would fully protect their equipment, none exists. Just as a house must be protected against different types of threats—burglary, arson, vandalism, hurricanes, mold, and termites—so too must a computer be protected from a variety of attacks. And just as protecting against termites is much different than protecting against a hurricane, there are several different defenses that must be in place for a computer to remain safe.

In this chapter, you will learn about computer security. You will start by looking at the types of computer attacks that occur today. Next, you will find out what defenses must be in place to keep desktop information secure. Because it's not possible to guarantee that defenses will be successful, the chapter concludes by looking at how to recover from an attack.

Attacks Using Malware

Malware is software that enters a computer system without the user's knowledge or consent and then performs an unwanted—and usually harmful—action. Malware is a general term that refers to a wide variety of damaging or annoying software programs. One way to classify malware is by its primary objective. Some malware has the primary goal of rapidly spreading its infection, while other malware has the goal of concealing its purpose. Another category of malware has the goal of making a profit for its creators.

There is much debate on how to classify the different types of malware. It should be noted that the three categories used here—spreading, concealing, and profiting—are not mutually exclusive. That is, spreading malware also tries to conceal itself, yet in comparison to other types of malware its main goal is to replicate itself.

Malware That Spreads

The two types of malware that have the primary objective of spreading are viruses and worms. These are also some of the earliest types of malware to have an impact on personal computer systems.

Virus A *biological virus* is an agent that reproduces inside a cell. When a cell is infected by a virus, the virus takes over the operation of that cell, converting it into a virtual factory to make more copies of it. The cell is forced to produce thousands of identical copies of the original virus very rapidly. Biologists often say that viruses exist only to make more viruses.

The polio virus can make over *one million* copies of itself inside one single infected human cell.

A **computer virus (virus)** is malicious computer code that, like its biological counterpart, reproduces itself on a single computer. A virus first inserts itself into a computer file (which can be either a data file or program). This can be done in several ways. For example, in an *appender infection*, the virus first attaches or "appends" itself to the end of a file. It then changes the beginning of the original file with a "jump" instruction pointing to the virus code. When the program is launched, the jump instruction redirects control to the virus. An appender infection is illustrated in Figure 3-1. A more sophisticated *Swiss cheese infection* injects portions of the code throughout the program's executable code instead of only at the end of the file (any overwritten original code is transferred and stored inside the virus code for proper execution of the host program after the infection). Figure 3-2 illustrates a Swiss cheese infection.

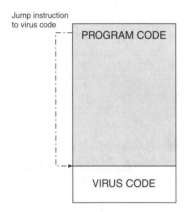

Figure 3-1 Appender infection
© Cengage Learning 2014

Figure 3-2 Swiss cheese infection
© Cengage Learning 2014

There are over 20 known methods that viruses use to infect a file. These vary in the level of sophistication and all are designed to avoid detection.

Each time the infected program is launched or the file is opened, either by the user or the computer's operating system, the virus performs two actions. First, it tries to reproduce itself by inserting its code into another file on the same computer. Second, it unloads a malicious payload and performs an action. Viruses have performed the following actions:

- Caused a computer to crash repeatedly
- Displayed an annoying message
- Erased files from a hard drive
- Made multiple copies of itself and consumed all of the free space in a hard drive
- Turned off the computer's security settings
- Reformatted the hard disk drive

Sometimes a virus will remain dormant for a period of time before unleashing its payload.

A virus can only replicate itself on the host computer on which it is located; it cannot automatically spread to another computer. Instead, it must typically rely on the actions of users to spread to other computers. Because viruses are attached to files, viruses are spread by a user transferring those files to other devices. For example, a user may send an infected file as an e-mail attachment or copy it to a universal serial bus (USB) flash drive and give the drive to another user. Once the virus reaches the other computer it begins to infect it. This means that a virus must have two "carriers": a file to which it attaches and a human being to transport it to other computers.

NOTE One of the first viruses found on a microcomputer was written for the Apple-II in 1982. Rich Skrenta, a ninth-grade student in Pittsburgh, wrote "Elk Cloner," which displayed his poem on the screen after every 50th use of the infected floppy disk. (Unfortunately, the program found its way onto the computer used by Skrenta's math teacher.)[1] In 1984, the mathematician Dr. Frederick Cohen introduced the term *virus* based on a recommendation from his advisor, who came up with the name from reading science fiction novels.

Unlike other malware, a virus is heavily dependent upon the user for its survival. First, the user must launch the program or open a file in order for the virus to begin replicating and unloading its payload. Second, the user must transmit the infected files or programs from one computer to another.

NOTE A molecular biologist noted several additional similarities between biological and computer viruses: both must enter their host passively (by relying on the action of an outside agent), both must be on the correct host (a horse virus cannot make a human sick, just as an Apple Mac virus cannot infect a Microsoft Windows computer), both can only replicate when inside the host, both may remain dormant for a period of time, and both types of viruses replicate at the expense of the host.

There are several types of computer viruses. A **program virus** infects program executable files. When the program is launched by double-clicking on its icon the virus is activated. A **macro virus** is written in a script known as a macro. A **macro** is a series of instructions that can be grouped together as a single command and are often used to automate a complex set of tasks or a repeated series of tasks. Macros can be written by using a macro language, such as Visual Basic for Applications (VBA), and are stored within the user document (such as in an Excel .xlsx worksheet). Once the user document is opened, the macro virus instructions execute and infect the computer.

NOTE Because of the risk of macro viruses, users should be cautious of opening any e-mail attachment because doing so could automatically launch a macro virus.

Worm The second type of malware that spreads is a worm. A **worm** is a malicious program designed to take advantage of vulnerability in an application or an operating system in order to enter a computer. Once the worm has exploited the vulnerability on one system, it immediately searches for another computer that has the same vulnerability. A worm uses a network to send copies of itself to other devices also connected to the network.

Some early worms were benign and designed simply to spread quickly and not corrupt the systems they infected. These worms only slowed down the network through which they were transmitted by replicating so quickly that they consumed all network resources. Newer worms can leave behind a payload on the systems they infect and cause harm, much like a virus. Actions that worms have performed include deleting files or allowing the computer to be remotely controlled by an attacker.

One of the first wide-scale worms occurred in 1988. This worm exploited a misconfiguration in a program that allowed commands e-mailed to a remote system to be executed on that system, and it also carried a payload that contained a program that attempted to determine user passwords. Almost 6,000 computers, or 10 percent of the devices connected to the Internet at that time, were affected. The worm was attributed to Robert T. Morris, Jr., who was later convicted of federal crimes in connection with this incident.

Although often confused with viruses, worms are significantly different. Table 3-1 lists the differences between viruses and worms.

Action	Virus	Worm
How does it spread to other computers?	Because viruses are attached to files, they are spread by a user transferring those programs to other devices.	Worms use a network to travel from one computer to another.
How does it infect?	Viruses insert their code into a file.	Worms exploit vulnerabilities in an application or operating system.
Does there need to be user action?	Yes	No
Can it be remote controlled?	No	Yes

Table 3-1 Difference between viruses and worms
© Cengage Learning 2014

Although viruses and worms are said to be self-replicating, where they replicate differs. A virus self-replicates *on* the local computer only. A worm self-replicates *between* computers (from one computer to another). This means that, if a virus infects Computer A, there will be multiple files on Computer A that are infected, but Computers B, C, and D are not affected. If a worm infects Computer A, there will be a single infection on it, but Computers B, C, and D may also be infected.

Malware That Conceals

Several types of malware have the primary objective of hiding their presence from the user, as opposed to rapidly spreading a virus or worm. Concealing malware includes Trojans, rootkits, backdoors, and arbitrary code execution.

Trojan According to ancient legend, the Greeks won the Trojan War by hiding soldiers in a large hollow wooden horse that was presented as a gift to the city of Troy. Once the horse was wheeled into the fortified city, the soldiers crept out of the horse during the night and attacked the unsuspecting defenders.

A computer **Trojan** is an executable program that contains hidden malware code. It typically is advertised as performing one activity but actually does something else (or it may perform both the advertised and malicious activities). Unlike a virus, which infects a system without the user's knowledge or consent, a Trojan program may be installed on the computer system with the user's approval; what the Trojan conceals is its malicious payload. For example, a user may download what is advertised as a free calendar program, yet when it is launched, in addition to installing a calendar, it also scans the computer for credit card numbers and passwords, connects through the network to a remote system, and then transmits that information to the attacker.

Some Trojans even try to distract the user to disguise the installation of malware. One Trojan opens a document that contains offensive political statements in order to divert the user's attention away from the computer's installation of the malware.

Trojans typically do not replicate themselves to the same computer (like a virus) or to another computer (like a worm). Whereas at one time viruses were the most active type of malware, today Trojans have become the most active type of malware.

Rootkit A **rootkit** is a set of software tools used by an attacker to hide the actions or presence of other types of malicious software, such as Trojans, viruses, or worms. Rootkits do this by hiding or removing traces of log-in records, log entries, and related processes. They also change the operating system to force it to ignore any malicious activity.

Originally the term *rootkit* referred to a set of modified and recompiled tools for the UNIX operating system. A root is the highest level of privileges available in UNIX, so a *rootkit* described programs that an attacker used to gain root privileges and to hide the malicious software.

One approach used by rootkits is to alter or replace operating system files with modified versions that are specifically designed to ignore malicious activity. For example, on a computer the anti-malware software may be instructed to scan all files in a specific directory. In order to do this, the software will ask for and receive a list of those files from the operating system. A rootkit, however, will change the operating system's ability to retrieve a list of files with its own modified instructions. These instructions ignore specific malicious files. The anti-malware software assumes that the computer will accurately provide it with a list of all files; it does not know that the computer is only displaying files that the rootkit has approved.

The fundamental problem with a rootkit is that users can no longer trust their computer; a rootkit may actually be in charge and hide what is occurring on the computer. The user and the operating system do not know that it is being compromised and is carrying out what it thinks are valid commands.

Backdoor A **backdoor** is software code that gives access to a program or service that circumvents normal security protections. Creating a legitimate backdoor is a common practice by a software developer, who may need to access a program or device on a regular basis, yet does not want to be hindered by continual requests for passwords or other security approvals. The intent is for the backdoor to be removed once the application is finalized. However, in some instances backdoors have been left installed, and attackers have used them to bypass security.

More commonly malware from attackers can install backdoors on a computer. This allows the attacker to return at a later time and bypass security settings.

Keylogger A **keylogger** silently captures and stores each keystroke that a user types on the computer's keyboard. This information can be later retrieved by the attacker or secretly transmitted to a remote location. The attacker then searches for any useful information in the captured text such as passwords, credit card numbers, or personal information.

A keylogger can be a small hardware device or a software program. As a hardware device, the keylogger is inserted between the computer keyboard and USB port, as shown in Figure 3-3. Because the device resembles an ordinary keyboard plug and because the computer keyboard port is often on the back of the computer, a hardware keylogger is often undetected. The device collects each keystroke and the attacker who installed the keylogger returns at a later time and physically removes the device in order to access the information it has gathered.

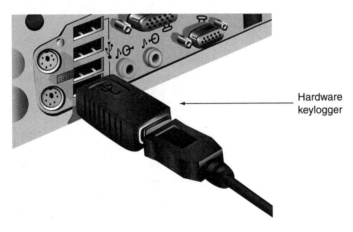

Hardware
keylogger

Figure 3-3 Hardware keylogger
© Cengage Learning 2014

A hardware keylogger with a 2-gigabyte (GB) capacity can capture over 2 billion keystrokes, which is the equivalent of over 1 million pages of text.

Software keyloggers are programs installed on the computer that silently capture sensitive information, as shown in Figure 3-4. Software keylogger programs hide themselves so that they cannot be detected by the user. An advantage of software keyloggers is that they do not require physical access to the user's computer as with a hardware keylogger. The software, often installed as a Trojan or by a virus, can routinely send captured information back to the attacker through the Internet.

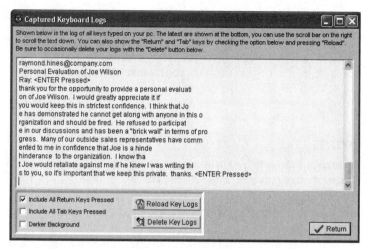

Figure 3-4 Information captured by a software keylogger

Source: Keyboard Collector

Some software keyloggers go far beyond just capturing a user's keystrokes. These programs can also make screen captures of everything that is on the user's screen every 30–60 seconds and even turn on the computer's Web camera to record images of the user!

Arbitrary Code Execution Consider a teacher who is manually grading a lengthy examination in her office by marking incorrect answers with a red pen. Because she is frequently interrupted from her grading by students, the teacher places a ruler on the test paper she is currently grading that indicates her "return point" where she should resume. Suppose that two devious students enter her office as she is grading. While one student distracts her attention, the second student silently slides the ruler down from question 4 to question 20, the last question on the test. When the teacher returns to her grading she would resume at the wrong "return point" and not look at any answers between questions 4 and 20.

This is similar to how an attacker attempts to compromise a computer. A storage area ("buffer") on the computer typically contains the memory location of the software program that was being executed when another function interrupted the process; that is, the storage buffer contains the "return address" where the computer's processor should resume once the new process has finished. By "overflowing" his own content into the buffer an attacker could wipe out the valid "return address" and substitute his own "return address." This new address would point to another area in the computer's memory area that contains his malware code, which the computer would then execute. This is called a **buffer overflow** attack.

Buffer overflow attacks are often the means by which an attacker will perform an **arbitrary code execution** (also called a **remote code execution**, or **RCE**) attack. As its name implies, an arbitrary code execution attack allows an attacker to gain control of the victim's computer to execute the attacker's commands, turning it into his own remote computer. Once under the attacker's control, the computer could perform virtually any command from the attacker, from accessing the computer's files to displaying objectionable content on the screen to erasing the entire contents of the hard drive.

In one arbitrary code execution attack, a user's computer can become infected if the user just *opens* a specially crafted file.

Malware That Profits

A third category of malware is that which is primarily intended to bring profit to the attackers. This includes botnets, spyware, adware, and scareware.

Botnet Whereas an attacker could use an arbitrary code execution attack as a "one time" attack to steal files or erase a computer's hard drive, often an attacker will take control of the computer so that it can follow the attacker's commands into the foreseeable future. In this case the infected "robot" (*bot*) computer is known as a **zombie**. When hundreds, thousands, or even hundreds of thousands of zombie computers are gathered into a logical computer network under the control of an attacker, this creates a **botnet**. Table 3-2 lists some of the attacks that can be generated through botnets.

Type of Attack	Description
Spamming	A botnet consisting of thousands of zombies enables an attacker to send massive amounts of spam. Some botnets can also harvest e-mail addresses.
Spreading malware	Botnets can be used to spread malware and create new zombies and botnets. Zombies have the ability to download and execute a file sent by the attacker.
Manipulating online polls	Because each zombie has a unique Internet Protocol (IP) address, each "vote" by a zombie will have the same credibility as a vote cast by a real person. Online games can be manipulated in a similar way.
Denying services	Botnets can flood a Web server with thousands of requests and overwhelm it to the point that it cannot respond to legitimate requests.

Table 3-2   Uses of botnets
© Cengage Learning 2014

Because of the multitasking capabilities of modern computers, a computer can act as a zombie while at the same time carrying out the tasks of its regular user. The user is completely unaware that his or her computer is being used for malicious activities.

Botnets are under the control of the attacker, known as a **bot herder**. After infecting a computer to turn it into a zombie, bot herders secretly issue commands to the zombie, known as *command and control (C&C)*. Today the C&C mechanism primarily uses the Hypertext Transfer Protocol (HTTP), which is the standard protocol for Internet usage. Using HTTP, botnet traffic may be more difficult to detect and block. A bot herder can make his zombies connect to a Web site that the bot herder operates and receive instructions for the next attack.

Some botnets even use blogs or social networking accounts for C&C. One bot herder sent specially coded attack commands through posts on the Twitter social networking service.

In many ways a botnet is the ideal base of operations for attackers:

- Zombies are designed to operate in the background, often without any visible evidence of their existence.

- Botnets provide a means for covering the tracks of the botnet herder. If any action is traced back, it ends at the hijacked computer of an innocent user.

- By keeping a low profile, botnets are sometimes able to remain active and operational for years.

- The growth of always-on Internet services, such as residential broadband, ensures that a large percentage of zombies in a botnet are accessible at any given time.

The number of botnets is staggering. One botnet controlled by a European bot herder contained 1.5 million zombies, and botnets of 100,000 zombies are not uncommon.[2] According to one security vendor one out of every three personal computers is infected with botnet malware, and 22 percent of the 1 billion computers worldwide connected to the Internet are actively under control of a bot herder.[3]

Botnets are widely recognized as the primary source of sending spam e-mail. The 10 largest botnets are responsible for generating 80 percent of all spam, or 135 billion spam messages each day.[4]

Spyware Spyware is a general term used to describe software that *spies* on users by gathering information without consent, thus violating their privacy. The Anti-Spyware Coalition defines spyware as tracking software that is deployed without adequate notice, consent, or control by the user.[5] This software is implemented in ways that impair users' control over:

- The use of system resources, including what programs are installed on their computers

- The collection, use, and distribution of personal or otherwise sensitive information

- Material changes that affect the user experience, privacy, or system security

Spyware usually performs one of the following functions on a user's computer: advertising, collecting personal information, or changing computer configurations. Table 3-3 lists different technologies used by spyware.

In addition to violating a user's privacy, spyware can also have negative effects on the computer itself:

- *Slow computer performance.* Spyware can increase the time to boot a computer or surf the Internet.

- *Create system instability.* Spyware can cause a computer to freeze frequently or even reboot.

Technology	Description	Impact
Automatic download software	Used to download and install software without the user's interaction	Can be used to install unauthorized applications
Passive tracking technologies	Used to gather information about user activities without installing any software	Can collect private information such as Web sites a user has visited
System modifying software	Modifies or changes user configurations, such as the Web browser home page or search page, default media player, or lower-level system functions	Changes configurations to settings that the user did not approve
Tracking software	Used to monitor user behavior or gather information about the user, sometimes, including personally identifiable or other sensitive information	Can collect personal information that can be shared widely or stolen, resulting in fraud or identity theft

Table 3-3 Technologies used by spyware
© Cengage Learning 2014

- *Add browser toolbars or menus*. Spyware may install new Web browser menus or toolbars.

- *Add shortcuts*. New shortcuts on the desktop or in the system tray may indicate the presence of spyware.

- *Hijack a home page*. An unauthorized change in the default home page on a Web browser can be caused by spyware.

- *Increase pop-ups*. Pop-up advertisements that suddenly appear are usually the result of spyware.

Harmful spyware is not always easy to identify. This is because not all software that performs one of the functions listed is necessarily spyware. With the proper notice, consent, and control, some of these same technologies can provide valuable benefits. For example, monitoring tools can help parents keep track of the online activities of their children while the children are surfing the Web, and remote-control features allow support technicians to remotely diagnose computer problems.

Adware Adware is a software program that delivers advertising content in a manner that is unexpected and unwanted by the user. The adware program may infect a computer as the result of a virus, worm, or Trojan. Once the adware is installed, it typically displays advertising banners, pop-up ads, or opens new Web browser windows at random intervals.

Users generally resist adware because:

- Adware may display objectionable content, such as that from gambling sites or pornography.

- Frequent pop-up ads can interfere with a user's productivity.

- Pop-up ads can slow a computer or even cause crashes and the loss of data.

- Unwanted advertisements can be a nuisance.

Some adware goes beyond affecting the user's computer. This is because adware programs can also perform a tracking function, which monitors and tracks a user's online activities and then sends a log of these activities to third parties without the user's authorization or knowledge. For example, a user who visits online automobile sites to view specific types of cars can be tracked by adware and classified as someone interested in buying a new car. Based on the order and type of Web sites visited, the adware can also determine whether the surfers' behavior suggests they are close to making a purchase or are also looking at competitors' cars. This information is gathered by adware and then sold to automobile advertisers, who send the users regular mail advertisements about their cars or even call the user on the telephone.

Scareware Scareware is software that displays a fictitious warning to the user in the attempt to "scare" the user into an action, such as purchasing additional software online to fix a problem that in fact does not exist. Scareware programs appear to be legitimate by mimicking the appearance of genuine software and—unlawfully—using legitimate trademarks or icons to misrepresent themselves.

Once installed on the user's computer, generally through social engineering or a Trojan, the scareware pretends to perform a security scan of the computer or an analysis of the hard drive. No matter what the condition of the computer, the scareware always reports that the computer is infected or the hard disk has serious problems. The scareware program shown in Figure 3-5 has supposedly scanned the user's computer and found numerous malware infections. The user is told to immediately purchase online the "full version" of the software to fix the problems. However, users who provide their credit card number to make the purchase find that an attacker simply captures this information and then uses the card number to make his or her own purchases.

Figure 3-5 Scareware
Source: Microsoft Security Intelligence Report

Uncle Greg had just finished describing to Abby the different types of attacks that a computer faces today. "I had no idea there were that many!" she said. "OK, so what do I do now? If antivirus software can't stop everything, do I need an anti-something for each one?"

Greg set down his coffee cup. "No, not really. There are some different protections that you'll want to install on your computer. But there are two things that I would consider to be really important. The first is to make sure your new computer will automatically install software patches." "Hey, Uncle Greg, remember who you're talking to. What's a 'patch'?" asked Abby. Greg laughed. "Sorry, I sometimes use too much computer-speak! Patches are software updates that fix software security problems on your computer. I can show you how to make sure your computer is set up to automatically install them, so you don't have to do anything."

"That sounds good," said Abby. "Now what's the second thing?" Greg said, "The second thing is something that everybody knows that they should do, but still very few people do it as regularly as they should. And when they do it it's usually done the wrong way. It's one of the most important protections you have against these attackers. Can you guess what it is?" Abby thought for a moment and said, "I'm afraid you've got me stumped. What is it?" Greg replied, "It's backing up everything on your computer. With all the new attacks that come out each day, the overwhelming odds are that your new computer could get infected. Having a good backup will protect you so you won't lose anything that's on your computer."

Abby smiled. "That's what I need. How do we get started?"

In many instances, the scareware embeds itself into the computer so that it cannot be closed, and rebooting the computer has no effect.

Computer Defenses

Because of the large number and different types of attacks and the fact that new attacks are being continually introduced, there are several security protections that a computer should have installed and configured to resist attacks. The defenses a user should implement include managing patches, installing antivirus software, configuring personal firewalls, using User Account Control, protecting against theft, creating data backups, and knowing the steps for recovering from an attack.

Managing Patches

Early operating systems were relatively simple programs whose job was to launch applications such as word processors or spreadsheet programs. Microsoft's first operating system, MS-DOS v1.0, was released in 1981 and had only 4,000 lines of code. It easily fit on a floppy disk that had a storage size of only 160,000 bytes. As more features and graphical user interfaces (GUIs) were added to operating systems they became more complex. Microsoft Windows 8 contains over 50 million lines of code and requires at least 20 GB of storage on the computer's hard drive. Because of the increased length and complexity of operating systems, unintentional vulnerabilities were introduced that could be exploited by attackers. In addition, new attack tools made what had been considered secure operating system functions and services vulnerable.

To address the vulnerabilities in operating systems that are uncovered after the software has been released, software vendors usually deploy a software "fix" to address the vulnerabilities. These fixes can come in a variety of formats. A security **patch** is a general software security update intended to cover vulnerabilities that have been discovered since the program was released. A **service pack** is software that is a cumulative package of all security updates plus additional features.

There is no universal agreement on the definition of these terms. For example, whereas most vendors and users refer to a general software security update as a patch, Microsoft calls it a *security update*.

Modern operating systems have the ability to perform automatic patch updates to their software. The computer interacts with the vendor's online update service and can take action with a patch based on the configuration option that is chosen. These options generally are similar to those for Microsoft Windows, as seen in Figure 3-6, and include:

- *Install updates automatically.* This option checks the Microsoft Web site every day at a user-designated time and, if there are any patches, automatically downloads and installs them.

- *Download updates but let me choose whether to install them.* The Download option automatically downloads the patches but does not install them, allowing the user to review and choose which patches to install.

- *Check for updates but let me choose whether to download and install them.* This option alerts the user that patches are available but does not download or install them. The user must go to the Microsoft Web site to review and install the patches.

- *Never check for updates.* This option disables automatic updates.

Microsoft releases its patches on the second Tuesday of each month, called "Patch Tuesday," unless the patch addresses a particularly serious vulnerability, and it is then released immediately.

Because of the importance of patches it is recommended that users configure their operating systems to install updates automatically. This provides the highest degree of performance.

Although operating systems have an integrated ability to perform automatic updates, applications such as word processors or graphics programs usually lack this capability, yet they may

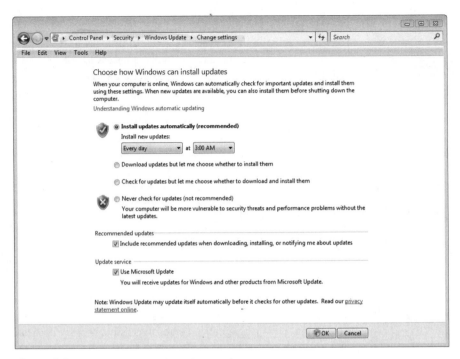

Figure 3-6 Windows automatic update options
Source: Microsoft Windows 7

have vulnerabilities that need to be patched. Recently operating system vendors have enhanced their automatic update capabilities to include updates from other vendors.

A growing trend among software vendors is to automatically download and install patches without any user intervention or options. The Google Chrome Web browser is automatically updated whenever it is necessary without even telling the user—and there are no user configuration settings to opt out of the updates.

Installing Antivirus Software

One of the first software security applications is **antivirus (AV)** software. This software can scan a computer's hard drive for infections as well as monitor computer activity and examine all new documents, such as e-mail attachments, that might contain a virus. If a virus is detected, options generally include cleaning the file of the virus, quarantining the infected file, or deleting the file. Figure 3-7 shows the settings of a typical AV program.

Most AV software identifies malware on a computer by matching it to a known pattern or "signature" of the malware. Thus, AV software on a computer must have its **signature files** regularly updated by downloads from the Internet.

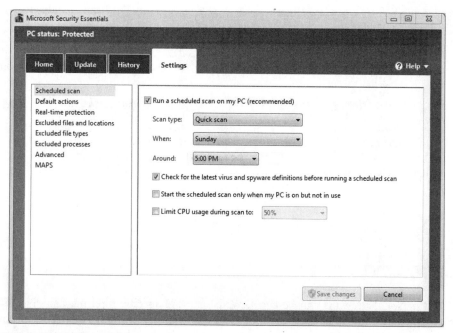

Figure 3-7 AV program settings
Source: Microsoft Security Essentials

NOTE

The flood of potential malware each month has increased to the point that the traditional signature-based method of detecting viruses and other malware may be reaching the breaking point. One antivirus software vendor receives over 200,000 submissions of potential malware each month. At this rate, the antivirus vendor would have to update and distribute its signature files every 10 minutes to keep users fully protected.

Antivirus software should be configured to constantly monitor for viruses and automatically check for updated signature files. In addition, the entire hard drive should be scanned for viruses on a regular basis.

BLOCK ATTACKS

Configuring Personal Firewalls

Commercial buildings, apartments, and other similar structures are required by both national and local building codes to have a firewall. In building construction, a firewall is usually a brick, concrete, or masonry unit positioned vertically through all stories of the building. Its purpose is to contain a fire and prevent it from spreading.

A software-based **personal firewall** runs as a program on a computer and serves a similar purpose: it is designed to prevent malware from spreading into the computer. It does this by examining the data coming into the computer from the Internet or the local network to which the computer is connected and blocks (*filters*) certain content. In addition to personal firewalls, more sophisticated network firewalls are also used. Table 3-4 compares these two types of firewalls.

Function	Personal Firewall	Network Firewall
Location	Runs on a single computer	Located on edge of the network
Scope of protection	Protects only computer on which it is installed	Protects all devices connected to the network
Type	Software that runs on computer	Separate hardware device
Filtering	Based on programs running on the computer	Provides sophisticated range of filtering mechanisms

Table 3-4 **Personal and network firewalls**
© Cengage Learning 2014

Network firewalls are covered in more detail in Chapter 5.

Although personal firewalls can be configured for more specific filtering, usually the settings for a personal firewall are based on the programs that are running on the local computer. Data can be allowed to enter the computer or sent from it based on the user granting or denying permission for a specific program to communicate through the network. By default, most programs are blocked by the personal firewall from sending or receiving data from the Internet or local network. Users can allow programs to communicate through the firewall. The settings for the Windows personal firewall are shown in Figure 3-8.

✅ Home or work (private) networks	Connected ⌄
Networks at home or work where you know and trust the people and devices on the network	
Windows Firewall state:	On
Incoming connections:	Block all connections to programs that are not on the list of allowed programs
Active home or work (private) networks:	🏠 Network
Notification state:	Notify me when Windows Firewall blocks a new program

Figure 3-8 Windows personal firewall settings
Source: Microsoft Windows 7

For most personal firewalls, inbound connections are blocked unless there is a specific firewall rule setting that allows them in. Outbound connections are allowed unless there is a rule that blocks them.

The recommended personal firewall settings are that the firewall be turned on for all network locations and connections. In addition, the firewall should block all inbound connections unless the user has specified exceptions to this rule for some known connections.

Using User Account Control (UAC)

A **user account** indicates the privilege level of a user; that is, it tells the computer which files and folders can be accessed and what configuration changes can be made to the computer. Microsoft Windows users can be assigned one of three different types of user accounts, each giving a different level of control over the computer:

- *Guest accounts.* **Guest accounts** are intended for users who need temporary use of a computer. There are very few settings that can be changed from a guest account.

- *Standard accounts.* A **standard account** is designed for everyday computing activities and allows for some settings to be modified.

- *Administrator accounts.* The highest level of user account is an **administrator account**. This provides the most control over a computer.

Modern operating systems contain a function that alerts the user to an event that the operating system is about to perform and may also ask explicit permission from the user to perform this task. This helps prevent a Trojan or other malware from secretly making changes or installing new software. In Microsoft Windows this security function is called **User Account Control (UAC)**. UAC provides information to users and obtains their approval before a program can make a change to the computer's settings.

When requesting approval from the user the UAC can perform two actions. First, it can temporarily switch to **secure desktop** mode in which the entire screen is temporarily dimmed. Secure desktop mode prevents an attacker from manipulating any UAC messages that appear on the screen. Second, a UAC dialog box appears. If the user has an administrator account the user must click *Continue* or *Yes* before UAC will allow any changes to be made or software installed, as shown in Figure 3-9. If the user's level is Standard or Guest, then the administrator password must be entered by another person before any changes are permitted.

Figure 3-9 UAC dialog box
Source: Microsoft Windows 7

The Windows UAC interface also provides extended information. A shield icon warns users if they attempt to access any feature that requires UAC permission. In addition, the UAC prompt includes a description of the requested action. The UAC prompts are color-coded to indicate the level of risk, from red (highest risk) to yellow (lowest risk).

There are four levels of UAC. These are listed and described in Table 3-5.

UAC level	Description	Explanation
Always notify	Users are notified before programs make changes to the computer or to Windows settings that require administrator permissions with secure desktop.	Highest level of security
Notify me only when programs try to make changes to my computer	Users are notified through the secure desktop before programs make changes to the computer that requires administrator permissions. Users will not be notified if they try to make changes to Windows settings that require administrator permissions.	Default setting
Notify me only when programs try to make changes to my computer (do not dim my desktop)	Users are notified before programs make changes to the computer that requires administrator permissions but not through secure desktop. Users will not be notified if they try to make changes to Windows settings that require administrator permissions.	Other programs might be able to interfere with the visual appearance of the dialog box and could be a security risk, if there are malicious programs running on the computer.
Never notify	Users are not notified before any changes are made to the computer. If the user account is administrator level, then programs can make changes to the computer without informing the users. If the user is a standard user any changes that require the permissions of an administrator will automatically be denied.	Least secure setting

Table 3-5 **Microsoft Windows UAC levels and descriptions**
© Cengage Learning 2014

It is recommended that the UAC level be set to *Always notify* to provide the highest degree of protection. In additions, users should be assigned standard accounts instead of administrative accounts. This helps provide a higher degree of security and prevent unauthorized software from being installed on the computer.

Creating Data Backups

One of the best defenses against attacks is frequently overlooked: it is to create **data backups** on a regular basis. Creating a data backup means copying files from a computer's hard drive onto other digital media that is stored in a secure location. Data backups protect against computer attacks because they can restore infected computers to their properly functioning state. Data backups can also protect against hardware malfunctions, user error, software corruption, and natural disasters.

There are several solutions to make creating backups easier. Modern operating systems can perform automated backups, and third-party software is also available that provides additional functionality.

There are two primary questions to consider when formulating a data backup strategy. The first question is *what* data should be backed up. All user-created files that cannot be easily or quickly recreated should be backed up. These include any personal files, such as documents created with a word processor, digital photos, personal financial data, and other similar information. However, should programs installed on the computer, such as the operating system or a word processor program, also be backed up? If these programs are readily available elsewhere or can be retrieved easily, such as from a DVD or downloaded online, there is little need to back them up along with the data files.

 The main reason to back up programs along with user data files is that it allows an infected computer to be completely restored more quickly from the backup instead of installing all of the programs individually from DVDs or online before restoring the user data files.

The second question is *where* the backup should be stored. Consider a user who installs a second hard drive in his computer to back up the data from the primary hard drive each night. This would allow for the primary hard drive to be restored quickly in the event of an infection or primary hard drive failure. However, what about a fire, tornado, or lightning strike? These events could destroy both the primary hard drive and the backup hard drive.

An alternative is to copy the data to an external portable device that could then be carried to a remote location. These types of devices include:

- *Portable USB hard drives.* These devices connect to the USB port of a computer and provide backup capabilities; they are fast, portable, and can store large amounts of data.

- *Disc storage.* DVD storage is compact, stable, inexpensive, and easy to transport to a remote location. The disadvantage to DVD storage is that it requires the user to be present during the backup process to continually "feed" discs into the drive if multiple discs are required. A larger-capacity Blu-ray device can hold significantly more data than a DVD. However, the time to record the information can still be lengthy.

- *Network-attached storage (NAS).* A *network attached storage (NAS)* device is similar to a portable USB hard drive except it has additional "intelligence" that allows all devices connected to the computer network to access it (instead of moving it from computer to computer). NAS devices are increasing in popularity among home network users. A disadvantage is the NAS, located in the same house or apartment as the computer, may be susceptible to the same natural disasters that the computer faces.

An alternative that may provide the best solution is online backups. There are several fee-based Internet services available that provide features similar to these:

- *Automatic continuous backup.* Once the initial backup is completed, any new or modified files are also backed up. Usually the backup software will "sleep" while the computer is being used and perform backups only when there is no user activity. This helps to lessen any impact on the computer's performance or Internet speed.

- *Universal access.* Files backed up through online services can be made available to another computer.

- *File feedback information.* A colored dot next to the filenames on the user's computer allows the user to see which files are backed up and which are not.

- *Optional program file backup.* In addition to user data files these services can as an option also back up all program and operating system files.

- *Delayed deletion.* Files that are copied to the online server will remain accessible for up to 30 days after they are deleted on the local computer. This allows a user to have a longer window of opportunity to restore a deleted file.

- *Online or disc-based restore.* If a file or the entire computer must be restored this can be done online. Some services also provide the option of shipping to the user the backup files on DVDs.

There are several services, some of which are free, that automatically back up any files that are placed in a designated folder on your computer. Although not as full-featured as online backup services, they do allow for backups of important data files.

MINIMIZE LOSSES

Recovering from an Attack

In spite of the best defenses, sooner or later an attack on a computer may be successful. Just as a homeowner cannot be absolutely certain that her house will never be broken into even if she has installed strong door locks, the same is true with computer security: the best defense is to "hope for the best but prepare for the worst."

Preparation is the key to recovering from an attack. For Microsoft Windows users it is important to create a *system repair disc* that can help repair Windows in the event of a serious error, such as errors caused by malware. In addition, there are several software AV vendors that offer free downloadable *rescue discs*. These are downloadable images that can be used to create a bootable DVD. When you insert this DVD into the computer's disc drive and restart the computer, the computer will bypass the infected hard drive and boot from the DVD, which will then automatically scan and disinfect the computer.

Chapter Summary

- Malicious software (malware) is software that enters a computer system without the owner's knowledge or consent and includes a wide variety of damaging or annoying software. One way to classify malware is by its primary objective: spreading, concealing, or profiting. Spreading malware includes viruses and worms. A computer virus is malicious computer code that reproduces itself on the same computer. A virus first inserts itself into a computer file (a data file or program) and then looks to reproduce itself on the same computer as well as unload its malicious payload. A worm is a program that is designed to take advantage of vulnerability in an application or an operating system in order to enter a system. Once the worm has exploited the vulnerability on one system, it immediately searches for another computer that has the same vulnerability.

- There are several types of concealing malware. A Trojan is a program advertised as performing one activity but actually does something else, either in addition to the advertised activity or as a substitute to it. A rootkit is a set of software tools used by an intruder to hide all traces of the malware. A backdoor is access to a program or a service that circumvents normal security protections. A keylogger silently captures and stores each keystroke that a user types on the computer's keyboard. A keylogger can be a small hardware device or a software program. Arbitrary code execution allows an attacker to gain control of the victim's computer to execute the attacker's commands, turning it into his own remote computer.

- Malware with a profit motive includes botnets, spyware, adware, and scareware. A computer under the remote control of an attacker is known as a zombie, and when many zombie computers are gathered into a logical computer network under the control of an attacker this creates a botnet. Spyware is a general term used for software that gathers information without consent, thus violating the user's privacy and personal security. Adware is a software program that delivers advertising content in a manner that is unexpected and unwanted by the user. Scareware is software that displays a fictitious warning to the user in the attempt to frighten the user into an action, such as purchasing additional software online to "fix" a nonexistent problem. Scareware programs appear to be legitimate by mimicking the appearance of genuine software.

- A security patch is a general software security update intended to cover vulnerabilities that have been discovered since the program was released. Modern operating systems, such as Apple Mac OS and Microsoft Windows, have the ability to perform automatic patch updates to their software. Applications such as word processors or graphics programs usually lack this capability yet may have vulnerabilities that need to be patched. Antivirus (AV) software can scan a computer's hard drive for infections as well as monitor computer activity and examine all new documents, such as e-mail attachments, that might contain a virus. If a virus is detected, options generally include cleaning the file of the virus, quarantining the infected file, or deleting the file.

- A software-based computer personal firewall runs as a program on a computer is designed to prevent malware from spreading into the computer. It does this by examining the data coming into the computer from the Internet or the local network to which the computer is connected and blocks certain content. Modern operating systems contain a function that alerts the user to an event that the operating system is about to perform and may also ask explicit permission from the user to perform this task. This helps prevent a Trojan or other malware from secretly making changes or installing new software. In Microsoft Windows this security function called User Account Control (UAC) and provides information to users and obtains their approval before a program can make a change to the computer's settings.

■ One of the best defenses against attacks is to create data backups on a regular basis. Creating a data backup is copying files from a computer's hard drive onto other digital media that is stored in a secure location and protect against computer attacks because they can restore infected computers to their properly functioning state.

■ In spite of the best defenses, sooner or later an attack on a computer may be successful. Preparation is the key to recovering from an attack. For Microsoft Windows users it is important to create a system repair disc that can help repair Windows in the event of a serious error, often which are caused by malware. In addition, there are several software AV vendors that offer free downloadable rescue discs. These are downloadable images that can be used to create a bootable DVD, which will then automatically scan and disinfect the computer.

Key Terms

administrator account   The highest level of user account and provides the most control over a computer.

adware   A software program that delivers advertising content in a manner that is unexpected and unwanted by the user.

antivirus (AV)   Software that can examine a computer for any infections as well as monitor computer activity and scan new documents that might contain a virus.

arbitrary code execution   An attack that allows an attacker to gain control of the victim's computer to execute the attacker's commands, turning it into his own remote computer.

backdoor   Software code that gives access to a program or a service that circumvents normal security protections.

bot herder   An attacker who controls a botnet.

botnet   A logical computer network of zombies under the control of an attacker.

buffer overflow   An attack that substitutes the "return address" pointer and points to another area in the computer's memory area that contains malware code

computer virus (virus)   Malicious computer code that, like its biological counterpart, reproduces itself on a single computer.

data backups   Copying files from a computer's hard drive onto other digital media that is stored in a secure location.

guest account   An account that is intended for users who need temporary use of a computer.

keylogger   Hardware or software that captures and stores each keystroke that a user types on the computer's keyboard.

macro   A series of instructions that can be grouped together as a single command and are often used to automate a complex set of tasks or a repeated series of tasks.

macro virus   A computer virus that is written in a script known as a macro.

patch   A general software security update intended to cover vulnerabilities that have been discovered.

personal firewall   Software that runs as a program on a computer is designed to prevent malware from spreading into the computer.

program virus   A computer virus that infects program executable files.

remote code execution (RCE)   Another name for arbitrary code execution.

rootkit   A set of software tools used by an attacker to hide the actions or presence of other types of malicious software.

scareware   Software that displays a fictitious warning to the user in the attempt to frighten the user into an action.

secure desktop   A mode in which the entire screen is temporarily dimmed to prevent an attacker from manipulating any UAC (User Account Control) messages that appear on the screen.

service pack   An operating system update that is a cumulative package of security patches or updates plus other features.

signature file   File that contains known patterns or sequences of bytes (strings) found in viruses; used by antivirus software to identify malware.

spyware   A general term used to describe software that spies on users by gathering information without consent, thus violating their privacy.

standard account   An account that is designed for everyday computing activities.

Trojan   An executable program advertised as performing one activity but actually does something else (or it may perform both the advertised and malicious activities).

user account   An account that indicates the privilege level of a user.

User Account Control (UAC)   A Windows security function provides information to users and obtains their approval before a program can make a change to the computer's settings.

worm   A malicious program designed to take advantage of a vulnerability in an application or an operating system in order to enter a computer.

zombie   An infected "robot" (bot) computer that is under the remote control of an attacker.

Review Questions

1. A _____ requires a user to transport it from one computer to another.

   a.   worm

   b.   rootkit

   c.   virus

   d.   Trojan

2. Each of the following is an action that a virus can take except _____.

   a. transport itself through the network to another device

   b. cause a computer to crash

   c. erase files from a hard drive

   d. make multiple copies of itself and consume all of the free space in a hard drive

3. Which of the following is a type of computer virus?

   a. Key virus

   b. Macro virus

   c. Remote virus

   d. Bootnet virus

4. Xi downloads a program that prints out coupons but in the background it silently collects her passwords. Xi has actually downloaded a _____.

   a. virus

   b. worm

   c. Trojan

   d. logic bomb

5. _____ is a general term used for describing software that gathers information without the user's consent.

   a. Adware

   b. Scrapeware

   c. Pullware

   d. Spyware

6. Each of the following is true regarding a keylogger except _____.

   a. hardware keyloggers are installed between the keyboard connector and computer keyboard or USB port

   b. software keyloggers are easy to detect

   c. keyloggers can be used to capture passwords, credit card numbers, or personal information

   d. software keyloggers can be designed to send captured information automatically back to the attacker through the Internet

7. The preferred method today of bot herders for command and control of zombies is to use _____.

   a. Internet Relay Chat (IRC)

   b. e-mail

   c. Hypertext Transfer Protocol (HTTP)

   d. spam

8. Each of the following is the reason why adware is scorned, except _____.

    a. it displays the attackers programming skills

    b. it displays objectionable content

    c. it can cause a computer to crash or slow down

    d. it can interfere with a user's productivity

9. An attacker who controls multiple zombies in a botnet is known as a _____.

    a. zombie shepherd

    b. rogue IRC

    c. bot herder

    d. cyber-robot

10. Each of the following is a typical feature of a fee-based Internet backup service except_____.

    a. backup to external hard drive

    b. universal access

    c. file feedback information

    d. delayed deletion

11. How many carriers must a virus have to replicate and attack?

    a. One

    b. Two

    c. Three

    d. Four

12. Which of the following is not a type of malware that attempts to conceal itself?

    a. Trojan

    b. Xbot

    c. Rootkit

    d. Back door

13. A _____ alters the operating system to hide its presence.

    a. worm

    b. virus

    c. rootkit

    d. trojan

14. A _____ is software code that gives access to a program or service that circumvents any normal security protections.

    a. court

    b. quantum

    c. service

    d. back door

15. Which of the following is an advantage of software keyloggers?

    a. They do not require physical access to the user's computer.

    b. They are cheaper.

    c. They are faster.

    d. They are larger.

16. An attacker that changes the computer's "return address" to point to malware has conducted _____ attack.

    a. buffer overflow

    b. memory allocation

    c. pointer

    d. resource management

17. Which of the following is an attack that allows an attacker to gain control of the victim's computer to execute the attacker's commands, turning it into his own remote computer?

    a. Arbitrary code execution

    b. Worm

    c. Virus

    d. Trojan

18. Each of the following is a characteristic of a personal firewall except _____.

    a. It is located on the edge of the network

    b. It only protects the computer on which it is installed.

    c. It is software that runs on the computer.

    d. It is based on programs running on the computer.

19. Which of the following user accounts provides the most control over a computer?

    a. Guest account

    b. Standard account

    c. Administrator account

    d. Closed account

20. Which level of UAC provides the lowest level of security?

   a. Always notify

   b. Never notify

   c. Notify on demand

   d. Universal notify

Hands-On Projects

Project 3-1: Test Antivirus Software

What happens when antivirus software detects a virus? In this project you download a virus test file to determine how your AV software reacts. The file downloaded is not a virus but is designed to appear to an antivirus scanner as if it were a virus.

You need to have antivirus software installed and running on your computer to perform this project.

1. Open your Web browser and enter the URL **www.eicar.org/86-0-Intended-use.html**

The location of content on the Internet such as this program may change without warning. If you are no longer able to access the program through the above URL then use a search engine to search for "EICAR AntiVirus Test File".

2. Read the "INTENDED USE" information. The file you will download is not a virus but is designed to appear to an antivirus scanner as if it were a virus.

3. Click **DOWNLOAD**.

4. Click the file **eicar.com**, which contains a fake virus. A dialog box may open that asks if you want to download the file. Wait to see what happens. What does your antivirus software do? Close your antivirus message and if necessary click **Cancel** to stop the download procedure.

5. Now click **eicar_com.zip**. This file contains a fake virus inside a compressed (ZIP) file. What happened? Close your antivirus message and, if necessary, click **Cancel** to stop the download procedure.

If your antivirus software did not prevent you from accessing the eicar_com.zip file, when the File Download dialog box appears, click **Save** and download the file to your desktop or another location designated by your instructor. When the download is complete, navigate to the folder that contains the file and right-click it. Then, click **Scan for viruses** on the shortcut menu (your menu command might be slightly different). What happened after the scan?

6. Click **eicarcom2.zip**. This file has a double-compressed ZIP file with a fake virus. What happened? Close your antivirus message and, if necessary, click **Cancel** to stop the download procedure.

7. If necessary erase any files that were saved to your computer.

8. Close all windows.

Project 3-2: Scan for Rootkits

In this project, you will download and install Kaspersky's TDSSKiller tool to help detect the presence of a rootkit.

1. Open your Web browser and enter the URL **support.kaspersky.com/viruses/solutions?qid=208283363**

The location of content on the Internet such as this program may change without warning. If you are no longer able to access the program through the above URL, then use a search engine to search for "Kaspersky TDSSKkiller".

2. Click **TDSSKiller.exe**.

3. Navigate to the location where the files were extracted and start the program by double-clicking **TDSSKiller.exe**. If you receive an Open File - Security Warning dialog box, click **Run**.

4. The **TDSSKiller** screen will appear.

5. Click **Start scan** to begin a scan of the computer for a rootkit.

6. When completed, TDSSKiller will display any threats that were detected. Note any threats that are detected.

7. Click **Close**.

8. Close all windows.

Project 3-3: Configure Microsoft Windows Security

It is important that security settings be properly configured on a computer in order to protect it. In this project, you will examine several security settings on a Microsoft Windows 7 computer.

This project shows how to configure Windows security for a home computer. If this computer is part of a computer lab or office, these settings should not be changed without the proper permissions.

1. Click **Start** and **Control Panel**.

2. Click **System and Security**.

3. Click **Action Center**.

4. If necessary expand the area under **Security**.

5. All of the indicators should say **On** or **OK** (with the exception of **Network Access Protection,** which may not be configured unless this computer is part of a school or business network). Note any indicators that say **Off.**

6. Now examine the UAC settings. Click **Change User Account Control** settings. Note that the UAC shield is displayed next to this option, indicating that the UAC dialog box may appear, depending upon the current configuration.

7. If the UAC dialog box appears, click **Yes** if you are running an administrator account. If you are not running as an administrator account, then you will need to have the password entered for you in order to continue.

8. The User Account Control Settings dialog box appears, as shown in Figure 3-10.

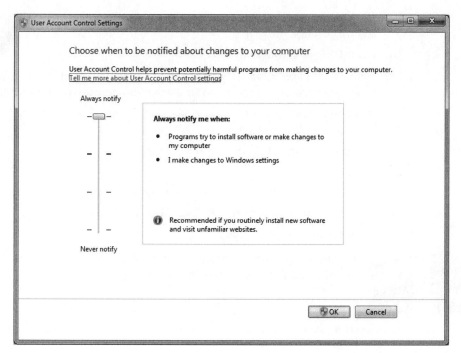

Figure 3-10 User Account Control dialog box
Source: Microsoft Windows 7

9. Move the slider bar through all of the settings. Read the information provided by each setting.

10. Now move the slider bar to the top setting, **Always notify me when.** Why is this the most secure setting?

11. Note what is contained on the **OK** button. What will clicking this button cause to happen? Click **OK** and then approve the UAC control.

12. Now check your personal firewall. Return to the **System and Security** window. Click **Windows Firewall.**

13. Expand the areas under your network connections (there may be more than one). Is the firewall active for all of these settings?

14. Click **Allow a program or feature through Windows Firewall.** A list of the current programs that have permission to send and receive data through your personal firewall is listed.

It is not advisable to turn off all of these permissions because they may have a negative impact on how you use your computer. You may want to ask your instructor or a computer professional for assistance on which if any of these permissions should be changed.

15. Click **Cancel.**

16. Click the back button to return to System and Security.

17. Click **Windows Update** to examine the current configuration status to receive patches.

18. Click **Change settings.**

19. Under **Important updates** what is this computer's current configuration? If necessary change it to **Install updates automatically (recommended).**

20. If necessary change **Install new updates:** to **Every day** and change the time to one that your computer will be on.

21. Be sure all of the check boxes are checked.

22. Click **OK.**

23. Click the back button to return to the System and Security page.

24. Finally, create a system repair disc. Click **Backup and Restore.**

25. Click **Create a system repair disc.**

Depending upon your computer you may need access to the original Windows installation disc to complete creating a system repair disc.

26. Insert a CD or DVD into the disc drive and click **Create disc.** Label and save this disc in a safe place.

27. Close all windows.

Project 3-4: Creating a Disk Image Backup

To back up programs and operating system files in addition to user files, one solution is to create a disk image. A disk image file is created by performing a complete sector-by-sector copy of the hard drive instead of backing up using the drive's file system. In this project, you download Macrium Reflect to create an image backup.

1. Use your Web browser to go to **www.macrium.com**.

It is not unusual for Web sites to change the location of where files are stored. If the URL above no longer functions, then open a search engine and search for "Macrium Reflect".

2. Click **DOWNLOADS** and then click **Download Now.** At the download site also click **Download Now.**

3. Run the file and then click **Trial installer. Select the edition** and then select **Professional.**

4. Click **Download.**

5. Accept the default settings to download, and install this program onto your computer. Launch the program by double-clicking on the icon.

6. When Reflect launches, click **Backup** if necessary.

7. Click **Create an image of the partition(s) required to backup and restore Windows.**

8. Under **Source** select the disk that contains the operating system and data for this computer.

9. Select the location to store the backup. You cannot store the backup on the same hard drive that you are creating the image on; you must store it on another hard drive in that computer or on an external USB hard drive. Under **Destination** select the appropriate location. Click **Next.**

10. Review the settings that are displayed. Note that, depending on the size of the data to be backed up and the speed of the computer, it will take several minutes to perform the backup. Click **Finish** and then **OK.** Click **OK** and then **Close.**

11. Leave Macrium Reflect open for the next project.

Project 3-5: Restoring a Disk Image Backup

It is important to test the steps necessary to restore a disk image in the event that a hard drive stops functioning. In this project, you will go through the steps of restoring the Macrium Reflect image backup created in Hands-On Project 3-4, although you will stop short of actually restoring the image.

1. Once the backup in Project 3-4 has finished, you will create a Rescue CD. This CD will allow you to boot your computer in the event that the hard drive becomes corrupt and restore the backup. Click **Other Tasks** and then **Create bootable Rescue media.**

2. Select **Linux – Select this option to create a Linux based recovery media.** Click **Next.**

3. Click **Finish.**

4. When prompted place a blank CD disk in the tray, and then click **OK.** Reflect will now create a recovery CD.

5. When the recovery CD has been created, close all windows.

6. Now boot from the recovery CD. Be sure the recovery CD is in the disk drive, and restart your computer. If it does not boot from the recovery CD, check the instructions for your computer to boot from a CD.

7. When the Restore Wizard dialog box is displayed, click **Next**.

8. In the left pane, click the location where you stored the image backup.

9. In the right pane, select the backup image that appears.

10. If you were actually restoring your image backup, you would continue to proceed. However, click the **Close** button.

11. Remove the CD.

12. Click **OK** to reboot your computer.

Case Projects

CASE PROJECTS

Case Project 3-1: Microsoft Safety Scanner

Microsoft offers a free tool that can scan a computer for malware and then remove it. Point your Web browser to **www.microsoft.com/security/scanner/ en-us/default.aspx**, and click **Download Now**. Follow the instructions to scan your computer. Were any problems found? Did you find this scanner easy to use? Would you recommend it to a friend? Write a one-paragraph summary on this tool.

Case Project 3-2: Online Backup Services

There are several good online backup services that can help make data backup easy for the user. Use a search engine to search for *online backup service reviews*, and select three different services. Research these services and note their features. Create a table that lists each service and compare their features. Be sure to also include costs. Which would you recommend? Why?

Case Project 3-3: Free Synchronization Storage

Although not as full-featured as online backup services, there are several free synchronization storage tools that allow users to back up data by synchronization: when you place a file in a designated folder, it is automatically stored to the remote site. Several of these sites offer free storage from 5 GB to unlimited space. Use a search engine to search for *free cloud synch storage*, and select three different services. Research these services and note their features. Create a table that lists each product and compare their features. Be sure to include storage space limits. How do they compare to online backup services? Which would you recommend? Why?

Case Project 3-4: AV Comparison

Select three different antivirus software products. What features does each have that are different from other vendors' products? What are each product's strengths and weaknesses? How much does it cost to be able to update the signature files for each product? What is the cost of each product? Which product would you recommend to others? Why? Write a one-page summary of your findings.

Case Project 3-5: Information Security Community Site Activity

The Information Security Community Site is a Course Technology/Cengage Learning information security course enrichment site. It contains a wide variety of tools, information, discussion boards, and other features to assist learners. Go to **community.cengage.com/infosec**. Click **Login** at the top of the page, and enter your sign-in name and password credentials that you created in Chapter 1. Visit the Discussions page by going to the **Students** tab and selecting the **Discussion Boards** link from the drop-down menu, where you can read the following question about penalties.

What should be the penalty for those who create viruses, worms, and other destructive malware? How should it be enforced? Record your responses on the Community Site discussion board.

Case Project 3-6: North Ridge Computer Consultants

North Ridge Computer Consultants (NRCC) is a local information technology company that specializes in security. In order to encourage students to enter the field of information security, NRCC often hires student interns to assist them with projects.

Athens Seafood is a regional chain of restaurants. Athens Seafood has been the victims of attacks that have affected its ability to serve customers. NRCC has been asked to help train their employees about the dangers of malware.

Create a PowerPoint presentation of at least eight slides that covers different types of malware attacks. Because the audience does not have a strong technical background, your presentation should be general in its tone.

References

1. "The First Computer Virus," accessed Mar. 3, 2011, http://www.worldhistorysite.com/virus.html.

2. Sanders, Tom, "Botnet operation controlled 1.5m PCs," *V3.CO.UK.* Oct. 21, 2005, accessed Mar. 3, 2011. http://www.v3.co.uk/vnunet/news/2144375/botnet-operation-ruled-million.

3. Acohido, Byron. "Hactivist attacks grow as governments get in on the action," *USA Today,* Jul. 25, 2012. Weber, Tim, "Criminals 'may overwhelm the web'," *BBC*

News, Jan. 25, 2007. http://www.usatoday.com/tech/news/story/2012-07-19/hactivism-anonymous-attacks/56464792/1.

4. Kassner, Michael, "The top 10 spam botnets: New and improved," *Tech Republic.* Feb. 25, 2010, accessed Mar. 3, 2011. http://www.techrepublic.com/blog/10things/the-top-10-spam-botnets-new-and-improved/1373.

5. "Anti-Spyware Coalition Definitions Document," *Anti-Spyware Coalition*, Nov. 12, 2007, accessed Mar. 3, 2011, http://www.antispywarecoalition.org/documents/definitions.htm.

Internet Security

After completing this chapter you should be able to do the following:

- Explain how the Internet and e-mail work
- Describe how attackers can use mobile code, cookies, and fraudulent digital certificates
- List the security risks with using e-mail
- Describe how to use Web browser settings to create stronger security
- List several different e-mail defenses

"This is weird," said Jamal. Chiara looked up from her computer and said, "What's weird?" Jamal and Chiara were in their school's computer lab waiting for their next class to begin. "I downloaded one file and everything was fine. But now I'm trying to download this file, and it's giving me a warning." Chiara moved her chair closer so she could see Jamal's screen. Jamal was trying to download the file *CoolFreeVideo.exe*, but a message had appeared that said, *This file is not commonly downloaded and could harm your computer.*

"Oh, we talked about that last Friday in our Introduction to Computers class when you were out sick," Chiara said. She went on to explain that the Web browser that Jamal was using had a security feature that checked any downloaded file against an online list of files that were known to be suspect. "It looks like the *CoolFreeVideo.exe* file has a negative rating, so the browser is warning you." Jamal leaned forward. "Is the reason why I didn't get the warning when I downloaded the first file was because it was OK?" "Probably," replied Chiara. "Our instructor said older browsers displayed a message like, *This file type can harm your computer so are you sure you want to do this?* before every file was downloaded. People got so used to the warning that always clicked *Yes* without even thinking."

Jamal moved his mouse. "Well, that makes sense. But why not let me download it and then give me a warning?" Chiara smiled and said, "That would be like closing the door *after* your dog ran out of your apartment! It's a whole lot better to block it from ever reaching your computer in the first place. What if you downloaded a dangerous file and your computer somehow didn't catch it?" "OK, I see what you mean," said Jamal.

Chiara continued, "Our instructor also said that downloading files was just one of the dangers when you're on the Internet. There are a whole lot more things to be worried about when you're surfing the Web." Jamal picked up his textbook and said, "You've got me curious now. What other things do I have to be worried about?"

The impact of the Internet on our world has been nothing short of astonishing. Although today's Internet has its roots all the way back in the late 1960s, it was only used by researchers and the military for almost a quarter of a century. With the introduction of Web browser software in the early 1990s, an incomprehensible amount of information was suddenly available at users' fingertips. Not only did it give unprecedented access to information, but the Internet also has created a collective force of awesome proportions. For the first time in human history, mass participation and cooperation across space and time is possible, empowering individuals and groups all over the world. The Internet is having a revolutionary impact on how we all learn, interact, and communicate.

But for all of the benefits that the Internet has provided, it also has become the primary pathway for attackers to reach our computers and personal information. When we connect a computer to the Internet to receive valuable information we also are exposing that computer to malicious attacks. An unprotected computer that is connected to the Internet can be infected in a matter of minutes, and the number of Internet-based attacks continues to increase dramatically each year.

In this chapter, you will learn about some of the attacks on computers that come through the Internet and what can be done to minimize those risks. First, you'll see how the Internet works and then you'll identify the types of risks with using it. After that, you'll examine the defenses that can be set up to make using this valuable tool a more enjoyable and productive experience.

How the Internet Works

The **Internet** is a worldwide set of interconnected computers, servers, and networks. There are two common misconceptions regarding it. First, the Internet is not made up of just individual devices (desktops, tablets, notebooks, smartphones, etc.) but instead is composed of networks to which devices are attached. The Internet is often called a global network of computer networks. Second, it is not owned or controlled by any single organization or government entity. Instead, these networks are operated by industry, governments, schools, and even individuals, who all loosely cooperate to make the Internet a global information resource.

Understanding how some of the basic Internet tools work helps to provide the foundation for establishing Internet security. The two main Internet tools that are used today are the World Wide Web and e-mail. It is through these tools that the overwhelming majority of Internet attacks occur.

The World Wide Web

The **World Wide Web (WWW)**, better known as the *Web*, is composed of Internet server computers on networks that provide online information in a specific format. The format is based on the **Hypertext Markup Language (HTML)**. HTML allows Web authors to combine text, graphic images, audio, video, and **hyperlinks** (which allow users to jump from one area on the Web to another with a click of the mouse button) into a single document. Instructions written in HTML code specify how a local computer's Web **browser** (a program for showing Web pages) should display the words, pictures, and other elements on a user's screen, as shown in Figure 4-1.

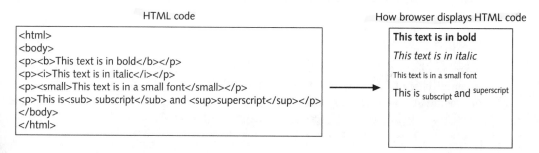

Figure 4-1 How a browser displays HTML code
© Cengage Learning 2014

The underlying HTML code for a Web page can be displayed in any browser.

Web servers distribute HTML documents based on a set of standards, or **protocols**, known as the **Hypertext Transfer Protocol (HTTP)**. HTTP is a subset of a larger set of standards for Internet transmission known as the **Transmission Control Protocol/Internet Protocol (TCP/IP)**.

The word *protocol* comes from two Greek words for *first* and *glue*, and originally referred to the first sheet glued onto a manuscript on which the table of contents was written. The term later evolved to mean an "official account of a diplomatic document" and was used in France to refer to a formula of diplomatic etiquette.

Internet transmissions reply on port numbers. A **port number** identifies the program or service that is being requested. For example, a Web browser on a computer that sends a request to a remote Web server would specify port 80, which is the standard port for HTTP transmissions. The Web server knows by the port number that the request is for an HTML document and responds by sending the entire HTML document (again using HTTP), which is stored on the user's local computer. The Web browser then displays the document. This process is illustrated in Figure 4-2.

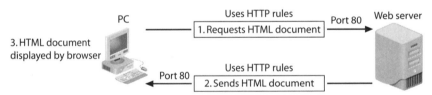

Figure 4-2 Web transmission using port numbers
© Cengage Learning 2014

The local computer does not view the HTML document on the Web server; rather, the entire document is transferred and then stored on the local computer before the browser displays it. This transfer-and-store process creates opportunities for sending different types of malicious code to the user's computer, and makes Web browsing a potentially risky security experience.

E-Mail

Since developer Ray Tomlinson sent the first e-mail message in 1971, e-mail has become an essential part of everyday life. It is estimated that over 100 trillion e-mails are sent annually, increasing at a rate of 10 percent each year. Three out of every four e-mails are sent by personal users (who send and receive an average of over 45 e-mails daily) while the rest are business-related (corporate users send and receive over 167 e-mails per day).[1]

E-mail systems use two TCP/IP protocols to send and receive messages: the **Simple Mail Transfer Protocol (SMTP)** handles outgoing mail, while the **Post Office Protocol (POP,** more commonly known as **POP3** for the current version) is responsible for incoming mail. The SMTP server listens on port number 25, while POP3 listens on port 110, as shown in Figure 4-3.

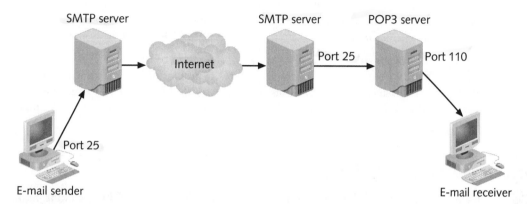

Figure 4-3 E-mail transport
© Cengage Learning 2014

An example of e-mail works is as follows:

1. The sender (*sender@source.com*) uses a stand-alone e-mail client such as Microsoft Outlook to compose and address the message to the receiver (*receiver@destination.com*) and then transmits the message by clicking the *Send* button in Outlook.

2. Outlook connects to the SMTP server at *mail.source.com* using port 25 and passes the message.

3. The SMTP server divides the "To" address into two parts: the recipient name (*receiver*) and the domain name (*destination.com*). If the domain name of the receiver is the same as the sender, the SMTP server hands the message to the local POP3 server for *source.com* using a program called the delivery agent. In this example, because the recipient is at another domain, the SMTP server at *source.com* connects through the Internet with the SMTP server at *destination.com* using port 25 and passes the e-mail message.

4. The SMTP server at *destination.com* recognizes that the domain name for the message is *destination.com*, so it hands the message via the delivery agent to the POP3 server for *destination.com*, which in turn puts the message in receiver's mailbox.

 If the SMTP server at *source.com* cannot connect with the SMTP server at *destination.com*, the message goes into a waiting queue at *source.com*, which periodically tries to resend the message, normally about every 15 minutes. After 4 hours, it sends an e-mail message to the sender indicating a problem. After five days, most servers stop attempting to send the message.

POP3 is a basic protocol that allows users to retrieve messages sent to the server by using an e-mail client to connect to the POP3 server and downloading the messages onto the local computer. After the messages are downloaded, they may be erased from the POP3 server.

IMAP (Internet Mail Access Protocol) is a more advanced mail protocol. With IMAP, the e-mail remains on the e-mail server and is not downloaded to the user's computer. Mail can be organized into folders on the mail server and read from any computer. IMAP users can work with e-mail while offline. This is accomplished by downloading e-mail onto the local computer without erasing the e-mail on the IMAP server. A user can read and reply to e-mail offline. The next time a connection is established, the new messages are sent and any new e-mail is downloaded. The current version of IMAP is **IMAP4.**

E-mail **attachments** are documents that are connected to an e-mail message, such as word processing documents, spreadsheets, or pictures. These attachments are encoded in a special format and sent as a single transmission along with the e-mail message itself. When the receiving computer receives the attachment, it converts it back to its original format.

Internet Security Risks

There are several risks that users face from using the Internet. These include mobile code, cookies, fraudulent digital certificates, drive-by downloads, redirecting Web traffic, and e-mail risks.

Mobile Code

In the early days of the Web, users viewed *static* content (information that does not change) such as text and pictures through a Web browser. As the Internet increased in popularity, the demand rose for content that can change—such as animated images or customized information—based on who is viewing it or the time of day. Because basic HTML code could not provide these functions, this dynamic content required special computer code to be downloaded and executed in the user's Web browser. This code, which is obtained from an external source outside of the user's security perimeter and is executed on the local computer without the user's express approval, is often called **mobile code**.

Mobile code can also be used by attackers to download and run their programs on the local computer. The most common examples of mobile code are JavaScript, Java, and ActiveX.

JavaScript JavaScript is the most popular mobile code. Because JavaScript cannot create separate "stand-alone" applications, the JavaScript instructions are embedded inside HTML documents. When a Web site that uses JavaScript is accessed, the HTML document that contains the JavaScript code is downloaded onto the user's computer. The user's Web browser then executes that code. Figure 4-4 illustrates how JavaScript works.

Because visiting a Web site that automatically downloads code (bypassing the personal firewall) to run on a local computer can be dangerous, several defense mechanisms are intended to prevent JavaScript programs from causing serious harm. JavaScript does not support certain capabilities. For example, JavaScript running on a local computer cannot read, write, create, delete, or list the files on that computer.

However, there are still security concerns with JavaScript. A malicious JavaScript program could capture and remotely transmit user information without the user's knowledge or authorization. For example, an attacker could capture and send the user's e-mail address to a remote source or even send a fraudulent e-mail from the user's e-mail account. Other

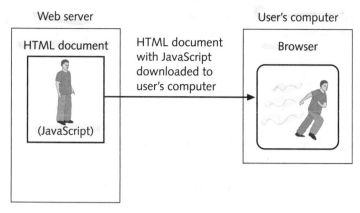

Figure 4-4 JavaScript
© Cengage Learning 2014

JavaScript attacks can be even more malicious. An attacker's JavaScript program could scan the user's network and then send specific commands to disable security settings.

Java Unlike JavaScript, **Java** is a complete programming language that can be used to create stand-alone applications. Java can also be used to create a smaller application called a **Java applet**. Whereas JavaScript is embedded in an HTML document, a Java applet is a separate program. Java applets are stored on the Web server and then downloaded onto the user's computer along with the HTML code, as shown in Figure 4-5. Java applets can perform interactive animations, mathematical calculations, or other simple tasks very quickly because the user's request does not have to be sent to the Web server for processing and then returned; instead, all of the processing is done on the local computer by the Java applet.

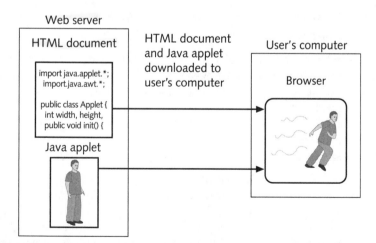

Figure 4-5 Java applet
© Cengage Learning 2014

In order to execute, Java applets require a software component to be added to a Web browser. This component is called a plug-in. A **plug-in** adds new functionality to the browser application so that users can play music and other multimedia content within the browser or view special graphical images that normally a browser could not play or display. The most widely used plug-ins for Web browsers are Java, Adobe Flash player, Apple QuickTime, and Adobe Acrobat Reader.

There are other types of components that add functionality to browsers. While a plug-in works within the browser, a helper application is started from the browser but runs as a separate application. Plug-ins are also different from extensions, which modify or add to existing functionality.

There are two types of Java applets. A **signed Java applet** has information that indicates the program is from a known source and has not been altered. An **unsigned Java applet** is a program that does not come from a trusted source. Unsigned Java applets run in a security **sandbox,** which is like a fence that surrounds the program and keeps it away from private data and other resources on a local computer. Unsigned Java applets cannot access specific resources on the computer (for example, run executable files, retrieve information stored on the system clipboard, or access printers), connect to or retrieve resources from another server, or change security settings. Signed Java applets can operate outside of the security sandbox if the user grants permission.

Because of the different ways in which Java applets can be signed, even signed Java applets should be considered as potentially harmful.

ActiveX ActiveX is not a programming language but a set of rules for how applications under the Microsoft Windows operating system should share information. **ActiveX controls** (also called add-ons) represent a specific way of implementing ActiveX and are sometimes called ActiveX applications. ActiveX controls can be invoked from Web pages through the use of a scripting language or directly by an HTML command.

An ActiveX control is similar to a Java applet in that it can perform many of the same functions. Unlike Java applets, however, ActiveX controls do not run in a sandbox but have full access to the underlying Windows operating system. Anything a user can do on a computer, an ActiveX control can do, such as deleting files or reformatting a hard drive. ActiveX controls are like miniature applications that can be run through the Web browser. They allow a Web site to interact directly with Windows and to perform functions that could not be performed using standard HTML code or scripting techniques.

To control the risks involved with ActiveX controls, Microsoft developed a registration system so that browsers can identify and authenticate an ActiveX control before downloading it. ActiveX controls can be signed or unsigned. A signed control provides a high degree of verification that the control was produced by the signer and has not been modified. However, signing does not guarantee the trustworthiness of the signer but only provides assurance that the control originated from the signer.

ActiveX poses a number of security concerns. First, the user's decision to allow installation of an ActiveX control is based on the *source* of the ActiveX control and not on the ActiveX control itself. The person who signed the control may not have properly assessed the control's safety and left open security vulnerabilities. Also, a control is registered only once per computer. If a computer is shared by multiple users, any user can download a control, making it available to all users on the machine. This means that a malicious ActiveX control can affect all users of that computer.

Cookies

HTTP does not have a mechanism for a Web site to track whether a user has previously visited that site. Any information that was entered on a previous visit, such as site preferences or the contents of an electronic shopping cart, is not retained so that the Web server can identify repeat customers. Instead of the Web server asking the user for the same information each time the site is visited, the server can store user-specific information in a file on the user's local computer and then retrieve it later. This file is called a **cookie.**

A cookie can contain a variety of information based on the user's preferences when visiting a Web site. For example, if a user inquires about a rental car at the car agency's Web site, that site might create a cookie that contains the user's travel itinerary. In addition, it may record the pages visited on a site to help the site customize the view for any future visits. Cookies can also store any personally identifiable information (name, e-mail address, work address, telephone number, and so on) that was provided when visiting the site; however, a Web site cannot gain access to information the user has stored on the local computer.

 Once a cookie is created on your computer then only the Web site that created the cookie can read it.

There are several different types of cookies:

- *First-party cookie.* A **first-party cookie** is created from the Web site that a user is currently viewing. For example, when viewing the Web site *www.cengage.com*, the cookie *CENGAGE* could be created and saved on the user's hard drive. Whenever the user returns to this site, that cookie would be used by the site to view the user's preferences and better customize the browsing experience.

- *Third-party cookie.* Some Web sites attempt to place additional cookies on the local hard drive. These cookies often come from third parties that advertise on the site and want to record the user's preferences. This is intended to tailor advertising to that user. These cookies are called **third-party cookies** because they are created by a third party (such as DoubleClick) that is different than the primary Web site.

- *Flash cookie.* A **Flash cookie** is named after the Adobe Flash player. Also known as *local shared objects* (LSOs), these cookies are significantly different from regular cookies. Flash cookies cannot always be deleted through the browser's normal configuration settings as regular cookies can. Typically, they are saved in multiple locations on the hard drive and can take up as much as 100,000 bytes of storage per cookie (about 25 times the size of a normal cookie). Flash cookies can also be used to reinstate regular cookies that a user has deleted or blocked. Known as *respawning*, the deleted cookie's unique ID can still be assigned to a new cookie using the data stored in a Flash cookie as a backup.

Cookies can pose both security and privacy risks. First-party cookies can be stolen and used to impersonate the user, while third-party cookies can be used to track the browsing or buying habits of a user. When multiple Web sites are serviced by a single marketing organization, cookies can be used to track browsing habits on all the client's sites. The marketing organization can track browsing habits from page to page within all the client sites and know which pages are being viewed, how often they are viewed, and the address of the viewing computer. This information can be used to infer what items the user may be interested in and to target advertising to the user.

Many Web sites use advertising and tracking features to watch what sites are visited in order to create a profile of user interests. When you visit a site it might create a unique identification number (like BTC081208) that is associated with your browser (they do not know your true identity). For example, this allows different ads to be displayed to baseball fans who are visiting spring training sites as opposed to those who are checking out tomorrow night's symphony performance. Not only will this tracking result in tailored ads being displayed as you surf, but it also will ensure that the same ads don't keep appearing over and over.

Fraudulent Digital Certificates

Consider Amanda who is making a purchase online by using her credit card. Because the Internet is an open network that allows virtually anyone to connect to it, it is critical to protect sensitive information—such as Amanda's credit card number—as it is being transported. Without this protection an attacker could "eavesdrop" on the transmission and steal Amanda's number.

An important means of protecting this information is to "scramble" it so that even if attackers access the data, they cannot read it. This scrambling is a process known as **cryptography** (from Greek words meaning *hidden writing*). Cryptography is the science of transforming information into a secure form while it is being transmitted or stored so that unauthorized persons cannot access it.

Cryptography's origins date back centuries. One of the most famous ancient cryptographers was Julius Caesar. In messages to his commanders, Caesar shifted each letter of his messages three places down in the alphabet, so that an *A* was replaced by a *D*, a *B* was replaced by an *E*, and so forth.

Changing the original text into a secret message using cryptography is known as **encryption**, while the reverse process—changing the scrambled encrypted message back into a readable form—is called **decryption**. An encryption **algorithm**, which consists of procedures based on a mathematical formula, is used to encrypt and decrypt the data. A **key** is a mathematical value entered into the algorithm to produce **ciphertext**, or text that is "scrambled." Just as a key is inserted into a lock to open or secure a door, in cryptography a unique mathematical key is input into the encryption algorithm to create the ciphertext. Once the ciphertext is transmitted and needs to be returned to its original state, the reverse process occurs with a decryption algorithm. The cryptography process is illustrated in Figure 4-6.

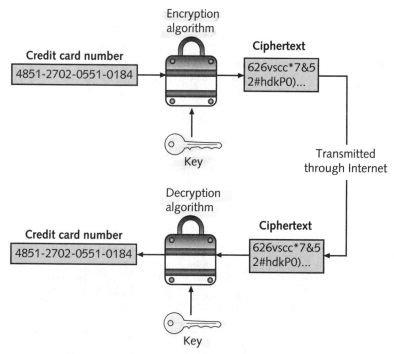

Figure 4-6 Cryptography process
© Cengage Learning 2014

One type of cryptography is called **public key cryptography** (also known as **asymmetric cryptography**). Public key cryptography uses two keys instead of only one. These keys are mathematically related and are known as the public key and the private key. The **public key** is known to everyone and can be freely distributed, while the **private key** is known only to the individual to whom it belongs. When Bob wants to send a secure message to Alice, he uses Alice's public key to encrypt the message. Alice then uses her private key to decrypt it. Public key cryptography is illustrated in Figure 4-7.

Because the public key is freely available to anyone, it would be possible for an attacker to substitute her own public key and then pretend to be a reliable source. To prevent this from occurring, digital certificates are used. A **digital certificate** is a technology that can associate a user's identity to a public key, in which the user's public key has been "digitally signed" by a trusted third party. This third party verifies the owner and that the public key belongs to that owner.

Web servers that accept confidential user information, such as a credit card number when making an online purchase, use digital certificates. The digital certificates perform two functions. First, they can ensure the authenticity of the Web server. Server digital certificates enable users connecting to the Web server to examine the identity of the server's owner. A user who connects to a Web site that has a digital certificate issued by a trusted third party can be confident that the data transmitted to the server is used only by the person or organization identified by the certificate. Second, digital certificates can ensure the authenticity of the cryptographic connection to the Web server. Sensitive connections to Web servers, such as when a user enters a credit card number to pay for an online purchase, need to be

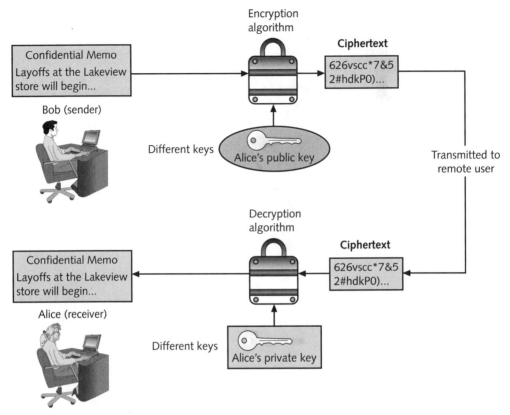

Figure 4-7 Public key cryptography
© Cengage Learning 2014

protected. Web servers can set up secure cryptographic connections so that all transmitted data is encrypted by providing the server's public key with a digital certificate to the client.

A server digital certificate ensures that the cryptographic connection functions as follows and is illustrated in Figure 4-8:

1. The Web server administrator generates an asymmetric pair of public and private keys for the server along with a server digital certificate that binds the public key with the identity of the server.

2. A user clicks on the *Pay Now* button to purchase merchandise.

3. The Web server presents its digital certificate to the user's Web browser. The browser examines the certificate's credentials and verifies that the third-party issuer is one that it recognizes (if the Web browser does not recognize the issuer it will issue a warning to the user).

4. The Web server's public key connected to the server's digital certificate is used to encrypt the credit card number on the user's computer, and then that encrypted data is transmitted to the Web server.

5. When the Web server receives the encrypted credit card data, it decrypts it using its private key.

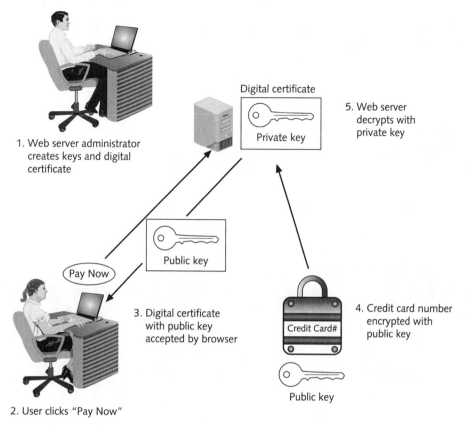

1. Web server administrator creates keys and digital certificate

Digital certificate

Private key

5. Web server decrypts with private key

Public key

Pay Now

3. Digital certificate with public key accepted by browser

Credit Card#

4. Credit card number encrypted with public key

Public key

2. User clicks "Pay Now"

Figure 4-8 Server digital certificate
© Cengage Learning 2014

A Web server digital certificate that both verifies the existence and identity of the organization and securely encrypts communications displays a sign to the user in the form of a padlock icon in the Web browser. Clicking the padlock icon displays information about the digital certificate along with the name of the site, as shown in Figure 4-9.

In recent years digital certificates, because of the valuable protection they afford, have come under different attacks:

- *Theft of valid digital certificates.* The theft of valid digital certificates from the trusted third parties that issue them has significantly increased. In one recent event, over 500 digital certificates were stolen from a Dutch firm. Further investigation revealed that these certificates were then used to validate a fake Google Gmail site (any users going to that site would have a padlock displayed that would trick them into thinking they were at the actual Gmail site). It is surmised that the attackers may have been part of a Middle Eastern government that wanted to spy on citizens in order to locate and crack down on dissidents. The government spies could log in to the fake Gmail mailboxes of the victims and read any stored e-mails as well as look at any documents created. In addition, the exact location of the victim could be determined.

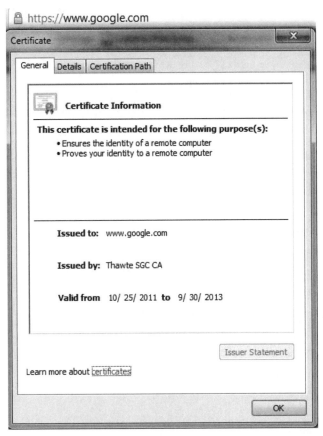

Figure 4-9 Padlock icon and certificate information
Source: Windows Internet Explorer 9

- *Creation of rogue digital certificates.* By creating a fictitious ("rogue") digital certificate, attackers can use them to pretend to be from a trusted third party. One recent piece of malware created a fake Microsoft code-signing digital certificate that allowed the attackers to distribute malware to Windows computers, which appeared as an update from Microsoft.

 To check on the validity of a digital certificate while surfing the Web you can click the padlock icon.

Drive-By Downloads

Most Internet users know that in order to avoid being infected while surfing they should not download any suspicious software. Yet what if just *viewing* a Web page could cause the computer to become infected? And what if that Web page was on a well-known and reputable Web site, such as a bank or a national retailer? Such occurrences, called **drive-by downloads,** are happening every day.

Attackers first identify a well-known Web site and then attempt to inject content by exploiting it through vulnerable applications like JavaScript. These vulnerabilities permit the attacker to gain direct access to the Web server's underlying operating system and then inject new content into the compromised Web site. The injected content is virtually invisible to the naked eye.

Technically speaking, the attackers use *zero pixel IFrame*. IFrame (short for *inline frame*) is an HTML element that allows for one HTML document to be embedded inside the main document. It is almost impossible to see a zero pixel IFrame.

When unsuspecting users visit an infected Web site, their browsers download code usually written in JavaScript that targets a vulnerability in the user's browser. If the script can run successfully on the user's computer, it will instruct the browser to connect to the attacker's own Web server to download malware, which is then automatically installed and executed on the user's computer. Unlike a traditional download that asks for the user's permission to perform an action, a drive-by download can be initiated simply by visiting a Web site.

CNET.com, ABC News' homepage, and Walmart.com have all at one time or another been infected with drive-by download malware.

Redirected Web Traffic

It is not uncommon for a user to make a mistake when typing a Web address into a browser. Table 4-1 lists some of the typical mistakes when attempting to enter the address *www.cengage.com*.

Type of Mistake	Example
Misspell the address	*www.cengag.com*
Omit a dot	*wwwcengage.com*
Omit a word	*www.cengage*
Incorrect punctuation	*www-cengage.com*

Table 4-1 Typical errors in entering Web addresses
© Cengage Learning 2014

Usually these mistakes result in the Web browser not being able to access the site and instead an error message is displayed. However, attackers can exploit a misaddressed Web name by registering the names of similar-sounding Web sites, such as *www.cengag.com*, *www.cengagge.com*, and *www.cengage.org*. When users attempt to enter *www.cengage.com* but makes a typing error they are instead directed to the attacker's Web site of that same name. Because this site is designed to look similar to the genuine site, users can be tricked into entering personal information that is then stolen.

Redirecting Web traffic is not limited to attackers. Several well-known Internet service providers (ISPs) automatically funnel misspelled addresses into their own Web site that contains a search feature.

E-Mail Risks

One of the more common means of distributing attacks is through e-mail. E-mail risks include spam, malicious attachments, and embedded hyperlinks.

Spam The amount of **spam**, or unsolicited e-mail, which goes through the Internet continues to escalate. Google estimates that 9 out of every 10 e-mail messages is spam.[2] The reason why users receive so many spam messages that advertise drugs, cheap mortgage rates, and items for sale is because sending spam is a lucrative business. It costs spammers very little to send millions of spam e-mail messages. In the past, spammers would purchase a list of valid e-mail addresses ($100 for 10 million addresses) and rent a motel room with a high-speed Internet connection ($85 per day) as a base for launching attacks. Today, however, almost all spam is sent from botnets: a spammer who does not own his own botnet can lease time from other attackers ($40 per hour) to use a botnet of up to 100,000 infected computers to launch a spam attack. Even if spammers receive only a very small percentage of responses, they still make a large profit. For example, if a spammer sent spam to 6 million users for a product with a sale price of $50 that cost only $5 to make, and if only 0.001 percent of the recipients responded and bought the product (a typical response rate), the spammer would make over $270,000 in profit.

A Russian-owned network was widely believed to be the hosting command and control center for five major botnets. When this network was disconnected from the Internet all of their botnets stopped functioning and spam volumes worldwide immediately fell by 75 percent.

Text-based spam messages that include words such as *Viagra* or *investments* can easily be trapped by **spam filters** that look for these words and block the e-mail. Because of the increased use of these filters, spammers have turned to another approach for sending out their spam. Known as **image spam**, it uses graphical images of text in order to circumvent text-based filters. Image spam cannot be filtered based on the content of the message because it appears as an image instead of text. These spam messages often include nonsense text so that it appears the e-mail message is legitimate (an e-mail with no text can prompt the spam filter to block it). Figure 4-10 shows an example of an image spam.

Beyond just being annoying, spam significantly reduces work productivity as users spend time deleting spam messages. Spam is also costly to organizations that must install and monitor technology to block spam. However, one of the greatest risks of spam is that it is used to widely distribute malware.

Malicious Attachments Another common means of distributing attacks is through e-mail attachments, or files that are sent with an e-mail message. Most users are unaware of the danger of attachments and routinely open any e-mail attachment that they receive, even if it is

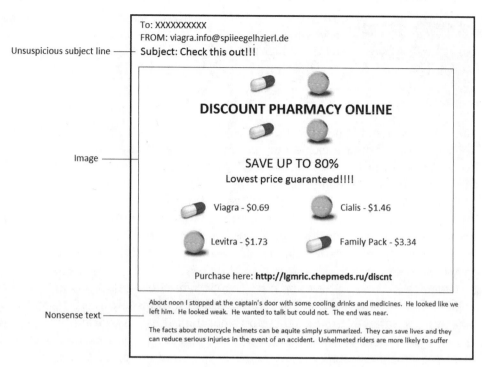

Unsuspicious subject line ——

Image ——

Nonsense text ——

Figure 4-10 Image spam
© Cengage Learning 2014

from an unknown sender. Attackers often include in the subject line information that entices even reluctant users to open the attachment, such as a current event (*Check out this info about yesterday's hurricane*) or information about the recipient (*Is this really you in this picture?*).

E-mail-distributed malware will often take advantage of information contained on the user's computer. For example, malware can replicate by sending itself as an e-mail attachment to all of the contacts in a user's e-mail address book. The unsuspecting recipients, seeing that an e-mail and attachment arrived from a "friend," typically with a provocative subject line, open the attachment and infect their computers.

If a file attached to an e-mail message contains a virus, the virus is launched when the file attachment is opened.

Embedded Hyperlinks Many e-mail messages have **embedded hyperlinks**, which are contained within the body of the message as a shortcut to a Web site. However, attackers can take advantage of embedded hyperlinks to direct users to the attacker's Web site instead. This "trickery" can be easily accomplished because an embedded hyperlink can display only words and not the actual address of the Web site. For example, an attacker could create an embedded hyperlink that appears legitimate to the reader (*Click here to log in to Online Account Services*) yet the underlying Web address to which the user is directed is the attacker's site. Even an embedded hyperlink that appears to be a legitimate

Security in Your World

"Chiara", said Jamal, "If you were trying to scare me you've done a pretty good job!" Chiara had just finished explaining to Jamal several of the types of attacks that can occur through the Internet. "But aren't these attacks rare? I mean, I don't hear my friends talking about being attacked."

Chiara smiled and said, "Well, I know you were in class the day when we talked about this. Remember our instructor said that right now about 25 percent of Internet users have infected computers, and most of them don't even know it? That's probably why your friends aren't telling you they've been attacked: they don't know that they have been!"

Jamal leaned back in his chair and said, "So what do we do?" Chiara took her book and opened it. "This says there are some security settings to configure your browser to make surfing safer. But one of the most important things is to use common sense. Just like my mother used to tell me not to drive around at night with my car doors unlocked, there are some basic Internet security things you can do to protect yourself."

"I feel like I'm surfing the Internet with my doors unlocked!" Jamal laughed. "Here, let me see what it says."

Web address (*www.onlineaccount.com*) can be crafted so that it goes to a different Web site (*www.attackers-dungeon.net*). The attacker's "look-alike" Web site asks the user to enter personal information, which the attacker captures and uses. In short, embedded hyperlinks can take users anywhere.

One organization distributed an e-mail from the IT security department that specifically warned users not to click on embedded hyperlinks because of the danger associated with them. However, at the bottom of the e-mail it said, "For more information click on this link"!

Internet Defenses

There are several defenses that can be used to protect against Internet attacks. These defenses include using configuring Web browser settings and using e-mail defenses.

Configuring Web Browser Settings

One of the best lines of defense against Internet attack is properly configuring the security settings on the Web browser. Modern Web browsers are highly customizable and allow the user to tailor the settings based on personal preferences. Beyond basic settings such as preferred home page and the size of displayed characters, browsers also allow the user to customize security and privacy settings.

Microsoft Internet Explorer (IE) is a typical Web browser that can be configured for security. This configuration of IE browser settings is performed by selecting security options to be turned on or off. IE Web browser defenses can be divided into four categories: advanced security settings, security zones, restricting cookies, and pop-up blockers.

Besides IE, other popular Web browsers include Firefox, Safari, Opera, and Chrome. Many of these browsers have settings similar to those illustrated in IE.

Advanced Security Settings Web browsers offer a wide range of configuration settings. For example, IE has over 60 configuration settings, many related to security. Figure 4-11 illustrates some of the security settings, several of which are described in the following list.

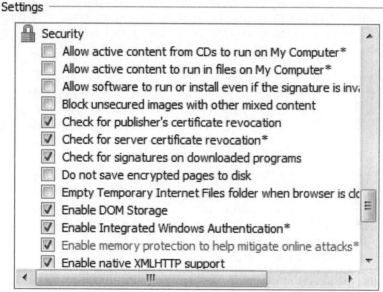

Figure 4-11 Internet Explorer security settings
Source: Windows Internet Explorer 9

- *Do not save encrypted pages to disk.* When a Web site is viewed, the actual HTML documents are sent from the Web server to the local computer and saved on the hard drive in an area known as Temporary Internet Files for the browser to display. A secure Web site may transmit sensitive information in a special encrypted form that prevents attackers from seeing the information while in transit. However, after the HTML document is saved on the hard drive, an attacker who could gain access to the computer may be able to retrieve it. This Web browser option prevents sensitive encrypted Web pages from being permanently saved on the hard drive.

- *Empty Temporary Internet Files folder when browser is closed.* To speed up processing, a Web browser first checks the hard drive on which the HTML documents are stored when they are received from the Web server. If the requested document is already stored, a Web browser only has to redisplay it and not request it again from the Web server. However, the stored information could be used by an attacker. This browser security option empties this folder whenever the browser is closed.

- *Warn if changing between secure and not secure mode.* While Web sites use the standard HTTP protocol for sending data through the Internet, this protocol is not secure and an attacker could view the contents of the transmission. An enhanced version of HTTP encrypts the data sent between the Web browser and the Web server so that it cannot be viewed by others. Turning on this option causes the Web browser to alert the user with a warning message when the Web server changes from secure to not secure mode.

Other advanced security settings restrict mobile code. For example, a setting that relates to Java applets, JavaScript, and ActiveX can disable, enable, or prompt the user before the code runs. However, disabling code may result in Web pages not being displayed properly.

Security Zones One of the drawbacks of the security configuration settings in Web browsers is that the user may not want to apply the same settings for accessing all Web sites. For example, a restrictive Web browser security setting that is set for online banking may prevent the same user from properly accessing a school's Web site to take an online exam.

One solution to this problem is to create Web zones. Some Web browsers allow the user to set customized security for these zones and then assign specific Web sites to a zone. For example, IE divides the Internet into four security zones, each of which can have a predefined (Low, Medium-low, Medium, or High) or customized security level, as shown in Figure 4-12. Table 4-2 lists the different IE Web zones.

Security zones can be used to defend against drive-by downloads.

Web sites can be assigned to one of these four zones. When that site is accessed, the security level for that zone is automatically invoked. This makes it easier to set browser security levels for different Web sites.

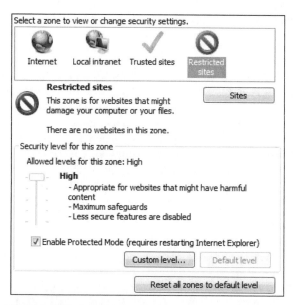

Figure 4-12 IE security zones

Source: Windows Internet Explorer 9

Zone	Description	Default Security Level
Internet	The default for all Web site sites. It prompts the user before downloading unsafe content and certain ActiveX controls are not downloaded.	Medium-high
Local intranet	Web pages from an organization's internal Web site are typically added to this zone. Most content will run without prompting the user.	Medium-low
Trusted sites	Web sites that are trusted not to pose any harm to a computer can be placed here.	Medium
Restricted sites	A Web site that is considered to be potentially harmful can be placed in the Restricted Sites zone.	High

Table 4-2 IE Web security zones

© Cengage Learning 2014

When a Web site that has been placed in one of the security zones is viewed, an icon representing that zone is displayed.

Restricting Cookies Restricting how cookies are created and used can also be done through configuring the Web browser. Most browsers allow users to configure cookies to one of the following types of settings:

- Allow all cookies to be set
- Block third-party cookies only

- Block sites from creating any cookies
- Keep cookies only until the browser is closed

Pop-Up blockers A pop-up blocker allows the user to limit or block most pop-ups. Whereas at one time these were separate programs, today they are a feature incorporated within a browser. Users can select the level of blocking, ranging from blocking all pop-ups to allowing specific pop-ups. When a pop-up is detected an alert can be displayed in the browser such as *Pop-up blocked; to see this pop-up or additional options click here.* The configuration settings for a typical browser pop-up blocker are shown in Figure 4-13. Users can select from having all pop-ups blocked, blocking most automatic pop-ups, or allow pop-ups from secure sites.

Figure 4-13 Pop-up blocker settings
Source: Windows Internet Explorer 9

E-Mail Defenses

There are security defenses that can be configured to protect attacks through e-mail. The most common are spam filtering, the security settings in client-based e-mail programs, and securing attachments.

Spam Filters Beyond being annoying and disruptive, spam can also pose a serious security risk: spammers can distribute viruses as attachments through their spam e-mail messages. Spam filtering applications can be implemented on both the user's local computer as well as at the corporate or the Internet service provider level. An **Internet service provider (ISP)** is a business from which users purchase Internet access.

Most users actually receive only a small amount of spam in their local e-mail inbox. The majority is blocked before it even reaches the user.

E-mail can be accessed through either a Web browser or by using the local e-mail client, which is a program that runs on the computer. E-mail clients can be typically configured to filter spam that has bypassed the organization's or ISP's spam filter. The e-mail client spam filtering settings often include these features to block spam:

- *Blocked senders.* A list of senders can be entered for which the user does not want to receive any e-mail, also known as a **blacklist**. Any message received from one of the senders is sent to the junk e-mail folder. Several databases of blacklists are available on the Internet that include known spammers and others who distribute malicious content, and some sites allow users to download the lists and automatically add them to their e-mail server.

- *Allowed senders.* A list of senders can be entered for which the user will accept e-mail, also known as a **whitelist**.

- *Blocked top-level domain list.* E-mail from entire countries or regions can also be blocked and treated as spam.

Microsoft Outlook automatically blocks over 80 different types of file attachments that may contain malware.

E-mail Security Settings In addition to spam filters on the local e-mail client, there are other security settings that can be configured through the e-mail client application. These include:

- *Read messages using a reading pane.* Most e-mail clients contain a **reading pane**, which allows the user to read an e-mail message without actually opening it. Received e-mail messages can be viewed safely in the reading pane because malicious scripts and attachments are not activated or opened automatically in the reading pane.

Although malicious attachments may be blocked by using the e-mail reading pane, messages and attachments from unknown or unsolicited senders should always be treated with caution.

- *Block external content.* E-mail clients can be configured to block external content in HTML e-mail messages that are received, such as hyperlinks to pictures or sounds. When a user opens an e-mail message or it is displayed in the reading pane, the computer downloads the external content so that the picture can be displayed or the sound played. Spammers often send out spam to a wide range of e-mail addresses, not knowing which e-mail addresses exist or are accurate. In order to determine which e-mail addresses are valid and actually exist, a spammer can note which e-mail accounts downloaded the external content and then add those e-mail accounts to their spam list. Blocking external content helps to prevent this.

- *Use an e-mail postmark.* Occasionally it may be necessary to send a legitimate e-mail message that could look like spam and the recipient's spam filter could reject it. Some e-mail clients, like Microsoft Outlook, have an e-mail postmark feature. When the user sends a message with "spamlike" characteristics, the e-mail client solves a computationally costly puzzle and then puts that information about the puzzle and solution into two fields in the e-mail message's header. The recipient of the message does not see this information, but if she is using a compatible e-mail client, it can use the contents of the message to determine that the message is valid and not spam.

Although the sender of a message using the e-mail postmark probably will not notice the slight delay on an individual message when the puzzle is being computed, a spammer who tried to add an e-mail postmark to all of his spam would significantly slow down his computer, thus making postmarking impractical for spammers.

Attachments Because e-mail attachments can contain malware, it is important to be wary regarding these types of files. With some e-mail clients, when an attachment is received with an e-mail message, the client will permit the user to preview the contents of the attachment without saving and opening it. This helps to protect the user from malicious code that may be embedded in the attachment because scripts and ActiveX controls are disabled during attachment preview.

Attachment protection is also becoming available in other applications. Beginning with Microsoft Office 2010, all Office attachments (Word, Excel, PowerPoint, etc.) are automatically opened in **Protected View**, which is a read-only mode that disables editing functions. This helps prevent a malicious attachment from installing malware when it is opened by an unsuspecting user. The following are reasons why a file would be opened by Office in Protected View:

- *The file was opened from an Internet location.* A file that originated from an Internet location, such as downloaded from a Web-based e-mail, could be unsafe.

- *The file was received as an Outlook attachment and your computer policy has defined the sender as unsafe.* Protected View indicates that the file was received from a potentially unsafe sender.

- *The file was opened from an unsafe location.* A file that is opened from an area that Office considers to be unsafe, such as the Temporary Internet Files folder, would create this message.

- *The file is blocked by File Block*. Selected older versions of Microsoft Office documents, such as Word 2.0 and Excel 2.0, can harbor malicious code and are automatically blocked.

- *File validation failure*. Office has detected a problem with the file, and editing it may harm the computer.

A color-coded warning indicator at the top of the Office document explains why it was opened in Protected View. Users can click on the *Enable Editing* button in order to accept the file for editing.

As with all warnings, it is recommended that the Protected View *Enable Editing* button not be clicked without giving any thought to the source of the document. Protected View is designed to make the user pause and think about the risks before proceeding.

Internet Security Best Practices

There are several Internet security best practices when using e-mail or surfing the Web. Table 4-3 summarizes several of these practices.

Attack	Defense	Comments
Mobile code (JavaScript, Java, and ActiveX) performs malicious action	Disable from running in Web browser through browser settings.	Some Web pages may not function properly if mobile code is disabled.
Third-party cookies used to track browsing	Restrict cookies in Web browser through browser settings.	Cookies can make Web browser easier by not having to reenter the same information.
Redirected Web traffic through misspellings	Double-check typed address before submitting.	Difficult to see misspellings in long addresses
Attacks through e-mail spam or infected attachments	Use spam filters, reading panes, preview attachments, and Protected View.	Can easily be set through e-mail client or application
Embedded hyperlinks sends user to attacker's Web site.	Do not click on embedded hyperlinks in an e-mail.	These hyperlinks can mask the actual destination.
Malware takes advantage of vulnerability in plug-in	Configure browser to prompt user for permission to run plug-in or disable all plug-ins.	Some functionality may be lost when plug-ins are disabled.
Drive-by downloads infect computer	Set up browser security zones.	Takes time to manage multiple sites
Compromised digital certificates can be used to capture information.	When the padlock icon appears click on it to check the certificate's validity.	Will not detect if the certificate has been stolen

Table 4-3 Internet security best practices
© Cengage Learning 2014

It is important to remember the tradeoff between security and convenience when deciding upon which of these practices to use on a daily basis. Although some users may consider one or more of these best practices as "intrusive," they are designed to make using the Internet safer.

Chapter Summary

- The Internet is a worldwide set of interconnected computers, servers, and networks. It is composed of networks to which devices are attached. These networks are operated by industry, governments, schools, and even individuals who all loosely cooperate. The World Wide Web (WWW) is composed of Internet server computers on networks that provide online information the Hypertext Markup Language (HTML) format. HTML allows Web authors to combine text, graphic images, audio, video, and hyperlinks into a single document. Instructions written in HTML code specify how a local computer's Web browser should display the various elements. Web servers distribute HTML documents based on a set of standards known as the Hypertext Transport Protocol (HTTP). E-mail systems use two protocols to send and receive messages: the Simple Mail Transfer Protocol (SMTP) handles outgoing mail, while the Post Office Protocol (POP3) is responsible for incoming mail.

- Dynamic Web content requires special computer code to be downloaded and executed in the user's Web browser. This code is called mobile code. JavaScript is the most popular mobile code. Because JavaScript cannot create separate "stand-alone" applications, the JavaScript instructions are embedded inside HTML documents. Java is a complete programming language that can be used to create stand-alone applications called Java applets. Java applets require a software component added to a Web browser called a plug-in. ActiveX controls represent a specific way of implementing ActiveX in Microsoft Windows and are sometimes called ActiveX applications. ActiveX controls can be invoked from Web pages through the use of a scripting language or directly by an HTML command. Each of these three types of mobile code has associated security risks.

- A cookie is a file that a Web server stores on the local computer that contains user-specific information. A first-party cookie is created from the Web site that a user is currently viewing, while a third-party cookie is created by another entity that is different from the primary Web site. A Flash cookie is named after the Adobe Flash player. Cookies can pose both security and privacy risks. A digital certificate is a technology that can associate a user's identity with a cryptographic public key, in which the user's public key that has been "digitally signed" by a trusted third party. This third party verifies the owner and that the public key belongs to that owner. Because of their importance, digital certificates have increasingly been the targets of attacks.

- A drive-by download can infect a user's computer a result of just viewing a Web page, without downloading any content from it. It is not uncommon for a user to make a mistake when typing a Web address into a browser. Attackers can exploit a misaddressed Web name by registering the names of similar-sounding Web sites and directing users to one of those sites.

■ One of the more common means of distributing attacks is through e-mail. Spam, or unsolicited e-mail, is widely used to distribute malware. Another common means of distributing attacks is through e-mail attachments, or files that are sent with an e-mail message. These files can contain malware and can infect a user's computer when they are opened. E-mail messages often contain embedded hyperlinks, which are contained within the body of the message as a shortcut to a Web site. Attackers can take advantage of embedded hyperlinks to direct users to the attacker's Web site instead. Some Web browsers allow the user to set customized security for these zones and then assign specific Web sites to a zone, which can have their own level of security. Restricting how cookies are created and used can also be done by configuring the Web browser. A pop-up blocker allows the user to limit or block most pop-ups and is a feature incorporated within a browser. Users can select the level of blocking, ranging from blocking all pop-ups to allowing specific pop-ups.

■ There are different defenses that can be used to protect against Internet attacks. One of the best lines of defense against Internet attack is properly configuring the security settings on the Web browser, which allows the user to customize security and privacy settings. One important setting is to restrict mobile code so that Java applets, Java-Script, and ActiveX are disabled or must prompt the user before the code runs.

■ There are security defenses that can be configured to protect against attacks through e-mail. E-mail clients can be typically configured to filter spam that has bypassed other spam filters. Most e-mail clients contain a reading pane that allows the user to read an e-mail message without actually opening it. Received e-mail messages can be viewed safely in the reading pane because malicious scripts and attachments are not activated or opened automatically in the reading pane. E-mail clients can also be configured to block external content in HTML e-mail messages that are received, such as hyperlinks to pictures or sounds. Because e-mail attachments can contain malware, it is important to be wary regarding these types of files. With some e-mail clients when an attachment is received with an e-mail message the client will permit the user to preview the contents of the attachment without saving and opening it. Attachment protection is also becoming available in other applications.

Key Terms

ActiveX   A set of rules for how applications under the Microsoft Windows operating system should share information.

ActiveX control   A specific way of implementing ActiveX.

algorithm   Procedures based on a mathematical formula used to encrypt and decrypt data.

attachments   Documents that are connected to an e-mail message, such as word processing documents, spreadsheets, or pictures.

blacklist   A list of senders from which the user does not want to receive any e-mail.

browser   A program for displaying Web pages.

ciphertext   Text that is scrambled so that it cannot be read by an unauthorized party.

cookie   A file created by a Web server and stored on the local computer that contains user's preferences.

cryptography   The science of transforming information into a secure form while it is being transmitted or stored so that unauthorized persons cannot access it.

decryption   Changing encrypted text back into its original format that can be read.

digital certificate   A technology that can associate a user's identity to a public key and that is digitally signed by a trusted third party.

drive-by download   An attack that results from a user visiting a specially crafted malicious Web page.

embedded hyperlinks   Links contained within the body of the message as a shortcut to a Web site.

encryption   Changing the original text into a scrambled message that cannot be read by unauthorized users.

first-party cookie   A cookie that is created from the Web site that a user is currently viewing.

Flash cookie   A cookie named after the Adobe Flash player.

hyperlinks   Links that allow users to jump from one area on the Web to another with a click of the mouse button.

Hypertext Markup Language (HTML)   A language that allows Web authors to combine text, graphic images, audio, and video into a single document.

Hypertext Transfer Protocol (HTTP)   A subset of a larger set of standards for Internet transmission.

image spam   Spam that uses graphical images of text in order to circumvent text-based filters.

IMAP (Internet Mail Access Protocol)   An advanced e-mail protocol.

IMAP4   The version of IMAP current at the time of writing.

Internet   A worldwide set of interconnected computers, servers, and networks.

Internet service provider (ISP)   A business from which users purchase Internet access.

Java   A complete programming language that can be used to create stand-alone applications.

Java applet   A smaller Java application that is a separate program.

JavaScript   A type of mobile code embedded within HTML documents that is downloaded and executed in the user's Web browser.

key   A mathematical value entered into an algorithm in cryptography.

mobile code   Special computer code that is downloaded and executed in the Web browser.

plug-in   A software component added to a Web browser that adds new functionality.

POP3   The version of the Post Office Protocol current at the time of writing.

pop-up blocker   A Web browser setting that limits or blocks most pop-ups.

port number   An identifier that indicates the program or service that is being requested.

Post Office Protocol (POP)   The protocol for e-mail that handles incoming mail.

private key   One key of public key cryptography that must be kept secret.

Protected View   A Microsoft Office function that automatically opens selected documents in a read-only mode that disables editing functions.

protocol   A set of standards.

public key cryptography (asymmetric cryptography)   Cryptography that uses two mathematically related keys instead of only one.

public key   One key of public key cryptography that is known to everyone and can be freely distributed.

reading pane   An e-mail client feature that allows the user to read an e-mail message without actually opening it.

sandbox   A software technology that surrounds a program and keeps it away from private data and other resources on a local computer.

signed Java applet   A Java applet that has information that indicates the program is from a known source and has not been altered.

Simple Mail Transfer Protocol (SMTP)   The protocol for e-mail that handles outgoing mail.

spam filters   Software that inspects e-mail messages to identify and stop spam.

spam   Unsolicited e-mail.

third-party cookie   A cookie that is created by a third party.

Transmission Control Protocol/Internet Protocol (TCP/IP)   The standards for Internet transmissions.

unsigned Java applet   A Java applet that does not come from a trusted source.

whitelist   A list of senders from which the user will accept e-mail.

World Wide Web (WWW)   A network composed of Internet server computers on networks that provide online information in a specific format.

Review Questions

1. Each of the following is true about the Internet except:
    a. It is a local network of computers and networks.
    b. It is composed of networks to which devices are attached.
    c. It is not controlled by a single organization or government entity.
    d. Industry, governments, schools, and individuals all loosely cooperate in the Internet's self-governance.

2. What is the format used to write World Wide Web pages?
    a. Hypertext Transport Protocol (HTTP)
    b. Transmission Control Protocol/Internet Protocol (TCP/IP)
    c. Microsoft Adobe Printer (MAP)
    d. Hypertext Markup Language (HTML)

3. A(n) _____ identifies the program or service that is being requested from a Web browser.
   a. key
   b. port number
   c. HTML flag
   d. HTTPS footer

4. Which of these protocols handles outgoing e-mail?
   a. Simple Mail Transfer Protocol (SMTP)
   b. Post Office Protocol (POP)
   c. Internet Mail Access Protocol (IMAP)
   d. Hypertext Transport Protocol (HTTP)

5. Each of the following is an example of mobile code except _____.
   a. VMware
   b. JavaScript
   c. Java
   d. ActiveX

6. A cookie that was not created by the Web site that attempts to access it is called a _____.
   a. first-party cookie
   b. second-party cookie
   c. third-party cookie
   d. resource cookie

7. Which of the follow mobile codes resides outside an HTML document as a separate program?
   a. Java applet
   b. JavaScript
   c. ActiveY
   d. JavaRun

8. A Java applet _____ is a barrier that surrounds the applet to keep it away from resources on the local computer.
   a. container
   b. playpen
   c. fence
   d. sandbox

9. A _____ is a list of e-mail addresses from senders from whom you do not want to receive messages.

    a. whitelist

    b. bluelist

    c. redlist

    d. blacklist

10. Which of the following is true about a cookie?

    a. It can contain a virus.

    b. It acts like a worm.

    c. It places a small file on the Web server computer sent from the browser.

    d. It can pose a security and privacy risk.

11. Bob's computer was infected from a drive-by download attack. What did Bob do to get infected?

    a. He opened an e-mail attachment.

    b. He viewed a Web site.

    c. He clicked "Download."

    d. He unknowingly sent a virus to a Web site.

12. What is required for a Java applet to run in a Web browser?

    a. An extension

    b. A plug-in

    c. A control

    d. An extender

13. How many keys are needed for public key cryptography?

    a. One

    b. Two

    c. Three

    d. No limit

14. What sign is displayed by the Web browser to show that a digital certificate is being used?

    a. Key

    b. Door

    c. Padlock

    d. Bar

15. Why should you not click on an embedded hyperlink?

   a. They are slow.

   b. They seldom work properly.

   c. They can take you to a different Web site other than what is being advertised.

   d. They can take up too much disk space on your computer.

16. A reading pane allows the user to read an e-mail message_____.

   a. after the attachment has been saved to the hard drive

   b. only one time

   c. without actually opening it

   d. from a remote location

17. Each of the following is an Internet zone in Internet Explorer (IE) except_____.

   a. Internet

   b. Extranet

   c. Trusted sites

   d. Restricted sites

18. Which Internet Explorer (IE) Web zone is the default?

   a. Internet

   b. Local intranet

   c. Trusted Internet

   d. Remote Web

19. Why would you want to block external content from downloading into your e-mail client?

   a. To prevent spammers from knowing that your e-mail address is valid

   b. To take advantage of the remote reading pane

   c. To slow down your e-mail client so you can read the message

   d. To prevent your computer's graphics processor utility buffer from filling too quickly

20. Which of the following is not an Internet security best practice?

   a. Restrict cookies in Web browsers through browser settings.

   b. Double-check spelling on a typed Web address before submitting.

   c. Do not click on embedded hyperlinks in an e-mail.

   d. Run mobile code to prevent attacks.

Hands-On Projects

Project 4-1: Test Browser Security

One of the first steps in securing a Web browser is to conduct an analysis to determine if any security vulnerabilities exist. These vulnerabilities may be a result of missing patches of out of date plug-ins. In this project, you will use a plug-in to scan the browser.

1. Open your Web browser and enter the URL **browsercheck.qualys.com**.

> The location of content on the Internet such as this program may change without warning. If you are no longer able to access the program through the above URL then use a search engine to search for "Qualys Browser Check".

2. Note that the Web browser you are currently using is listed on this Web page.
3. Click **FAQ**.
4. Read the information on this page about what the Qualys browser check plug-in will do.
5. Return to the home page.
6. Click **Install Plugin**.
7. Check the box **I have read and accepted the Service User Agreement**.
8. Click **Continue**.
9. Follow your browser's instructions to install the plug-in.
10. After the plug-in is installed, a button may appear on the Web page that says **Update Plugin**. If it appears, click on the button to update the plug-in.
11. The plug-in should begin to scan your browser. If it does not automatically start click **Scan**.
12. An analysis of the browser's security will appear, like that shown in Figure 4-14.
13. If there are any security issues detected, click the **Fix It** buttons to correct the problem. Follow the instructions on each page to correct the problems.
14. Return to the Qualys scan results page.
15. If you have more than one Web browser on your computer under **Scan Options**, click **All Browsers and Plugins** and then click **Re-Scan**. This will scan all browsers on the computer.
16. Under **Detected Browsers**, click the appropriate browser to review and correct any security problems.
17. Close all windows.

Figure 4-14 Browser security scan results

Source: Qualys Browser scan at https://browsercheck.qualys.com

Project 4-2: Set Web Browser Security

Web browsers can provide protections against attacks. In this project, you will use the Windows Internet Explorer (IE) Version 9 Web browser.

1. Start **Internet Explorer**.

2. Click the **Tools** icon and then click **Internet options** to display the Internet Options dialog box. Click the **General** tab, if necessary.

3. First remove all of the HTML documents and cookies that are in the cache on the computer. Before erasing the files, look at what is stored in the cache. Under **Browsing history**, click the **Settings** button and then click the **View files** button to see all of the files. If necessary, maximize the window that displays the files.

4. Click the **Last Checked** column heading to see how long this information has been on the computer.

5. Next, select a cookie by locating one in the **Name** column (it will be something like *cookie: windows_7@microsoft.com*). Double-click the

name of the cookie to open it. If you receive a Windows warning message, click **Yes.** What information does this cookie provide? Close the cookie file and open several other cookies. Do some cookies contain more information than others?

6. Close the window listing the cookie files to return to the Settings dialog box. Click the **Cancel** button.

7. In the Internet Options dialog box under Browsing History, click **Delete.**

8. In the Delete Browsing History dialog box, click **Delete All** and then **Yes.**

9. Close the Internet Options dialog box.

10. Click the **Tools** icon and then click **Manage Add-ons.**

11. Under Add-on Types there are the different add-on categories. Select an add-on that has been added to this browser and view its name, publisher, version, and type in the details section of the window.

12. Close the dialog box.

13. Click the **Tools** icon and then **Internet Options.**

14. Click the **Security** tab to display the security options. Click the **Internet** icon. This is the zone in which all Web sites are placed that are not in another zone. Under **Security level for this zone** move the slider to look at the various settings.

15. Click **Custom level** and scroll through the ActiveX security settings. Would you consider these sufficient? Click **Cancel.**

16. Now place a Web site in the **Restricted** zone. Click **OK** and return to your Web browser. Go to **www.bad.com** and view the information on that site. Notice that the status bar displays an Internet icon, indicating that this Web site is in the Internet zone. Click your **Home** button.

17. Click the **Tools** icon and then click **Internet Options** to display the Internet Options dialog box again. Click the **Security** tab and then click **Restricted sites.** Click **Sites,** enter **www.bad.com,** click **Add,** and then click **OK.** Now return to that site again. What happens this time? Why?

18. Click the **Privacy** tab. Drag the slider up and down to view the different privacy settings regarding cookies. Which one should you choose? Choose one and then click **Apply.**

19. Click **Close.**

20. IE 9 also offers tracking protection. Click the **Tools** icon and then click **Safety.**

21. Click **Tracking Protection.**

22. Click the **Enable** button in this new window.

23. There are two ways to add sites from which you will be protected. You can visit the Web site that has added a script or cookie onto your computer and then click the **Settings** button to add or remove the site. Another option is to download a list of sites. Go to **ie.microsoft.com/testdrive/Browser/Tracking ProtectionLists/Default.html**

The location of content on the Internet, such as this program, may change without warning. If you are no longer able to access the program through the above URL, then use a search engine to search for "Internet Explorer 9 TPL".

24. Click **Privacy choice**.

25. Notice that there are two choices for blocking sites. Read the information about each. If you choose to add this feature, follow the directions.

26. Close all windows.

Project 4-3: Manage Flash Cookies

Adobe Flash cookies are significantly different than regular cookies. Flash cookies can also be used to reinstate regular cookies that a user has deleted or blocked. Adobe Flash version 10.3 was the first version to allow Flash cookies to be deleted through the browser's normal configuration settings as regular cookies can. However, cookies created by any version of Flash can be managed through the Adobe Web site. In this project, you will change the settings on Flash cookies.

1. Use your Web browser to go to **www.macromedia.com/support/documentation/en/flashplayer/help/settings_manager02.html**

The location of content on the Internet, such as this program, may change without warning. If you are no longer able to access the program through the above URL, then use a search engine to search for "Adobe Flash Global Privacy Settings Panel".

2. The Global Privacy Settings panel is displayed. The first tab in the Global Privacy Settings is for Camera and Microphone. Click **Always ask ...** and then click **Confirm**.

3. Click the next tab, which is the **Global Storage Settings**. Uncheck **Allow third-party Flash content to store data on your computer**.

4. Click the **Global Security Settings** tab. Be sure that either **Always ask** or **Always deny** is selected.

5. Click the **Website Privacy Settings** tab. This regards privacy settings for a camera or microphone. Click **Delete all sites** and then **Confirm**.

6. Close all windows.

Project 4-4: Viewing Digital Certificates

In this project, you will view digital certificate information using Microsoft Internet Explorer.

1. Use your Web browser to go to **www.google.com**.

2. Note that there is no padlock icon in the browser address bar, indicating that no digital certificates are used with this site. To verify this click **Page** and then

Properties. The Protocol: is HTTP and the Connection: is Not Encrypted. Why do you think digital certificates are not used here? Should they be?

3. Click the **Certificates** button. What message appears? Click **OK** and then click **OK** in the Properties dialog box.

4. Now use your Web browser to go to **gmail.google.com.** This is the Web interface to the Google e-mail facility. Note the padlock icon in the browser address bar indicating that digital certificate is now being used. Click the padlock icon to view the **Website Identification** window.

5. Click **View certificates.**

6. Note the general information displayed under the **General** tab.

7. Now click the **Details** tab. The fields are displayed for this X.509 digital certificate.

8. Click **Valid to** to view the expiration date of this certificate.

9. Click **Public key** to view the public key associated with this digital certificate. Why is this site not concerned with distributing this key? How does embedding the public key in a digital certificate protect it from impersonators?

10. Click the **Certification Path** tab. Because Web certificates are based on the distributed trust model there is a "path" to the root certificate. Click the root certificate and click the **View Certificate** button. Click the **Details tab** and then click **Valid to.** Why is the expiration date of this root certificate longer than that of the Web site certificate? Click **OK** and then click **OK** again to close the Certificate window.

11. Now view all the certificates in this Web browser. Click **Tools** and **Internet Options.**

12. Click the **Content** tab.

13. Click the **Certificates** button.

14. Click **Trusted Root Certificate Authorities** to view the root certificates in this Web browser. Why are there so many?

15. Close all windows.

Project 4-5: Viewing Revoked Digital Certificates

Digital certificates that have been revoked are listed in the Web browser. In this project, you will view any untrusted certificates on your computer.

1. Click **Start,** type **Run,** and then press Enter.

2. Type **CERTMGR.MSC** and then press Enter.

3. In the left pane, expand **Trusted Root Certification Authorities.**

4. In the right pane, double-click **Certificates.** These are the CAs approved for this computer.

5. In the left pane, expand **Intermediate Certification Authorities.**

6. Click **Certificates** to view the intermediate CAs.

7. Click **Certification Revocation List.**

8. In the right pane, all revoked certificates will display. Select a revoked certificate and double-click it, as illustrated in Figure 4-15.

Figure 4-15 Revoked digital certificates
Source: Windows Internet Explorer 9

9. Double-click one of the revoked certificates. Read the information about it and click fields for more detail if necessary. Why do you think this certificate has been revoked? Close the Certificate Revocation List by clicking the **OK** button.

10. In the left pane, expand **Untrusted Certificates**.

11. Click **Certificates**. The certificates that are no longer trusted are listed in the right pane.

12. Double-click one of the untrusted certificates. Read the information about it and click fields for more detail if necessary. Why do you think this certificate is no longer trusted?

13. Click **OK** to close the Certificate dialog box.

14. Close all windows.

Case Projects

Case Project 4-1: Compare Browser Security

Of the most popular Web browsers—IE, Firefox, Safari, Opera, and Chrome—which is the most secure? Using the Internet, research the security features of each of these browsers. Create a table that lists the different security features. In your opinion, is there one browser that is more secure than the rest? Is there a browser that is the least secure? Give reasons for your conclusion

Case Project 4-2: Using IE Security Zones

Although security zones can help provide a higher degree of security, do they hinder browsing too much? For three days, use IE to create security zones for your Web surfing, and place sites that you visit in your zones. Then, write a paper on your experience. Was it easy or hard to use security zones? What difficulties did you encounter? What could be done to encourage the average user to take advantage of zones? Create a one-page summary of your work with security zones

Case Project 4-3: Do Not Track

Some Web browsers now offer a "Do Not Track" feature that allows users to opt out of tracking by Web sites they do not visit and third-party cookies. Use the Internet to research Do Not Track. What are its advantages for users? What are the arguments against it by marketers and Web browser venders? Would you be willing to pay for this feature? Write a one-page paper on your research.

Case Project 4-4: Fraudulent Digital Certificates

The growing use of fraudulent digital certificates has many security experts concerned, since it is a technology that is very important to using the Internet for secure transactions. Research at least two recent incidences of attackers or governments using fraudulent digital certificates. How did they use them? What was the reason? How did Web browser vendors react? What did they do to stop these fraudulent certificates? Write a one-page summary of your findings.

Case Project 4-5: Information Security Community Site Activity

The Information Security Community Web site is an online companion to this textbook. It contains a wide variety of tools, information, discussion boards, and other features to assist learners. In order to gain the most benefit from the site you will need to set up a free account.

The Information Security Community Site is a Course Technology/Cengage Learning information security course enrichment site. It contains a wide variety of tools, information, discussion boards, and other features to assist learners. Go to **community.cengage.com/infosec**. Click **Login** at the top of the page and enter your sign-in name and the password credentials that you created in Chapter 1. Visit the Discussions page by going to the **Students** tab and selecting the **Discussion Boards** link from the drop-down menu, where you can read the following case study.

How would you restrict spam? Should it be done by technology or passing laws (remember that domestic laws would not apply to spammers who lived outside the country)? Should all spammers be required to register with a central agency? What should be the penalty for violating your proposal? Record your responses on the Community Site discussion board.

Case Project 4-6: North Ridge Computer Consultants

North Ridge Computer Consultants (NRCC) is a local information technology company that specializes in security. In order to encourage students to enter the field of information security, NRCC often hires student interns to assist them with projects.

Dawn's Interior Designs (DID) provides design services to a variety of clients in the area. A competitor recently was the victim of a successful attack that exposed the personal information of their customers and generated bad publicity for that company. DID wants to avoid what happened to their competitor, yet they are aware that many of their employees do not know how to use the Internet and e-mail safely. DID has contacted NRCC to create a training manual for their employees.

Create a two-page Word document that summarizes the risks that users face when using the Internet and e-mail, and that also provides a bulleted list of steps that users should take in order to stay secure. Because the employees do not have a strong technical background, your paper should be general in its tone.

References

1. "Communication fatigue disrupts marketing message," *The Globe and Mail*, Jul. 20, 2012, accessed Aug. 25, 2012. <http://www.theglobeandmail.com/report-on-business/small-business/sb-marketing/advertising/communication-fatigue-disrupts-marketing-messages/article4402374/>.

2. "What percentage of total internet traffic is spam?," *Skeptics*, Apr. 15, 2011, accessed Aug. 28, 2012. <http://skeptics.stackexchange.com/questions/2175/what-percentage-of-total-internet-traffic-is-spam>.

© Shutterstock.com

chapter 5

After completing this chapter you should be able to do the following:

- Define Wi-Fi and Bluetooth and explain how they work
- Describe the various attacks that can be launched against a wireless network
- List the defenses for a home Wi-Fi network
- Describe how to use a public wireless network securely
- List the types of mobile device security for laptops, tablets, and smartphones

"Hi, Katelyn. Paul told me that you were stopping by," said Mrs. Taggart. Katelyn and Mrs. Taggart's son Paul had been friends since elementary school, and both were now attending the local college, where Katelyn was majoring in computer information systems. "You just can't seem to get rid of me, can you?" laughed Katelyn.

"Hey, Mom, look at this," said Paul. Paul adjusted the screen of Katelyn's computer so his mother could see it. "What is all of this?" asked Mrs. Taggart. Paul replied, "Katelyn is showing me some fascinating software." Katelyn explained that in her wireless technologies course at the college they were studying wireless network security. The project for this week was to download two free wireless applications from the Internet and use them. "This first program," said Katelyn, "captures and decodes unprotected wireless transmissions right out of the air so you can read them." "Watch this," said Paul. He opened a Web site on his laptop computer that was connected to the Taggart's home Wi-Fi network and started typing. Lines of information appeared in rapid succession at the top of Katelyn's screen. "That's what's being transmitted," Katelyn said. "But now show her the other part," said Paul. Katelyn clicked on one of the lines of information and at the bottom of the screen the words that Paul was typing suddenly started appearing on Katelyn's computer. "This program can show what anybody who uses your Wi-Fi network is sending and receiving," said Katelyn. "That's really interesting," said Mrs. Taggart.

"But now look at this," said Paul. He used his Web browser to navigate to his school e-mail account, and entered his username and password. "Show her," said Paul. Katelyn clicked on another line and Paul's username and password appeared. "Katelyn says that because our Wi-Fi network is not protected, almost anything we type can be seen by anybody else," said Paul. Mrs. Taggart laughed and said, "But they would have to be inside our house to see that." "No, they wouldn't," replied Paul. Mrs. Taggart looked at Katelyn. "He's right," Katelyn said. "When I first got here Paul and I walked down the street with my laptop past three houses and we still were able to pick up your wireless signal. I—or anybody with this program—could be down the street and see what's being sent and received on your Wi-Fi network and you would never know it." Mrs. Taggart looked concerned. She worked as a contract employee for a financial services firm and used their home Wi-Fi network with her own laptop and new tablet computer. "You mean they can see anything I do as well?" she asked. "Yes," said Katelyn, "Unless the network is protected, anybody can see it."

"And," said Paul, "The other program Katelyn showed me can detect how many other Wi-Fi networks in our neighborhood are sending out signals. Did you know that we can pick up over 15 wireless networks from our neighborhood just sitting right here?" Katelyn added, "Of those 15 guess how many networks are protected to prevent anyone from seeing what's being transmitted? Only three of them!"

Mrs. Taggart sat down. "Katelyn, I had no idea. How can we protect our network?"

A *disruptive technology* is a radical technology or innovation that fills a new role that an existing device or technology could not. Examples of disruptive technologies, along with those that they replaced in the last 150 years, include steamships (which replaced sailing ships), telephones (which replaced telegraphs), automobiles (which replaced horses), word processors (which replaced typewriters), and the Internet (which, increasingly, is replacing libraries). These disruptive technologies have had a profound impact on society, altering the way people live, work, and play.

Today, another disruptive technology is changing our world: mobile devices and the wireless networks that support them. Thanks to tablets, laptops, and smartphones, it is no longer necessary to use a desktop computer tethered by cable to a network in order to surf the Web, check e-mail, or access inventory records. Mobile devices and wireless networks have made mobility possible to a degree rarely even imagined before. Travelers using their mobile devices can have access to the Internet while waiting in airports, traveling on airplanes and trains, and working in their hotel rooms. At work, businesses have found that employees who have wireless access to data during meetings and in conference rooms can significantly increase their productivity. Free wireless Internet connections are available in restaurants across the country, and in some arenas and stadiums fans can even order concessions on their mobile devices and have them delivered to their seats. There is hardly a sector of the economy that has not been dramatically affected by mobile devices and wireless technology.

Statistics confirm the popularity of mobile devices. The growth of worldwide shipments of personal computers has slowed while the growth of portable devices has dramatically increased. It is estimated that by 2015 annual PC growth will be only 1.4 percent while the growth of portable devices will increase by 11.3 percent.[1] And users have become increasingly attached to their mobile devices. A new dictionary word has recently been introduced to reflect this: *nomophobia* is the fear of not being with your mobile phone!

Just as users have flocked to mobile devices and wireless networks, so too have attackers. Mobile devices have seen an increase in malware and attacks directed at them. Wireless data networks have become a prime target for attackers, since penetrating such networks may result in an open path to the many devices connected to them. Just as it is important for users to protect their desktop computers, it is also critical to protect their mobile devices and associated wireless networks.

In this chapter, you will examine some of the attacks on wireless data networks and mobile devices that use them. First, you will explore the types of attacks that a wireless network faces along with the attacks directed at mobile devices using these networks. Then, you will learn how to protect wireless networks at home and how to use public wireless networks safely. You will also look at how to protect the mobile devices themselves.

Mobile Attacks

There are several types of attacks that are directed toward mobile devices. Understanding the attacks directed toward wireless networks that support these devices is equally important.

Attacks through Wireless Networks

There are two major types of wireless networks that are popular today among users. These networks are Wi-Fi and Bluetooth.

Wi-Fi Networks Wi-Fi networks have become commonplace today. Understanding what Wi-Fi is, the equipment needed to operate on a Wi-Fi network, and the attacks that this type of network faces are all important.

What Is Wi-Fi? **Wi-Fi** (*wireless fidelity*) is a wireless data network technology that is designed to provide high-speed data connections for mobile devices. This type of network is technically known as a **wireless local area network (WLAN)**. Devices such as laptop computers, tablets, smartphones, wireless printers, and game consoles that are in range (up to 350 feet or 107 meters) of a centrally located connection device in a Wi-Fi network can send and receive information using radio frequency (RF) transmissions at speeds up to 600 million bits per second (Mbps).

 Wi-Fi networks are different from the cellular telephony networks that are designed, installed, and maintained by the wireless telephone carriers. These networks use standards such as *3G* and *4G LTE* for both voice and data communications and charge users accordingly for this coverage. Wi-Fi networks, in comparison, are set up and maintained by users and are faster than cellular telephony networks although they have a smaller geographical area of coverage.

The rapid growth of Wi-Fi has been nothing short of phenomenal. According to some estimates, by 2014 there will be 1.4 billion devices shipped annually that support wireless data standards, and these devices will transmit the amount of data traffic equal to almost one billion DVDs. By mid-2011 one quarter of all households around the world, or 439 million households, were using wireless data technology, with South Korea leading the way with over 80 percent of its households using wireless (the U.S. was eighth with 61 percent). It is estimated that by 2016 over 800 million households will have Wi-Fi wireless data technology installed.[2]

In the field of computer networking and wireless communications, the most widely known and influential organization is the **Institute of Electrical and Electronics Engineers (IEEE)**. The IEEE and its predecessor organizations date back to 1884. The IEEE is one of the leading developers of global standards in a broad range of industries such as energy, biomedical and healthcare, and transportation. It is currently involved in developing and revising over 800 standards.

 Some of the IEEE standards apply to circuits and devices, communication and information technology, control and automation, electromagnetics, geoscience, ocean technology, remote sensing, instrumentation measurement and testing, optics, power and energy, and signal processing.

The IEEE has been responsible for establishing standards for Wi-Fi networks. Table 5-1 lists the different standards and their characteristics.

Wi-Fi Equipment The list of equipment needed for a Wi-Fi wireless network is surprisingly short. Each mobile device (laptop, tablet, smartphone, etc.) must have a **wireless client network interface card adapter** (or *wireless adapter*) to send and receive the wireless signals. For early laptop computers these wireless adapters were external devices that connected to the computer's Universal Serial Bus (USB) and had an external antenna, as illustrated in Figure 5-1. However, today they are internal devices built into mobile devices. In addition to this wireless adapter, special software is needed that translates data between the wireless card and the computer.

Name	Year Ratified	Maximum Speed	Comments
802.11	1997	2 Mbps	No longer used today because of its slow speed
802.11b	1999	11 Mbps	Quickly became widely popular but rarely found today due to its slow speed
802.11a	1999	54 Mbps	Mainly used in business environments
802.11g	2003	54 Mbps	Combines the best features of 802.11b and 802.11a and is still used today
802.11n	2009	600 Mbps	Most widely used type of wireless network
802.11ac	Projected 2013	3,600 Mbps	Designed primarily for wireless video delivery

Table 5-1 IEEE standards for Wi-Fi networks
© Cengage Learning 2014

All operating systems today include this software that will automatically scan the airwaves, detect any Wi-Fi networks in the area, and either offer the user the option of connecting to that network or automatically connect based on previous preferences set by the user.

Figure 5-1 External USB wireless adapter
© Oleksiy Mark/www.Shutterstock.com

The other equipment needed for a home-based Wi-Fi network is a **wireless broadband router.** This device, illustrated in Figure 5-2, actually combines several networking technologies. It typically is connected to the user's modem that is in turn connected to an Internet connection. The wireless router acts as the "base station" for the wireless devices, sending and receiving wireless signals between all devices as well as providing the "gateway" to the external Internet. A home Wi-Fi network is shown in Figure 5-3. Note that the wireless router in this figure supports both wired devices (PC and printer) as well as wireless devices (laptop and tablet) so that *all* the devices can be accessible on the network. This allows, for example, the wireless tablet to print to the wired printer. In addition, all wired and wireless devices can share the Internet connection.

Figure 5-2 Wireless broadband router
© vetkit/www.Shutterstock.com

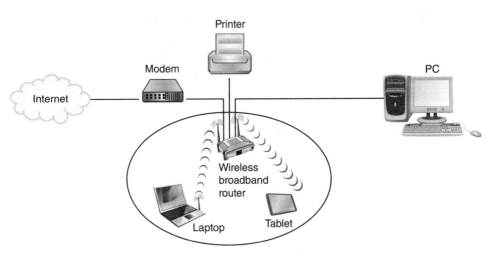

Figure 5-3 Home Wi-Fi network
© Cengage Learning 2014

In an office setting, instead of using a wireless broadband router, a more sophisticated device known as an **access point (AP)** is used. Whereas most homes or apartments would have only one wireless router, businesses typically have multiple APs (often into the hundreds). Because the wireless signal can only be transmitted for several hundred feet, multiple APs are used to provide "cells" or areas of coverage. As the user moves (called *roaming*) from one cell to another with their wireless device a *handoff* occurs so that the AP to which the user is closest now becomes the new base station. Cells of coverage are shown in Figure 5-4.

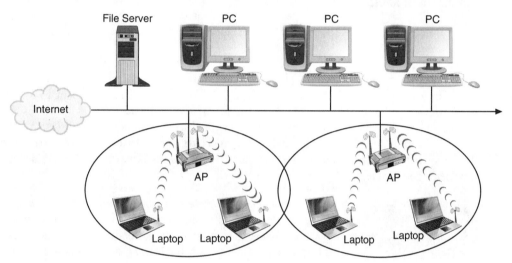

Figure 5-4 Wi-Fi cells
© Cengage Learning 2014

Attacks on Wi-Fi Attacks against home Wi-Fi networks are relatively easy, for several reasons. First, most home users overlook the fact that the signal emanating from a wireless broadband router is not confined to the house or apartment. That signal can be picked up outside of the building, in some cases hundreds of feet away. Second, many home users are unaware how to configure security on their router. Third, some users consider Wi-Fi security an inconvenience because they underestimate the risks. Home users face several risks from attacks on their insecure wireless networks, such as:

- *Stealing data.* On a computer connected to the home Wi-Fi network, an attacker could access any folder with file sharing enabled. This essentially provides an attacker full access to sensitive data from the computer.

- *Reading wireless transmissions.* Usernames, passwords, credit card numbers, and other information sent over the Wi-Fi network could be captured by an attacker.

- *Injecting malware.* Because attackers might access the network behind a firewall, they could inject Trojans, viruses, and other malware onto the user's computer.

- *Downloading harmful content.* In several instances, attackers have accessed a home computer through an unprotected Wi-Fi network, downloaded child pornography to the computer, and then turned that computer into a file server to distribute the content. When authorities traced the files back to that computer, the unsuspecting owner was arrested and his equipment confiscated.

Attackers can easily identify unprotected home wireless networks through **war driving**. War driving is searching for wireless signals from an automobile or on foot using a portable computing device.

War driving is derived from the term *war dialing*. When telephone modems were popular in the 1980s and 1990s, an attacker could program the device to randomly dial telephone numbers until a computer answered the call. This random process of searching for a connection was known as war dialing, so the word for randomly searching for a wireless signal became known as war driving.

When using a free or fee-based Wi-Fi network in a coffee shop, airport, or school campus there are also security concerns. These networks are rarely protected (in order to allow easy access by users), so attackers can easily read any wireless transmissions sent to and from the user's device. In addition, an attacker can set up an **evil twin**. An evil twin is an AP or another computer that is set up by an attacker designed to mimic an authorized Wi-Fi device. A user's mobile device may unknowingly connect to this evil twin instead of the authorized device so that attackers can receive any sensitive transmissions or directly send malware to the user's computer.

The popularity of free Wi-Fi wireless networks is projected to skyrocket, in part because of the end of unlimited smartphone and tablet data plans. Many wireless telephone carriers are ending all unlimited data plans, or offering unlimited plans but slowing the transmission speed after users have used a specific amount of data bandwidth. Many users opt to find a free Wi-Fi network when possible in order to not exceed their data plan limits.

Bluetooth Bluetooth is another common wireless technology. Bluetooth is a short-range wireless technology designed for interconnecting computers and peripherals, handheld devices, and cell phones. It can be used for almost any short-range application where low cost is essential. Unlike Wi-Fi that can provide coverage of up to several hundred feet at 600 Mbps, most Bluetooth devices have a range of only 33 feet (10 meters). Also, the rate of transmission is only 1 million bits per second (Mbps).

The current version is Bluetooth v4.0 (a subset is known as Bluetooth Low Energy), but all Bluetooth devices are backward compatible with previous versions.

Bluetooth technology enables users to connect wirelessly to a wide range of computing and telecommunications devices. Figure 5-5 shows a Bluetooth management screen on a Bluetooth-enabled laptop with a mouse and a smartphone connected. Other types of Bluetooth-enabled product pairings are listed in Table 5-2.

The original Bluetooth standard was designed as a simple cable replacement for computers and other devices.

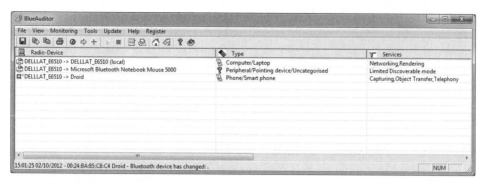

Figure 5-5 Bluetooth pairings
Source: BlueAuditor

Category	Bluetooth Pairing	Usage
Automobile	Hands-free car system with cell phone	Drivers can speak commands to browse the cell phone's contact list, make hands-free phone calls, or use its navigation system.
Home entertainment	Stereo headphones with portable music player	Users can create a playlist on a portable music player and listen through a set of wireless headphones or speakers.
Photography	Digital camera with printer	Digital photos can be sent directly to a photo printer or from pictures taken on one cell phone to another phone.
Computer accessories	Computer with keyboard and mouse	A small travel mouse can be linked to a laptop or a full-size mouse and keyboard that can be connected to a desktop computer.
Gaming	Video game system with controller	Gaming devices and video game systems can support multiple controllers, while Bluetooth headsets allow gamers to chat as they play.
Medical and health	Blood pressure monitors with smartphones	Patient information can be sent to a smartphone, which can then send an emergency phone message if necessary.

Table 5-2 Bluetooth products
© Cengage Learning 2014

 Bluetooth is also finding its way into unlikely devices. A Victorinox Swiss Army pocketknife model has Bluetooth technology that can be used to remotely control a computer when projecting a Power-Point presentation. The pocketknife also serves as a 32 GB USB flash drive. Since pocketknives cannot be carried onto an airplane, one version of the pocketknife lacks a sharp blade.

Because of the "on-the-fly" nature of Bluetooth pairings, attacks on wireless Bluetooth technology are not uncommon. Two Bluetooth attacks are bluejacking and bluesnarfing. **Bluejacking** is an attack that sends unsolicited messages to Bluetooth-enabled devices.

Usually bluejacking involves sending text messages, but images and sounds can also be transmitted. Bluejacking is usually considered more annoying than harmful because no data is stolen. However, many Bluetooth users resent receiving unsolicited messages. **Bluesnarfing** is an attack that accesses unauthorized information from a wireless device through a Bluetooth connection, often between cell phones and laptop computers. In a bluesnarfing attack the attacker copies e-mails, calendars, contact lists, cell phone pictures, or videos by connecting to the Bluetooth device without the owner's knowledge or permission.

Attacks on Mobile Devices

Attacks focused on mobile devices are common. These include attacks against laptops as well as tablets and smartphones.

Laptops Laptop computers face the same attacks as desktop computers. These include viruses, worms, Trojans, rootkits, backdoors, keyloggers, Arbitrary Code Execution, spyware, adware, and scareware.

An additional risk that laptop computers face, as well as all mobile devices, is theft. Because of their portable nature laptops can be fairly easily lost or stolen, and any unprotected data on the laptop could be retrieved by the thief. The follow data illustrates the problem:

- A laptop is stolen on average once every 50 seconds. The location where the most laptops are stolen in North America is Chicago, followed by Houston, Detroit, and Los Angeles.[3]

- One-third of all laptops stolen in the United States go missing from public schools. Residential property is the second most common location.[4]

- Consumer-owned laptops are most often stolen in August and September (as students return to school) and November and December (during holiday shopping).[5]

Laptop theft is especially prevalent at airports. The airport with the highest number of thefts is Atlanta, followed by Miami, Orlando, Chicago, Los Angeles, and San Francisco. Table 5-3 lists the top five areas where airport laptop theft occurs.

Area of Airport	Percentage of Laptops Stolen
Luggage/storage area	29%
Terminal/boarding area	22%
Other	19%
Airplane	18%
Check-in/security	12%

Table 5-3 Top five areas for airport laptop theft[6]
Source: Absolute Software

Almost one-third of all laptops stolen or left behind at airport security are never recovered.[7]

Tablets and Smartphones The popularity of tablet computers and smartphones continues to rise. A **feature phone** is a traditional cellular telephone that includes a limited number of features, such as a camera, an MP3 music player, and ability to send and receive **short message service (SMS)** text messages. Many feature phones are designed to highlight a single feature, such as the ability to take high-quality photos or provide a large amount of memory for music storage. A **smartphone** has all the tools that a feature phone has but also includes an operating system that allows it to run third-party applications (*apps*). Because it has an operating system, a smartphone offers a broader range of functionality. Users can download apps that perform a wide variety of functions for productivity, social networking, music, and so forth, much like a standard computer. Because of this ability to run apps, smartphones are essentially handheld personal computers. As the popularity of smartphones has increased, the sales of feature phones have decreased. Table 5-4 lists the worldwide market share of smartphones and feature phones.

Year	Percentage of Smartphone Market Share	Percentage of Feature Phone Market Share
2011	35	46
2012	46	41
2013	54	38
2014	58	35
2015	62	33
2016	67	28

Table 5-4 **Smartphone versus feature phone worldwide market share** [8]
Source: HIS iSuppli Market Research

Tablet computers are portable computing devices with screen sizes ranging from 5 to 10 inches (127 to 254 millimeters), compared to notebook computers whose screens typically range from 10 to 17 inches (254 to 432 millimeters). Designed for user convenience, tablets are thinner, lighter, easier to carry, and more intuitive to use. Whereas laptops are designed for performance, tablets are focused on ease of use. Like smartphones, tablet computers have an operating system that allows them to run third-party apps. The most popular operating systems include Apple iOS, Google Android, and Microsoft Windows. It is estimated that by 2016 the number of tablets shipped will overtake laptop shipments.[9]

Tablets are purchased more often in mature markets like the United States, while laptops sell better in emerging markets. This is because laptops are often the only computing devices in a household in emerging markets, whereas in mature markets tablets supplement existing computer resources.

Tablets and smartphones have increasingly been the target of attackers. Malware that is specifically directed at tablets and smartphones is sometimes referred to as **mobile malware**. It includes many of the same types of attacks that can be directed at desktop computers, such as Trojans, viruses, worms, and arbitrary code execution.

In addition, there are unique dangers that mobile devices face. For example, an attacker could infect a smartphone and cause it to repeatedly dial a premium-rate telephone number that charges a substantial fee for the call (either the attacker owns the number or is given a percentage kickback by the owner for the volume of calls). It is not unusual for hundreds or even thousands of dollars to be charged to a victim's cell phone bill by this type of attack. Another attack takes advantage of a mobile device that has had its built-in limitations and protections removed by the owner. This practice, known as **jailbreaking**, installs a standard administration-level "root" password that allows full access to all of the device's functions. An attacker who can remotely access the mobile device can then use the standard password to exploit it.

There are a variety of means by which an attacker can infect a mobile device:

- *Infected app.* Apps are often posted on an "app store." These online stores are managed by the operating system vendors and provide a means for users to purchase (some apps are free) and download an app. Although some of these vendors screen the apps to determine if they contain malware, other vendors do not. Also, even screened apps with infecting malware have been able to slip past the review process and be posted on an app store.

- *Unofficial app store.* There are many unofficial app stores from which users can download apps (sometimes called *sidelining*). Generally, the apps on these sites are not previewed and may contain malware.

- *Connection to another computer.* Although tablets and cell phones do not have the wide array of connection interfaces that desktop computers do, all of these devices have a means to connect to a desktop or laptop computer, typically through a USB or wireless connection. An infected desktop computer can transmit malware to a mobile device through this connection.

- *Attachment.* E-mail or SMS text message attachments can contain malware. When the attachment is opened it may infect the device.

- *Wi-Fi and Bluetooth connection.* Because all mobile devices use Wi-Fi and often Bluetooth for network connectivity, attacks can be distributed through these networks.

Mobile Defenses

Despite the fact that there are many different attacks directed at mobile devices and wireless networks, there are several defenses that can be utilized for protection. These defenses can be broken down into defenses for wireless networks and defenses for protecting the wireless devices.

Wireless Network Security

Reducing the risk of attack through wireless networks is an important security step. This involves securely configuring a home wireless network to repel attackers and also following secure practices for using a public wireless network safely.

Home Wi-Fi Security Configuring a Wi-Fi wireless broadband router in order to provide the highest level of security protection is an important step. Configuring the router includes securing it and turning on Wi-Fi Protected Access 2 (WPA2) Personal. In addition, there are other steps that can also be taken.

"That should do it," said Katelyn. She had just finished helping Mrs. Taggart configure her wireless broadband router. "Katelyn, I had no idea there were so many different options on this router," said Mrs. Taggart. "Look at these." She pointed at the screen and read several of the settings. "This one says 'Fragmentation length.' And what is 'CTS/RTS Threshold' and 'Short preamble mode'? How would anybody know what to do unless they had someone like you to help them?" she asked. Katelyn moved the mouse and said, "I know what you mean. The problem is that those options you're looking at are about changing how the wireless signals are transmitted. There isn't any reason why anybody would change those unless they're having a transmission issue. But people look at those and can easily get overwhelmed and think that configuring the security on their router is really complicated, so they don't even try."

"And," said Paul, "I think most people just don't know what to do about security on the router. It's actually not that hard. You did in less than five minutes." Katelyn smiled and said, "It really isn't hard at all. It just takes a few minutes to make your wireless network safe."

"Katelyn, I can't thank you enough," said Mrs. Taggart. "I'm glad to help," Katelyn replied. "Now, can I show you a couple of things about your new tablet? There are some security settings on it that are good to have turned on. And there's a new app out for this tablet that does a 'remote wipe' that you might be interested in." Paul picked up the tablet to hand to Katelyn and asked, "What's a remote wipe?" Katelyn took the tablet and said, "If you ever lose the tablet or it gets stolen you can remotely erase your data so the thief can't get it. Some companies require all of their users to have it on their mobile devices."

Mrs. Taggart leaned forward in her chair. "That is exactly what I need. Can you show me how to install it?"

Securing the Wireless Router The first step in securing a Wi-Fi wireless broadband router is essential but is frequently overlooked. It involves "locking down" the device by creating a password to protect its internal configuration settings. Most wireless routers come preconfigured with a default password, and these passwords are well known by attackers. Protecting the router with a strong password prevents attackers from accessing the wireless router and turning off any security settings.

To secure the wireless router the address of the router and the default password must first be known. This information is included in the documentation of the wireless router, can be obtained through the vendor's Web site, or can be determined by examining the network settings. The wireless router's Internet Protocol (IP) address, such as *192.168.1.1*, can be entered into a Web browser on a computer connected to the wireless network, which then displays the router's login screen. Once the default password is entered, access will be granted to the configuration settings of the router where a new password can be entered.

In addition, most routers also permit remote management of the router's configuration settings through the Internet. There are several router configuration options for remote management. The typical settings, as illustrated in Figure 5-6, are as follows:

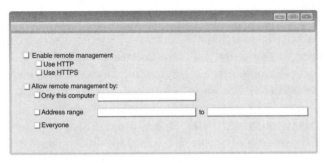

Figure 5-6   Wireless router remote access settings
© Cengage Learning 2014

- *Enable remote management.* This setting permits users to access the router's configuration settings from another location through the Internet. The *Use HTTPS* option will encrypt the transmissions so that an attacker cannot view them.

- *Allow remote management by:.* This option designates which devices can perform remote management. It can be one device (*Only this computer*), multiple devices (*Address range*), or all devices (*Everyone*).

 Some newer wireless routers provide remote management and wireless network access via an app installed on a smartphone or tablet. This app lets users check to see if a computer, mobile device, gaming console, media player, or other device is attached to the wireless network. In addition, e-mail alert notifications can be sent to warn owners of a security intrusion attempt into the network or whenever a security update is available. Also, if there is a video camera connected to the network, users can view the video transmissions remotely through the app.

Unless remote management is essential, it is recommended that this feature be disabled. Turning remote management off adds a stronger degree of security, because it limits access to the configuration settings of the wireless router to only the local computer connected to it.

 **Turning on Wi-Fi Protected Access 2 (WPA2) Personal** The wireless signal that comes from a wireless broadband router can be picked outside of the building where the router is located, in some cases hundreds of feet away. On an unsecured wireless network, virtually anyone can access the Wi-Fi signal to read transmissions and to access the network. This makes it critical to perform two key security tasks: to encrypt the signal so that no one can

read any information being sent and received, and to prevent unauthorized users from accessing the network.

Although these two tasks may seem daunting, they can easily be accomplished by turning on **Wi-Fi Protected Access 2 (WPA2) Personal.** WPA2 provides the optimum level of wireless security and has been mandatory for all certified wireless devices manufactured since March 2006.

Despite the fact that WPA2 Personal provides the optimum level of wireless security and has been mandatory since 2006, there are still a surprising number of Wi-Fi networks that do not implement it. In a recent analysis by this author, 23 different Wi-Fi networks were discovered in one residential neighborhood, but only three used the secure WPA2 Personal setting. In another test, 26 wireless networks were found with six running WPA2 Personal, three were using a weaker form of security, and 17 were completely unprotected.

Turning on WPA2 Personal involves turning it on at the wireless router and then entering a key value on each authorized device that has been preapproved to join the Wi-Fi network. In the wireless router configuration settings there are two steps that must be performed. First, the WPA2 Personal security option, which may be labeled as *WPA2-PSK [AES]*, is turned on by clicking the appropriate option button. Second, a key value, sometimes called a *preshared key (PSK)*, *WPA2 shared key*, or *passphrase*, must be entered. This key value can be from 8 to 63 characters in length. This is illustrated in Figure 5-7.

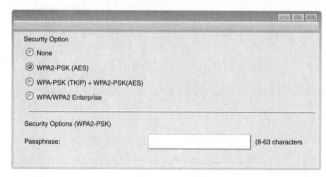

Figure 5-7 WPA2 Personal wireless router settings
© Cengage Learning 2014

After turning on WPA2 Personal on the wireless router and entering a key value, the same key value must also be entered on each mobile device that has permission to access the Wi-Fi network. A mobile device that attempts to access a wireless network with WPA2 Personal will automatically ask for the key value. After this value is entered the device can access the wireless network. Once the key value is entered, the mobile device can retain the value and does need to ask for it again.

Because of a security weakness it is important that key values exceed 20 characters in length. It is recommended that they be as long as possible because of the damage that can result from a key value being cracked by an attacker.

As a means of simplifying turning on WPA2 Personal, many devices now support **Wi-Fi Protected Setup (WPS)** as an optional means of configuring security. There are two common WPS methods. The PIN method utilizes a personal identification number (PIN) printed on a label on the wireless router or displayed through a software setup wizard. The user types in the PIN on the mobile device (such as a tablet or laptop computer), and the security configuration automatically occurs, as illustrated in Figure 5-8. This is the mandatory model and all devices certified for WPS must support it.

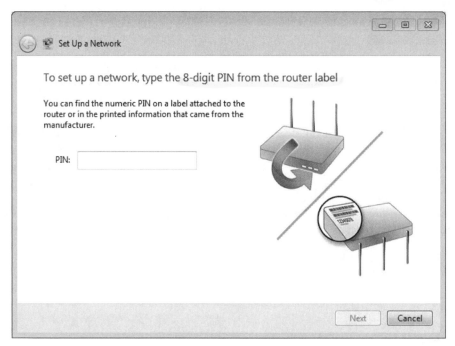

Figure 5-8 WPS PIN method
Source: Microsoft Connect Now

In late 2011 it was revealed that there are significant security design and implementation flaws in WPS using the PIN method. It is recommended that either the manual configuration method described above be used or that WPS be disabled on the wireless router and only turned on temporarily when adding a new device to the Wi-Fi network.

The second method is the push-button method: the user pushes a button (usually an actual button on the wireless router and a virtual one displayed through a software setup wizard on the wireless device), and the security configuration takes place. Support for this model is mandatory for wireless routers and optional for connecting devices.

Over 700 wireless devices have been certified to run WPS.

BLOCK ATTACKS

Other Security Settings Although securing the wireless router with a strong password and turning on WPA2 Personal are the most effective Wi-Fi security settings, there are other security settings that are widely promoted. Unfortunately, some of these only provide a marginal degree of additional security or no additional security at all. These weak Wi-Fi security settings include:

- *Disabling SSID broadcasts.* The **Service Set Identifier (SSID)** in a Wi-Fi network serves as the network name identifier. Wireless routers continually advertise their presence by broadcasting their SSID. For a degree of protection, some wireless security sources encourage users to configure their wireless routers to prevent the SSID from being broadcast but instead require the user to manually enter the SSID on the wireless device (this assumes that only authorized users have been given the SSID). Although not advertising the SSID might seem to provide protection, in reality it does not. This is the case because, even when the SSID is turned off from being broadcast, it can still be easily discovered in other transmissions sent by the wireless router.

- *Restricting users by MAC address.* A **Media Access Control (MAC) address** is a unique hardware number that is "burned in" to each wireless network interface card adapter. Mobile devices can be restricted from entering the network based on their MAC address (called *MAC address filtering*). Restrictions can be implemented in one of two ways: a device can be allowed into the network ("Let this specific device in") or a device can be blocked from accessing the network ("Keep this specific device out"). However, the MAC address—like the SSID—can be determined from other information sent by the Wi-Fi router so that an attacker can readily circumvent MAC address filtering.

- *Limiting the number of users.* Wireless routers can be configured so that the number of users can be restricted. Wireless users are "leased" a temporary IP address from the wireless router while they are connected to the network, and a maximum number of "leases" can be set to match the number of authorized devices on the network: if there are four network devices, then the maximum number of leases can be set to four. Presumably if an attacker is able to breach the wireless security protections and gain access to the network, she would not receive a lease since the maximum number would already be distributed. However, this would hold true only if all of the approved network devices were currently connected to the wireless network; if one of the wireless devices leaves the network (a very common occurrence), then a lease is available to the attacker.

However, there are two additional settings that can add a stronger degree of security to supplement WPA2 Personal:

- *Changing the SSID.* All wireless routers come with a default SSID. An attacker who picks up a Wi-Fi signal and can read the SSID will immediately know the type of wireless router being used and can exploit any weaknesses of that type of router. The SSID on the wireless router should be changed from its default value to an anonymous value that does not identify the owner or location of the network. For example, *Taggart_Network* or *1234_Main_St* would not be good SSIDs; a better choice might be something like *MyWireNet599342*.

5

- *Turning on guest access.* Most wireless routers allow for a separate guest network to be set up in addition to the main Wi-Fi network. This serves to isolate the main network from the guest network. The guest network can be configured so that any user who connects to the separate guest network can only access the Internet directly and other devices in the same network. Another option restricts guests to only Internet access; they cannot access any other network devices, such as a printer.

One semiconductor manufacturer is designing wireless network card interface adapters to automatically connect without any user intervention to any free Wi-Fi wireless network whose signal is detected. This means that a user who walks by a local coffee shop with his or her laptop in standby mode stored a backpack would silently and automatically connect through the Wi-Fi to check for new e-mail and other updates. Many security researchers are afraid this could result in many "silent" attacks on users who pick up a signal from a malicious Wi-Fi network.

Public Network Security Security steps can also be taken regarding wireless networks in a public setting. These include disabling Bluetooth and using caution when using open Wi-Fi connections.

Disabling Bluetooth When using a smartphone or tablet that supports Bluetooth, it is advisable to disable Bluetooth and turn on this service only as necessary. To prevent bluesnarfing, Bluetooth devices should be turned off when not being used or when in a room with unknown people. Another option is to set Bluetooth on the device as *undiscoverable*, which keeps Bluetooth turned on in a state where it cannot be detected by another device.

Using Public Wi-Fi Public Wi-Fi networks, such as those in a coffee shop, library, restaurant, or airport, should be used with caution. Because the signals are rarely if ever encrypted, any attacker in the area can easily read any transmissions. The following is a list of sound practices when using public Wi-Fi:

- *Watching for an evil twin.* Attackers will often impersonate a legitimate Wi-Fi network by creating their own look-alike network, tempting unsuspecting users to connect with the attacker's network instead. Many attackers create a direct **ad hoc network**, a peer-to-peer network that connects a wireless device directly to another wireless device, such as the victim's laptop directly to the attacker's laptop. For example, an attacker who sets up an ad hoc network may name it *Free Wireless Network* or *Free Airport Wireless* in the hopes that an unsuspecting user will connect directly to the attacker's computer. Once the connection is made, the attacker can inject malware into the user's computer or steal data from it. One defense is to note that the icons for an ad hoc network are different from the icons for a network using a wireless router. This is illustrated in Figure 5-9.

Attacker ad hoc network

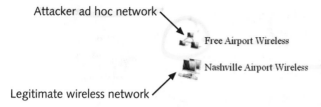

Legitimate wireless network

Figure 5-9 Ad hoc networks use a different icon than Wi-Fi networks using a router
© Cengage Learning 2014

- *Limiting the type of work.* It is advisable to not use a public Wi-Fi for much more than Web surfing or watching online videos. Accessing online banking sites or sending confidential information such as a Social Security number could be intercepted by an attacker if not properly protected.

- *Using a virtual private network.* A **virtual private network** (VPN) uses an unsecured public network, such as the Internet, as if it were a secure private network. It does this by encrypting all data that is transmitted between the remote device and the network. This ensures that any transmissions that are intercepted will be indecipherable. VPNs can be software-based or hardware-based. Software-based VPNs, in which the VPN software is running on the mobile device itself, are common. A wireless user can "tunnel" through the less-than-secure public Wi-Fi network using a VPN, relying on its security advantages. For example, a user may access a public wireless hotspot at an airport or coffee shop and use VPN to "tunnel" through it to reach a secure corporate network.

- *Using sites with digital certificates.* Because digital certificates can be used to encrypt transmissions, it is advisable to use sites that implement digital certificates when accessing public Wi-Fi.

 Digital certificates are covered in Chapter 4.

Mobile Device Security

There are several steps that can be used to secure mobile devices. These can be divided into security for laptop devices and security for tablets and smartphones.

Laptops There are two common security functions for protecting laptops. These are protecting against physical theft and encrypting the information contained on the laptop.

 **Protecting against Physical Theft** The portability of laptops computers also has a downside: they can easily be stolen. Most laptop computers have a special steel bracket security slot built into the case. A **cable lock** can be inserted into the security slot of a portable device and rotated so that the cable lock is secured to the device, while a cable connected to the lock can then be secured to a desk or chair. A cable lock is illustrated in Figure 5-10.

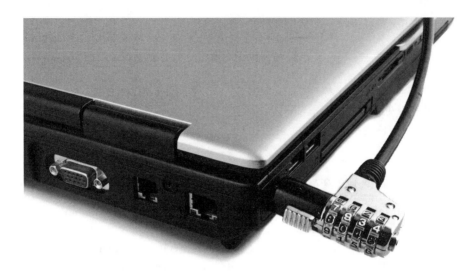

Figure 5-10 Cable lock
© O.Bellini /www.Shutterstock.com

However, many smaller devices like tablets lack a security slot for a cable lock. As an option, tracking software is available that can be installed on the device to identify its location in the event that it is stolen. By hiding itself, this software can report back to the owner the internal computer addresses, nearby networking equipment, and the name of the wireless network to which the thief has connected the device. Devices that have built-in Web cameras can also be instructed to take pictures, presumably of the thief.

One of the drawbacks of software tracking is that the tracking company could trace the location of any device on which the software is installed—whether it was stolen or not—without the owner's permission. Now there are free and open source systems for tracking the location of a laptop that do not depend upon a proprietary central service that you have to trust. When the free or open source software is installed on a laptop, no one besides the owner (or an agent of the owner's choosing) can track the device.

Encrypting Data Another protection is to encrypt sensitive data that is stored on a laptop computer. Unlike public key cryptography or asymmetric cryptography that uses two keys, most encryption for data stored on a laptop uses **private key cryptography** (also called **symmetric cryptography**). Private key cryptography uses same single key to encrypt and decrypt a document and is illustrated in Figure 5-11.

Cryptography can be applied through either software or hardware. Encryption software can be used to encrypt or decrypt files one by one. However, this can be a cumbersome process. Instead, protecting groups of files, such as all files in a specific folder, can take

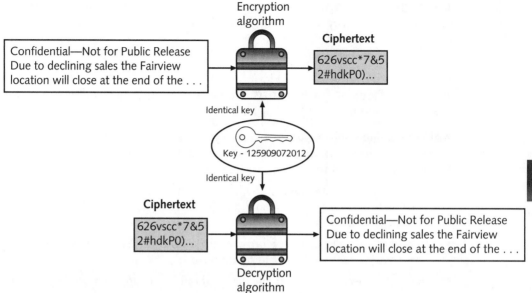

Figure 5-11 Private key cryptography
© Cengage Learning 2014

advantage of the operating system's file system (a *file system* is a method used by operating systems to store, retrieve, and organize files). Cryptography can also be applied to entire disks. This is known as **whole disk encryption** and protects all data on a hard drive.

Software encryption suffers from the same fate as any application program: it can be subject to attacks to exploit its vulnerabilities. As another option, cryptography can be embedded in hardware to provide an even higher degree of security. One example of hardware encryption is encrypted hardware-based USB devices, such as flash drives, which can be used to prevent these types of attacks. This drive resembles a standard USB flash drive, but it has several significant differences:

- Encrypted hardware-based USB drives will not connect to a computer until the correct password has been provided.

- All data copied to the USB flash drive is automatically encrypted.

- The external cases are designed to be tamper-resistant, so attackers cannot disassemble the drives.

- Administrators can remotely control and track activity on the devices.

- Compromised or stolen drives can be remotely disabled.

Just as an encrypted hardware-based USB flash drive will automatically encrypt any data stored on it, self-encrypting hard disk drives (HDDs) can also encrypt all files stored on them. When the computer or other device with a self-encrypting HDD is initially powered up, the drive and the host device perform an authentication process.

Tablets and Smartphones Protecting tablets and smartphones involves configuring the devices with security in mind and also being aware of risks when downloading and installing apps. In addition, there are several "best practices" that should be followed to provide the highest degree of protection.

Configuring Devices for Security Mobile devices have several different security-related settings that should be used. These include:

- Users should apply any security updates to their mobile devices frequently. If available, the automatic update option should be selected so that any updates can be applied as soon as they are available.

- Users should enable **auto-lock**, which password-protects the device when it has not been used for a set period of time. In addition, devices should be configured so they are locked by a strong password.

- When using the device's Web browser the auto-complete features that remember usernames or passwords should be disabled.

- The Web browser on the mobile device should be configured properly for security as well.

Using Apps Apps pose some of the biggest risks for mobile devices. When using apps users should consider the following:

- Download apps only from reputable sources. Be sure to read the reviews and check the feedback on apps before installing them.

- Do not download third-party apps but instead use apps from reputable developers.

- Download and install an antivirus (AV) app as it becomes available and keep it up to date.

- For critical data an encryption app should be used to keep the portable data secure while in transit.

- Download and install a **remote wipe** app that can erase the contents of the device if lost or stolen.

- Install and use tracing and tracking software to identify the location of the device.

One of the latest trends from security software vendors is a suite of anti-malware protection products that offer protection for a variety of devices, both desktop and mobile, for a single price. A user can purchase the suite and protect, for example, a Windows desktop and laptop computer, a Mac, an Android smartphone, and an iPad. In addition, a Web-based management interface lets users review online which devices are protected by which software, install software directly from the vendor's site, and even configure the protection settings remotely.

Best Practices A list of "best practices" for using mobile devices securely includes the following:

- Take appropriate physical security measures to prevent the theft of mobile devices.
- Never leave a mobile device unattended.
- Report lost or stolen devices immediately.
- Use appropriate sanitization and disposal procedures for mobile devices. Users should delete all information stored in a mobile device before discarding, exchanging, or donating it.
- Back up data stored on the mobile device on a regular basis.
- Be cautious when opening e-mail and text message attachments or clicking on links.
- Do not call telephone numbers contained in unsolicited e-mails or text messages.
- Do not jailbreak a mobile device.
- Be aware of current threats affecting mobile devices.

Chapter Summary

- Wi-Fi is the common term used to describe a wireless data network that is designed to provide high-speed data connections for mobile devices (the technical term is wireless local area network, or WLAN). Mobile devices within range of a centrally located connection device in a Wi-Fi network can send and receive information using radio frequency (RF) transmissions at speeds that range up to 600 million bits per second (600 Mbps). The Institute of Electrical and Electronics Engineers (IEEE) has been responsible for establishing standards for Wi-Fi networks.

- Each mobile device must have a wireless client network interface card adapter to send and receive the wireless signals. These interface cards are generally built into mobile devices. In addition a wireless broadband router is needed for a home-based Wi-Fi network. This router acts as the "base station" for wireless devices, sending and receiving wireless signals between all devices as well as providing the "gateway" to the external Internet. In an office setting, instead of using a wireless broadband router a more sophisticated device known as an access point (AP) is used.

- There are several different attacks that can launched against home Wi-Fi networks, such as stealing data, reading wireless transmissions, injecting malware, and downloading harmful content. In a public Wi-Fi network an attacker can set up an evil twin to mimic an authorized Wi-Fi device. A user's mobile device may unknowingly connect to this evil twin instead of the authorized device so that attackers can receive any transmissions or directly send malware to the user's computer.

- Bluetooth technology is a short-range wireless technology designed for interconnecting computers and peripherals, handheld devices, and cell phones. Bluetooth uses short-range RF transmissions and provides rapid "on-the-fly" device pairings. Two Bluetooth attacks are bluejacking and bluesnarfing. Bluejacking is an attack that sends unsolicited messages to Bluetooth-enabled devices. Bluesnarfing is an attack that accesses unauthorized information from a wireless device through a Bluetooth connection, often between cell phones and laptop computers.

- Laptop computers face the same attacks as desktop computers. These include viruses, worms, Trojans, rootkits, backdoors, keyloggers, Arbitrary Code Execution, spyware, adware, and scareware. An additional risk that laptop computers (as well as other mobile devices) face is theft.

- A feature phone is a traditional cellular telephone that includes a limited number of features, such as a camera, an MP3 music player, and ability to send and receive short message service (SMS) text messages. A smartphone has all the tools that a feature phone has but also includes an operating system that allows it to run third-party applications (*apps*). Tablet computers are portable devices with smaller screen sizes and are designed for user convenience. Tablets and smartphones have increasingly been the target of attackers.

- Mobile malware is specifically directed at tablets and smartphones. It includes many of the same types of attacks that are directed at desktop computers (Trojans, viruses, worms, and arbitrary code execution), plus threats unique to mobile devices. For example, an attacker could infect a smartphone and cause it to repeatedly dial a premium-rate telephone number that charges a fee for the call. Another attack takes advantage of a mobile device that has had its built-in limitations and protections removed by the owner (jailbreaking). An attacker who can remotely access the mobile device can then exploit it. A mobile device can be infected through an infected app, by downloading an app from an unofficial app store, by a connection to another computer, through an attachment, and through a wireless connection.

- Configuring a Wi-Fi wireless broadband router to provide the highest level of security protection is an important step in securing a wireless network. The first step in securing a Wi-Fi wireless broadband router involves "locking down" the device by creating a password to access its internal configuration settings. In addition, most routers also permit remote management of the router's configuration settings through the Internet. Unless remote management is essential it is recommended that this feature be disabled.

- Another important step in securing a Wi-Fi network is turning on Wi-Fi Protected Access 2 (WPA2) Personal. Turning on WPA2 Personal involves turning it on at the wireless router and then entering a key value on each authorized device that has been preapproved to join the Wi-Fi network. As a means of simplifying turning on WPA2 Personal many devices now support Wi-Fi Protected Setup (WPS) as an optional means of configuring security. Although securing the wireless router with a strong password and turning on WPA2 Personal are the most effective Wi-Fi security settings, there are other security settings that are widely promoted. Unfortunately, some of these only provide a marginal degree of additional security or no additional security at all.

- When using a smartphone or tablet that supports Bluetooth it is advisable to disable Bluetooth and turn on this service only as necessary. Public Wi-Fi networks, such as those in a coffee shop, library, restaurant, and airport, should be used with caution. Because the signals on public Wi-Fi networks are rarely if ever encrypted, any attacker in the area can easily read any transmissions.

- One way of protecting laptop computers is to install a cable lock to secure the device to a desk or chair. Another protection is to encrypt sensitive data that is stored on a laptop. Protecting tablets and smartphones involves configuring the devices with security in mind and also being aware of risks when downloading and installing apps. In addition, there are several "best practices" that should be followed to provide the highest degree of protection for your mobile devices.

Key Terms

access point (AP) A more sophisticated device used in an office setting instead of a wireless broadband router.

ad hoc network A direct peer-to-peer network that connects a wireless device directly to another wireless device.

auto-lock A mobile device setting that locks down the device when it has not been used for a set period of time.

bluejacking An attack that sends unsolicited messages to Bluetooth-enabled devices.

bluesnarfing An attack that accesses unauthorized information from a wireless device through a Bluetooth connection.

Bluetooth A short-range wireless technology designed for interconnecting computers and peripherals, handheld devices, and cell phones.

cable lock A device that can be inserted into the security slot of a portable device to protect it from theft.

evil twin An AP or another computer that is set up by an attacker designed to mimic the authorized Wi-Fi device.

feature phone A traditional cellular telephone that includes a limited number of features.

Institute of Electrical and Electronics Engineers (IEEE) The most widely known and influential organization in the field of computer networking and wireless communications. The IEEE sets wireless networking standards.

jailbreaking Removing the built-in limitations and protections of a mobile device.

Media Access Control (MAC) address A unique hardware number that is "burned in" to each wireless network interface card adapter.

mobile malware Malware that is specifically directed at tablets and smartphones.

private key cryptography (symmetric cryptography) Cryptography that uses same single key to encrypt and decrypt sensitive information.

remote wipe A cellular phone app that can erase the contents of the device if it is lost or stolen

Service Set Identifier (SSID) The network name identifier in a Wi-Fi network.

short message service (SMS) A service that provides the ability to send and receive text messages.

smartphone A cellular phone that has an operating system that allows it to run third-party applications.

tablet computer Portable computing device with a screen size that ranges from 5 to 10 inches (127 to 254 millimeters), designed for user convenience.

virtual private network (VPN) A technology that uses an unsecured public network, such as the Internet, as if it were a secure private network.

war driving Searching for wireless signals from an automobile or on foot using a portable computing device.

whole disk encryption Cryptography that can be applied to entire disks.

Wi-Fi (*wireless fidelity*) A wireless data network that is designed to provide high-speed data connections for mobile devices.

Wi-Fi Protected Access 2 (WPA2) Personal A security setting that provides the optimum level of wireless security.

Wi-Fi Protected Setup (WPS) A simplified and optional method for configuring WPA2 Personal wireless security.

wireless broadband router A device used for a home-based Wi-Fi network that combines several networking technologies.

wireless client network interface card adapter A device that allows a mobile device to send and receive wireless signals.

wireless local area network (WLAN) The technical name for a Wi-Fi network.

Review Questions

1. The technical name for a Wi-Fi network is:

   a. Wireless local area network (WLAN)

   b. Bluetooth

   c. Wireless personal area network (WPAN)

   d. Wireless Ultraband (WU)

2. Which of the following IEEE Wi-Fi networks is the fastest?

   a. 802.11

   b. 802.11a

   c. 802.11x

   d. 802.11c

3. Which of the following is false about a wireless broadband router?

   a. It is usually found in a large business with hundreds of wireless users.

   b. It typically is connected to the user's modem.

   c. It sends and receives wireless signals between all wireless devices.

   d. It combines several networking technologies.

4. When a user moves from one cell of coverage to another cell in a Wi-Fi network this is called _____.

   a. migrating

   b. roaming

   c. handshaking

   d. traveling

5. Which of the following is not a risk that someone would face using an unprotected home Wi-Fi network?

   a. An attacker could steal sensitive data from a computer on the wireless network.

   b. The information contained in wireless transmissions could be captured and read.

   c. An attacker could take control of the user's keyboard over the network.

   d. Malware could be injected into computers connected to the Wi-Fi network.

6. The maximum range a Bluetooth wireless signal travels is about _____ feet.

   a. 10

   b. 33

   c. 128

   d. 350

7. _____ is an attack that sends unsolicited messages to Bluetooth-enabled devices.

   a. Bluejacking

   b. Bluestealing

   c. Bluesnarfing

   d. Bluesending

8. Which of the following devices does not have an operating system that allows it to run third-party applications?

   a. Tablet

   b. Smartphone

   c. Feature phone

   d. Laptop

9. Which of the following is not a feature of a tablet computer?

   a. Performance and power

   b. Light weight

   c. 5- to 10-inch screen size

   d. Easy to use

10. _____ is the process of bypassing the built-in limitations and protections of a mobile device.

    a. Twisting

    b. Jailbreaking

    c. Rooting

    d. Cracking

11. Why should you not download apps from an unofficial app store?

    a. Apps are always inferior on an unofficial app store.

    b. It always takes longer to download the app than from an approved store.

    c. It deprives the developers of any royalties.

    d. The apps on these sites are generally not previewed and may contain malware.

12. What is the first step in securing a Wi-Fi wireless broadband router?

    a. Creating a password to protect its internal configuration settings

    b. Disabling all wireless connections

    c. Turning on short preamble packets

    d. Monitoring the Wi-Fi signal with a remote telemonitor

13. What provides the optimum level of wireless security for a home Wi-Fi network?

    a. Placing the wireless router in a box

    b. Using a good SSID

    c. Strong passwords on wireless devices

    d. Turning on Wi-Fi Protected Access 2 (WPA2) Personal

14. What technology is designed to simplify securing a Wi-Fi network?

    a. Wi-Fi Vault

    b. Wi-Fi Secure Transmission (WFST)

    c. Wi-Fi Protected Setup (WPS)

    d. Wi-Fi Protected Access (WPA) Corporate

15. Which of the following can add a stronger degree of security to a Wi-Fi network?

    a. Disable SSID broadcasts

    b. Restrict users by MAC address

    c. Limit the number of users

    d. Turning on guest access

16. Each of the following is a sound security practice when using a public Wi-Fi network except_____.

   a. watching out for an evil twin

   b. using the network for less than one hour per day

   c. using a virtual private network (VPN)

   d. not using the network when entering confidential information on a Web site

17. Cryptography that uses one key instead of two is called _____.

   a. public key cryptography

   b. private key cryptography

   c. single key cryptography

   d. remote key cryptography

18. Each of the following is an advantage of an encrypted hardware-based USB flash drive except:

   a. They automatically connect to the computer when the drive is inserted.

   b. All data is automatically encrypted.

   c. The cases are tamper-resistant.

   d. They can be remotely disabled.

19. _____ protects a mobile device when it has not been used for a set period of time.

   a. Auto-lock

   b. Screen refresh

   c. Manager tie down (MTD)

   d. Remote security

20. Which of the following is *not* a best practice for using a mobile device?

   a. Back up data stored on the mobile device on a regular basis.

   b. Do not jailbreak a mobile device.

   c. Wait 24 hours before reporting a lost device.

   d. Be aware of current threats affecting mobile devices.

Hands-On Projects

Project 5-1: Download and Install a Wireless Monitor Gadget

Most Wi-Fi users are surprised to see just how far their wireless signal will reach, and if the network is unprotected this makes it easy for an attacker hiding several hundred feet away to break into the network. There are several tools available that will show the different wireless signals from Wi-Fi networks that can be detected. Some of these tools are in the form of a gadget, which is a small, mini-application that runs on the desktop and provides easy access to commonly used information and tools. In this project, you will download and install the Xirrus Wi-Fi Monitor gadget. You will need a computer with a wireless network interface card adapter, such as a laptop, to complete this project.

1. Use your Web browser to go to **www.xirrus.com/library/wifitools.php.**

It is not unusual for Web sites to change the location of where files are stored. If the URL above no longer functions then open a search engine and search for "Xirrus Wi-Fi Monitor gadget".

2. Scroll down to the section **Download Gadget.**

3. Under **Gadget for Windows 7 and Vista** click **Download Gadget v1.2.**

4. Click **Save** and specify the location for the download, if necessary.

5. When the download has finished, open the download file, and if necessary, unzip it.

6. Double-click the application file. Click **Allow** if asked.

7. Click the **Install** button.

8. Minimize all open windows to expose the gadget on the desktop.

9. Move the mouse pointer over the gadget to display the gadget's configuration options.

10. Click the gadget's **Larger size** button to increase the gadget's size.

11. Click the gadget's wrench to open the gadget's option screen.

12. If necessary, under **Sweep Type** select **Radar.**

13. Under **Display Units** select dBm. Click **OK.**

14. On the gadget click **Show networks …**

15. Click the name of a wireless network under the **SSID** column. The signal strength of the network you clicked should appear on the radiation chart.

16. Click the name of another wireless network and note its strength.

17. Are you surprised by the number of wireless network signals you can detect? Do you think the different owners of these networks are aware that their signal is accessible?

18. Close all windows.

Project 5-2: Downloading and Installing an Advanced Wireless Detection Application

Although gadgets can provide limited information, there are other tools that can be used to detect much more information from Wi-Fi signals. In this project, you will download and install advanced wireless detection software.

1. Use your Web browser to go to **www.vistumbler.net**.

It is not unusual for Web sites to change the location of where files are stored. If the URL above no longer functions, then open a search engine and search for "Vistumbler".

2. Next to **Download EXE:** click Vistumbler v**XX** (where *XX* is the latest version).

3. Follow the prompts to download and install Vistumbler on your computer.

4. If the program does not launch after the installation is complete, click **Start** and then click **Vistumbler**.

5. Expand the window to full screen.

6. Click **Scan APs.** If no networks appear, click **Interface** and then select the appropriate wireless NIC interface. How many Wi-Fi networks can you detect?

7. Note the columns **Signal** and **High Signal**. These indicate the strength of the signal being detected.

8. Click **View**.

9. Click **Show Signal dB (Estimated)**. The columns **Signal** and **High Signal** now provide the estimated strength using another measurement.

10. Click **Graph 1**.

11. Click one of the APs displayed at the bottom of the screen. Allow Vistumbler to accumulate data over several minutes. What information is displayed on this graph?

12. Click **Graph 2**.

13. Click another one of the APs displayed at the bottom of the screen. Allow Vistumbler to accumulate data over several minutes. What information is displayed on this graph? How is this different from the previous graph? How could an attacker use this information?

14. Now carry the laptop to another location. What happens to these graphs as you move?

15. Click **No Graph** to return to the previous screen.

16. Close all windows.

Project 5-3: Viewing Bluetooth Devices Using Blueauditor

Just as many users are surprised to learn that their Wi-Fi signal travels well beyond the walls of their house or apartment, many Bluetooth users are surprised to discover how their signal can easily be detected by another device. In this project you will install software to view Bluetooth devices in the area that can be detected by the computer. To complete this project, you will need a computer that has either built-in Bluetooth technology or a Bluetooth USB adapter. (If you are already using a Bluetooth mouse or similar device on a computer that does not have integrated Bluetooth, you will have a Bluetooth

USB adapter.) In addition, you will need a separate Bluetooth device, such as a Bluetooth mouse, keyboard, or smartphone that supports Bluetooth.

1. Turn on or install the Bluetooth mouse, keyboard, or similar device on the computer.

2. Go to **www.wifiauditor.com**.

It is not unusual for Web sites to change the location of where files are stored. If the URL above no longer functions, then open a search engine and search for "Blueauditor".

3. Click **Download Blueauditor**.

4. When the file finishes downloading, launch the setup file to install Blueauditor.

5. When the installation is complete, start Blueauditor if necessary.

6. Click **Monitoring**.

7. Click **Run**.

8. Click **Run** in the **Devices Search Parameters Dialog** box.

9. Wait several seconds for the Bluetooth device to appear. What information about the device is transmitted through this Bluetooth network? Are you surprised at the level of detail that is transmitted?

10. Scroll across to identify the different information.

11. Add another Bluetooth device to the Bluetooth network, such as a smartphone that supports Bluetooth. It may be necessary to both turn on the Bluetooth capabilities and to make the device discoverable. Then, move the device close to the computer so that it can be detected.

12. What information about this device is transmitted through the Bluetooth network? How could an attacker use this information?

13. Close all windows.

Project 5-4: Configuring a Password and WPA2 Personal

The ability to properly configure a wireless router or AP for strong security is important. In this project, you will use an online emulator from D-Link to configure the two important security settings.

Although your wireless router may be different, this emulator provides an overview of how the configuration settings a typical Wi-Fi wireless router may look.

1. Use your Web browser to go to **support.dlink.com/emulators/dap1522/**.

It is not unusual for Web sites to change the location of where files are stored. If the URL above no longer functions, then open a search engine and search for "D-Link DAP-1522 emulator".

2. Click **DAP-1522 AP Mode.**

3. The emulated login screen will appear. Click **Login** without entering a password.

4. An emulated Setup screen displaying what a user would see when configuring an actual DAP-1522 is displayed.

5. Click **Maintenance.**

6. Under the section **ADMIN PASSWORD** is where a new password would be entered to enter the configuration settings. Why is this important?

7. Click **SETUP.**

8. Under **Manual Wireless Network Setup** click the button **Manual Wireless Network Setup.**

9. Under **Wireless Security Mode** click the down arrow in the **Security Mode:** options. What are the choices listed? Click **WPA-Personal.**

10. Under **WPA** click the down arrow next to **WPA Mode:.** Select **WPA2 Only.**

11. Click the down arrow next to **Cipher Type:.** Select **AES**, which is the highest level of security.

12. The **Passphrase** box under **PRE-SHARED KEY** is where you would enter the key value. Because it is important that this value be strong, it is recommended that you use an password generation program. Leave this D-Link site link up and open another tab on your Web browser.

13. Go to **www.grc.com/passwords.htm.**

14. Under **63 random printable ASCII characters,** select that value and copy it into your clipboard by right-clicking and selecting **Copy.**

15. Return to the D-Link page.

16. Click in the **Passphrase** box, and paste this value from the clipboard by right-clicking and selecting **Paste.**

Because the passphrase has to be entered only once on the AP and once on each wireless device it does not have to be a passphrase that must be committed to memory. Instead, it can be a long and complicated passphrase to enhance security. Under normal circumstances the passphrase now would be entered on each wireless device and saved in a password management application so it can be retrieved when needed.

17. Remain in the emulator for the next project.

Project 5-5: Configuring Additional Security Settings

In this project you will configure additional security settings on an emulated wireless router. If you have not done so already, complete the steps to access the online emulator as described in Project 5-4.

1. Under **WI-FI PROTECTED SETUP (ALSO CALLED WNC 2.0 IN WINDOWS VISTA)** note that it is enabled by default. Is this good or bad? Why?

2. Uncheck the box next to **Enable:**.

3. Under **WIRELESS NETWORK SETTINGS** what is the default name of the **Wireless Network Name?** Why should this be changed?

4. Change the Wireless Network Name to a more secure name using the criteria discussed in this chapter.

5. Note the two options under **Visibility Status**. What are they? What happens when you set this to **Invisible?** Why does it only provide a weak degree of security protection?

6. Click **ADVANCED** on the horizontal menu bar.

7. If necessary, click **MAC ADDRESS FILTER** in the left pane to display the MAC Address Filter screen.

8. In the **MAC FILTERING SETUP** section, click the down arrow below **Configure MAC Filtering Below.**

9. Click **Turn MAC filtering ON and ALLOW computers listed to access the network**. This will allow you to configure the device for preventing specific computers from accessing the network.

10. Now you need to enter the MAC address of your computer. To find your computer's MAC address, click **Start** and type **CMD** in the search bar, and press **Enter** to launch the command prompt window.

11. Type **ipconfig/all** and press **Enter**.

12. Scroll through the information listed and locate the **Physical Address** of the wireless network adapter.

13. Return to the DAP-1522 emulator and enter this information.

14. Click the **Add** button and then click **Save Settings**. Note that in this emulator the actual MAC address will not be listed under the MAC FILTERING RULES.

15. Why would this only provide a weak degree of security?

16. Close all windows.

Case Projects

CASE PROJECTS

Case Project 5-1: Compare Wireless Routers

Use the Internet to identify four different brands of wireless broadband routers. Create a table that lists each device, its features, available security, and costs. Below the table, write a paragraph describing which you would choose for your home use and why.

Case Project 5-2: Survey of Wireless Users

Create a short survey to administer to wireless users regarding how they would typically use a free wireless network in a restaurant or coffee shop. Include questions such as, "What precautions do you take when using a free wireless network?" "Can you list the dangers in using an open wireless network?" "Do you ever purchase anything that requires you to type in a credit card number while using a free wireless network?" and "Do you know how to spot an evil twin?" Ask five friends or acquaintances for their responses. Based on these responses, give a grade of "A" through "F" to each wireless user. Now take the test yourself and give yourself a similar rating. What improvements can you make in using a free wireless network?

Case Project 5-3: Is War Driving Legal?

Use the Internet to research the legality of war driving. Is it considered illegal? Why or why not? If it is not illegal, do you think it should be? What should be the penalties? Create a report on your research.

Case Project 5-4: Attacks on Wireless Medical Devices

Many medical devices use wireless technology, yet they lack the necessary security protections. At a recent security conference a security researcher, who was himself a diabetic, demonstrated a wireless attack on an insulin pump that could change the delivery of insulin to the patient. A security vendor found that they could scan a public space from up to 300 feet (91 meters) away, find vulnerable pumps made by a specific medical device manufacturer, and then force these devices to dispense fatal insulin doses. And another researcher "hacked" into a defibrillator used to stabilize a heartbeat and reprogrammed it. He also disabled its power-save mode so the battery ran down in hours instead of years. These attacks on wireless medical devices have prompted different areas of the federal government, such as the national Information Security and Privacy Advisory Board (ISPAB), the Food and Drug Administration (FDA), the National Institute of Standards and Technology (NIST), and Department of Homeland Security (DHS) to issue warnings. Use the Internet to research the current state of these attacks and proposed defenses. Should the vendors who make these wireless medical devices be forced to add security features to their devices? What should be the penalty if they do not? And what should be the penalty for an attacker who manipulates a wireless medical device?

Case Project 5-5: Securing a Mobile Device

Select a mobile device that you own or would like to have. Use the Internet to research its available security settings. Then create a document that lists the different settings, why they should be used, and how they are configured.

Case Project 5-6: Information Security Community Site Activity

The Information Security Community Site is a Course Technology/Cengage Learning information security course enrichment site. It contains a wide variety of tools, information, discussion boards, and other features to assist learners. Go to **community.cengage.com/infosec**. Click **Login** at the top of the page and enter your sign-in name and password credentials that you created in Chapter 1. Visit the Discussions page by going to the **Students** tab and selecting the **Discussion Boards** link from the drop-down menu, where you can read the following case study.

A federal lawsuit was recently filed in Massachusetts by a producer of videos. The producer accused over 50 people in Massachusetts of illegally downloading and sharing movies. The illegal downloads were traced to IP addresses belonging to both named individuals and to several unknown persons. The complaint alleges that each of the defendants was directly responsible for (1) downloading and sharing the movie, or (2) contributing to the piracy through their negligence of failing to secure their wireless network. The lawsuit says, "Defendants failed to adequately secure their Internet access, whether accessible only through their computer when physically connected to an Internet router or accessible to many computers by use of a wireless router. Defendants' negligent actions allowed others to unlawfully copy and share Plaintiff's copyrighted Motion Picture, proximately causing financial harm to Plaintiff and unlawfully interfering with Plaintiff's exclusive rights in the Motion Picture." In other words, this case poses the question of whether users who leave their wireless networks unprotected can be held liable if someone uses that network to illegally download copyrighted content, even if they don't have the owner's permission to use the wireless network.

The attorney for the plaintiffs referred to a 1932 case. In this case two barges being towed by two tugboats sunk during a storm. The owners of the tugboats were sued because they had failed to install radios in their tugs, which would have alerted the captains to the storm. Even though there was no legal requirement in 1932 that they have radios in their tugboats, an appellate court held that the owners were negligent. Why? Because even though they didn't have to have radios, they should have known better. This same standard, says the attorney, applies to this movie case: the owners of unsecured wireless routers should have known better than to leave their wireless networks open.

What do you think? Is this a valid argument? Should Wi-Fi owners be held liable if they do not secure their wireless networks and another person uses that network for an illegal activity? Why or why not? Record your responses on the Community Site discussion board.

Case Project 5-7: North Ridge Computer Consultants

North Ridge Computer Consultants (NRCC) is a local information technology company that specializes in security. In order to encourage students to enter the field of information security, NRCC often hires student interns to assist them with projects.

A recent high-profile attack was started as a result of a homeowner's Wi-Fi network not being secured. This has prompted the local neighborhood association to take steps to inform its residents the dangers of unprotected wireless networks and how to secure them. The association contacted NRCC to ask them to make a presentation at their monthly meeting.

Create a PowerPoint presentation of at least eight slides that lists the dangers of an unprotected Wi-Fi network and what are the steps to be taken to protect it. Because most of the residents do not have a technical background your presentation should more practical than technical.

References

1. "IDC lowers PC outlook at shipments decline in second quarter ahead of fall production updates," *IDC*, Aug. 23, 2012, accessed Sep. 1, 2012. <http://www.idc.com/getdoc.jsp?containerId=prUS23660312>.

2. "One in four households in the world use Wi-Fi," *Huffington Post*, Apr. 11, 2012, accessed Sep. 6, 2012. <http://www.huffingtonpost.com/2012/04/11/one-in-four-households-in-the-world-use-wi-fi_n_1419014.html>.

3. "Absolute Software 2011 Computer Theft Report," *Absolute Software*, May 23, 2012, accessed Sep. 2, 2012. <http://blog.absolute.com/absolute-software-2011-computer-theft-report/>.

4. *Ibid.*

5. *Ibid.*

6. "Computer theft report infographic," *Absolute Software*, Aug. 29, 2012, accessed Sep. 2, 2012. <http://blog.absolute.com/computer-theft-report-infographic/>.

7. "Op-Ed: A reporter's worst nightmare," *News is my Business*, Aug. 20, 2012, accessed Sep. 2, 2012. <http://newsismybusiness.com/op-ed-a-reporters-worst-nightmare/>.

8. "Smartphones see accelerated rise to dominance," *HIS iSuppli Market Research*, Aug. 28, 2012, accessed Sep. 3, 2012. <http://www.isuppli.com/Mobile-and-Wireless-Communications/News/Pages/Smartphones-See-Accelerated-Rise-to-Dominance.aspx>.

9. "Tablet computer sales will overtake notebooks by 2016," *VB/Mobile*, Aug. 15, 2012, accessed Sep. 3, 2012. <http://venturebeat.com/2012/08/15/tablet-computer-sales-will-overtake-notebooks-by-2016/>.

© Shutterstock.com

chapter 6

Workplace Security

After completing this chapter you should be able to do the following:

- Define physical access and list the tools used to restrict it

- Describe how tokens and cards can be used for security

- Explain what a security policy is and list several different policies

- Define technology and procedural access control

- List the steps to be taken to prepare for a crisis

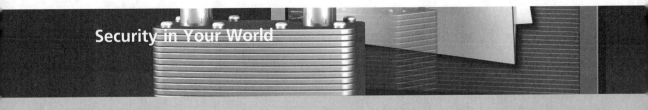

"Are you nervous?" asked Zhi. She was meeting Stefan at the local coffee shop one afternoon before he started his new job the next day. Stefan had been working as an intern at a large corporation while he was in his last year of college. Stefan had done such a good job that the corporation decided to hire him full time even before he finished school, but with the stipulation that he still had to graduate. "Yes, I am a little nervous," he said. "Even though I have been there for several months, I'll be in a new department with a different supervisor."

"You'll do just great," said Zhi. "Do you know what they have planned for you tomorrow?" Stefan set down his cup on the table. "They told me it would be mostly orientation all day. I'm sure that there's a big difference between being an intern and being a full-time employee regarding everything you need to know," he said. Zhi laughed and said, "The biggest difference will be a full-time paycheck!"

Stefan smiled. "I do know that I'll be assigned a new access card so that I can enter and leave the building. And they will probably give me a temporary token until they phase those out," he said. Zhi sat back in her chair. "Are they really that concerned about security? It seems to me that just about anybody can enter that building. I remember when I met you over there for lunch a couple of weeks ago nobody stopped me," she said. "They seem to be very concerned about security," said Stefan. "And the reason you were not stopped is because we met in the public cafeteria. If you had tried to go up the elevator, you never would have made it."

"That sounds pretty strict," said Zhi. "What are they trying to hide?" Stefan said, "I don't know that they're trying to hide anything but they're just trying to protect everyone. You can't just walk around and go in and out of conference rooms or offices. You have to use your access card every time you want to enter one."

"Wow!" Zhi said. "What other kind of security do they have there?"

Attacks directed against businesses and organizations are widespread. One of the reasons why these are such tempting targets is that a successful attack that breaches the security of an organization can expose hundreds of computers to an attacker instead of just one or two computers in a home network. Information in customer databases (credit card numbers, data on the company's latest research, and the costs charged by suppliers, for example) is all extremely valuable and is highly sought after by attackers.

Many of the security defenses that should be used by employees at work are the same as home security defenses—such as not clicking embedded hyperlinks or opening attachments from unknown senders—nevertheless, there is a significant difference in home security and the security in an organization. The primary difference is who is responsible for creating and establishing the levels of security: in a home network the *user* sets up the security while in a business it is the *organization* that does it. Rarely would employees be given the freedom to create their own desired level of security on an office computer.

What this means for employees working in an office environment is that it is important to know *what* to expect at the office in terms of security instead of *how* to configure devices for protection. Although all organizations are different, there is a common core of security protections that almost all organizations follow.

In this chapter you will explore what to expect in terms of security as an employee at the workplace. First you look at physical security that involves physical access to the facility and to computer systems. Next, you will look at security provisions that restrict access to data. Finally, you will look at crisis preparedness procedures.

Restricting Physical Access

Restricting physical access in an office environment generally involves restricting access to facilities as well as to computer systems.

Access to Facilities

Restricting physical access to facilities involves limiting access to the areas in which sensitive equipment or resources are located. These types of restrictions include hardware locks, proximity readers, mantraps, video surveillance, and fencing.

Hardware Locks Residential hardware locks for doors generally fall in four categories. Most residences have keyed entry locks (use a key to open the lock from the outside), privacy locks (lock the door but have access to unlock from the outside via a small hole; typically used on bedroom and bathroom doors), patio locks (lock the door from the inside but cannot be unlocked from the outside), and passage locks (latch a door closed yet do not lock it; typically used on hall and closet doors). The standard keyed entry lock, shown in Figure 6-1, is the most common type of door lock for keeping out intruders, but its security

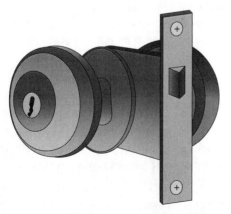

Figure 6-1 Residential keyed entry lock
© Cengage Learning 2014

is minimal. Because it does not automatically lock when the door is closed, a user may mistakenly think a door is locked when it is not. Also, a thin piece of plastic such as a credit card can sometimes be wedged between the lock and the door casing to open it, or the knob itself can be broken off with a sharp blow, with a hammer, for example, and then the door can be opened.

Door locks in commercial buildings are different from residential door locks. For rooms that require enhanced security, a lever coupled with a **deadbolt lock** is common. This lock extends a solid metal bar into the door frame for extra security, as shown in Figure 6-2. Deadbolt locks are much more difficult to defeat than keyed entry locks. The lock cannot be broken from the outside like a preset lock, and the extension of the bar prevents a credit card from being inserted to "jimmy" it open. Deadbolt locks also require that a key be used to both open and lock the door.

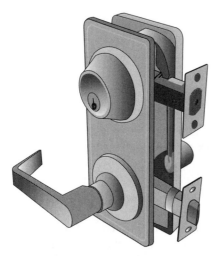

Figure 6-2 Deadbolt lock
© Cengage Learning 2014

The categories of commercial door locks include storeroom (the outside is always locked, entry is by key only, and the inside lever is always unlocked), classroom (the outside can be locked or unlocked, and the inside lever is always unlocked), store entry double cylinder (includes a keyed cylinder in both the outside and inside knobs so that a key in either knob locks or unlocks both at the same time), and communicating double cylinder lock (includes a keyed cylinder in both outside and inside knobs and the key unlocks its own knob independently).

However, any residential or commercial door locks that use keys can be compromised if the keys are lost, stolen, or duplicated. To achieve the best security when using keyed door locks, most organizations use key management procedures such as:

- Change locks immediately upon loss or theft of keys.
- Inspect all locks on a regular basis.

- Issue keys only to authorized persons.

- Keep records of who uses and turns in keys.

- Keep track of keys issued, with their number and identification, for both master keys and duplicate keys.

- Master keys should not have any marks identifying them as masters.

- Secure unused keys in a locked safe.

- Set up a procedure to monitor the use of all locks and keys and update the procedure as necessary.

- When making duplicates of master keys, mark them "Do Not Duplicate," and wipe out the manufacturer's serial numbers to keep duplicates from being ordered.

Because of the difficulties in managing keys for hundreds or thousands of users, an alternative to a key lock is a more sophisticated door access system using a **cipher lock**, as shown in Figure 6-3. Cipher locks are combination locks that use buttons that must be pushed in the proper sequence to open the door. Although cipher locks may seem similar to a combination padlock, they have more intelligence. A cipher lock can be programmed to allow a certain individual's code to be valid on specific dates and times. For example, an employee's code may be valid to access the computer room from only 8:00 AM to 5:00 PM Monday through Friday. This prevents the employee from entering the room late at night when most other employees are gone. Cipher locks also keep a record of when the door was opened and by which code.

Figure 6-3 Cipher lock
© Cengage Learning 2014

A disadvantage of cipher locks is that they can be vulnerable to shoulder surfing, so users should be careful to conceal which buttons they push.

Proximity Readers Instead of using a key or entering a code to open a door, a user can display an object (sometimes called a *physical token*) to identify herself. One of the most common types of physical tokens is an *ID badge*. ID badges originally contained a photograph of the bearer and were visually screened by security guards. Later ID badges contained a magnetic stripe that was "swiped" or a barcode identifier that was scanned to identify the user.

However, when verifying hundreds or thousands of users at a time, swiping or scanning ID badges can result in a bottleneck. New technologies do not require that an ID badge be visually exposed. Instead, the badge emits a signal identifying the owner; the signal is then detected as the owner moves near a **proximity reader**, which receives the signal. This makes it unnecessary for the bearer to remove the badge from a pocket or purse.

ID badges that can be detected by a proximity reader are often fitted with tiny *radio frequency identification (RFID) tags*. RFID tags, as shown in Figure 6-4, can easily be affixed to the inside of an ID badge and can be read by an RFID proximity reader as users walk through a turnstile with the badge in their pocket.

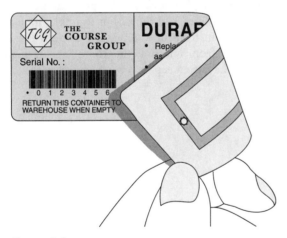

Figure 6-4 RFID tag
© Cengage Learning 2014

RFID tags on ID badges are passive and do not have their own power supply; instead, the tiny electrical current induced in the antenna by the incoming signal from the transceiver provides enough power for the tag to send a response. Because it does not require a power supply, passive RFID tags can be very small (only 0.4 mm × 0.4 mm and thinner than a sheet of paper); the amount of data transmitted is limited to typically just an ID number. Passive tags have ranges from about 1/3 inch to 19 feet (10 millimeters to 6 meters). Active RFID tags must have their own power source.

Mantraps A **mantrap** is designed to separate a nonsecure area from a secure area. A mantrap device monitors and controls two interlocking doors to a small room (a vestibule), as shown in Figure 6-5. When in operation, only one door is able to be open at any time.

Mantraps are used at high-security areas where only authorized persons are allowed to enter, such as sensitive data-processing rooms, cash handling areas, and research laboratories.

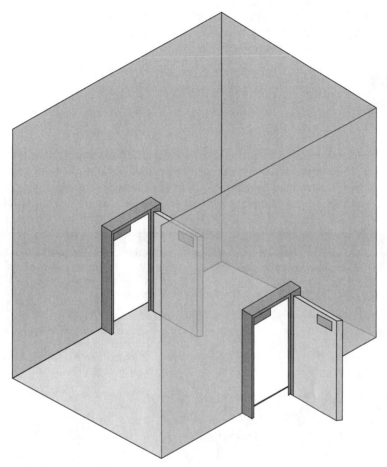

Figure 6-5 Mantrap
© Cengage Learning 2014

Before electronic security was available, vestibules with two locked doors were used to control access to sensitive areas. An individual attempting to gain access to a secure area would give his credentials to a security officer; the security officer would then open the first door to the vestibule and ask the individual to enter and wait while his credentials were being checked. If the credentials were approved, the second door would be unlocked; in the event that the credentials were fraudulent, the person would be trapped in the vestibule (a "mantrap") and could only exit through the first door.

Video Surveillance Monitoring activity with a video camera can also provide a degree of security. Using video cameras to transmit a signal to a specific and limited set of receivers is called **closed circuit television (CCTV)**. CCTV is frequently used for surveillance in areas that require security monitoring such as banks, casinos, airports, and military installations.

Some CCTV cameras are fixed in a single position pointed at a door or a hallway. Other cameras resemble a small dome and allow the security technician to move the camera 360 degrees for a full panoramic view. High-end video surveillance cameras are motion-tracking and will automatically follow any movement.

CCTV cameras are now widely deployed in many public areas and are monitored by the police and governmental agencies.

Fencing   Securing a restricted area by erecting a barrier, called **fencing**, can be an effective method for maintaining security. However, standard chain link fencing offers limited security because it can easily be circumvented by climbing over it or cutting the links. Most modern perimeter security consists of a fence equipped with other deterrents as are listed in Table 6-1.

Technology	Description	Comments
Anti-climb paint	A nontoxic petroleum gel-based paint that is thickly applied and does not harden, making any coated surface very difficult to climb.	Typically used on poles, down-pipes, wall tops, and railings above head height (8 feet or 2.4 meters).
Anti-climb collar	Spiked collars that extends horizontally for up to 3 feet (1 meter) from the pole to prevent anyone from climbing; serves as both a practical and visual deterrent.	Spiked collars are for protecting equipment mounted on poles like CCTV or in areas where climbing a pole can be an easy point of access over a security fence.
Roller barrier	Independently rotating large cups (in diameter of 5 inches or 115 millimeters) affixed to the top of a fence prevents the hands of intruders from gripping the top of a fence to climb over it.	Often found around public grounds and schools where a nonaggressive barrier is important.
Rotating spikes	Installed at the top of walls, gates, or fences; the tri-wing spike collars rotate around a central spindle.	Can be painted to blend into fencing.

Table 6-1   Fencing deterrents

© Cengage Learning 2014

Access to Systems

Passwords are commonly used to restrict access to computer systems. However, their weakness is that they should be committed to memory. Another type of authentication credential is based on the approved user having a specific item in his possession. The most common items are tokens and cards.

Tokens   A significant increase in the level of security when accessing sensitive data can be achieved by using a token. A **token** is typically a small device (usually one that can be affixed to a keychain) with a window display, as shown in Figure 6-6. The token and a corresponding authentication server share a unique algorithm (each user has a different algorithm). The token generates a code from the algorithm once every 30 to 60 seconds. This code is valid for only a brief period of time (the time it is displayed on the token). When the user logs in she enters her username along with the code (or a variation of it) currently being displayed on the token. When the authentication server receives it the server looks up the algorithm associated with that specific user, generates its own code, and then compares it with what the user entered. If they are identical, the user is authenticated. This process is illustrated in Figure 6-7. Instead of the user presenting a password (what she knows) a token introduces another form of authentication, namely what the person has (a token).

Figure 6-6 Token
© Cengage Learning 2014

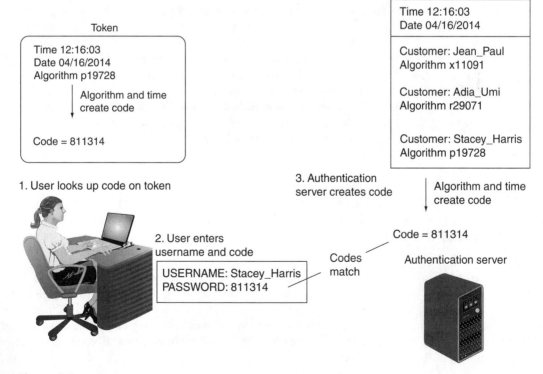

Figure 6-7 Code generation and comparison
© Cengage Learning 2014

The code is not transmitted to the token; instead, both the token and authentication server have the same algorithm and time setting.

Tokens have several advantages over passwords. First, standard passwords are static in nature: they do not change unless the user is forced to create a new password. Because passwords do not change frequently, this can give an attacker a lengthy period of time in which to crack and then use the password. In contrast, tokens produce dynamic passwords that change frequently and are called *one-time passwords (OTP)*. An attacker who steals the code would have to use it within the token's time limit (usually 60 seconds) before it expires.

As an additional level of security, many token systems randomly ask the user to wait until the code changes and then enter that new code. This ensures that the code has not been stolen (but it does not protect against the theft of the token itself).

Second, a user might not know if an attacker has stolen his password, and confidential information could be accessed without the user knowing it was taking place. If a token is stolen, it would become obvious and steps could immediately be taken to disable that account.

There are several variations of token systems. Some systems use the code displayed on the token as a replacement for a password, while others require a password along with the code. A more secure system requires the user to create a personal identification number (PIN), which is then combined with the code to create a single passcode (for example, if a user has the PIN 1694 and the code currently displayed is 190411, he will enter 1694190411 as the passcode). Because this approach uses both what a user knows (the password) and what the user has (the token), it is called **multifactor authentication** and uses more than one type of authentication credential. Using just one type of authentication, like a password, is called **single-factor authentication**.

Because of the wide popularity of cell phones, these devices are rapidly replacing tokens. A code can be sent to a user's cell phone through an app on the device or as a text message instead of using a token.

Cards There are several types of cards that can be used to authenticate individuals. A **smart card**, as illustrated in Figure 6-8, contains an *integrated circuit chip*, which can hold information, which can then be used as part of the authentication process. Smart cards can either be contact cards, which contain a tell-tale "pad" allowing electronic access to the contents of the chip, or contactless cards that do not require physical contact with the card itself.

"What's the notebook that you're reading?" asked Zhi. After Stefan's first day on the job, he and Zhi had gotten together again at the coffee shop. "This is just some light reading," laughed Stefan. He went on to explain that it contained the security policies of his employer. "That certainly doesn't look like the college's security policy that we had to read for our computer class," said Zhi. Stefan shook his head. "No, it's nothing like it at all. These are very detailed and they outline exactly what you can and cannot do. I was surprised at how much it covers—and it's very long, too."

Zhi look over his shoulder at the index. "There are a whole lot of security policies listed there. I thought a security policy was just one document like ours at school," she said. "Nope," said Stefan as he picked up a pencil. "We have many different security policies, and I have to read through all of them tonight." Zhi pulled up a chair to the table. "Can you show me what some of them are?"

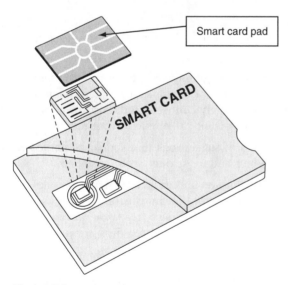

Figure 6-8 Smart card
© Cengage Learning 2014

Restricting Data Access

Whereas restricting physical access limits an employees' admission to the facilities, restricting data access limits what an employee can see and do with the organization's data stored on its computer systems. Restricting data access involves two elements of access control, namely technology access control and procedural access control. Both of these restrictions should be clearly outlined in the organization's security policy.

Security Policies

Security policies are essential elements in an organization's overall security platform. It is important to know what a security policy is along with the different types of policies.

What Is a Security Policy? At its core, a security policy is a document that outlines the protections that should be enacted to ensure that the organization's assets face minimal risks. At one level, a security policy can be viewed as a set of management statements that defines an organization's philosophy about how to safeguard its information. At a more technical and detailed level, a security policy can be seen as the rules for computer access and specifically how these will be carried out. In short, a **security policy** is a written document that states how an organization plans to protect the company's information technology assets. Security policies, along with the accompanying procedures, standards, and guidelines, are key to implementing information security in an organization. Having a written security policy empowers an organization to take appropriate action to safeguard its data.

Although these definitions cover a broad scope, they are not conflicting but are complementary. They reflect the different approaches to viewing a security policy.

There are several different terms used to describe the "rules" that a user follows in an organization:

- *Standard.* A standard is a collection of requirements specific to the system or procedure that must be met by everyone. For example, a standard might describe how to secure a computer at home that remotely connects to the organization's network. Users must follow this standard if they want to be able to connect.

- *Guideline.* A guideline is a collection of suggestions that should be implemented. These are not requirements to be met but are strongly recommended.

- *Policy.* A policy is a document that outlines specific requirements or rules that must be met. A policy is considered the correct tool for an organization to use when it is establishing security. This is because a policy applies to a wide range of hardware or software (and is not a standard) and a policy is required (it is not just a guideline).

An organization's information security policy can serve several functions:

- It can be an overall intention and direction, formally expressed by the organization's management. A security policy is a vehicle for communicating an organization's information security culture and acceptable information security behavior.

- It details specific risks and how to address them, and provides controls that executives can use to direct employee behavior.

- It can help to create a security-aware organizational culture.

- It can help to ensure that employee behavior is directed and monitored to ensure compliance with security requirements.

An effective security policy must carefully balance two key elements: trust and control. There are three approaches to trust:

- *Trust everyone all of the time.* This is the easiest model to enforce because there are no restrictions. However, this is impractical because it leaves systems vulnerable to attack.

- *Trust no one at any time.* This model is the most restrictive, but is also impractical. Few individuals would work for an organization that did not trust its employees.

- *Trust some people some of the time.* This approach exercises caution in the amount of trust given. Access is provided as needed with technical controls to ensure the trust is not violated.

A security policy attempts to provide the right amount of trust by balancing no trust and too much trust. Deciding on the level of trust may be a delicate matter; too much trust may lead to security problems, while too little trust may make it difficult to find and keep good employees.

Control is the second element that must be balanced. One of the goals of a security policy is to implement control. Deciding on the level of control for a specific policy is not always clear. The security needs and the culture of the organization play a major role when deciding what level of control is appropriate. If policies are too restrictive or too hard to implement and comply with, employees will either ignore them or find a way to circumvent the controls. Management must commit to the proper level of control that a security policy should address.

Because security policies are a balancing act between trust and control, not all users have positive attitudes toward security policies. Users sometimes view security policies as a barrier to their productivity, a way to control their behavior, or useless requirements that are difficult to follow. This is particularly true if in the past security policies did not exist or were loosely enforced.

Security Policy Subpolicies Because a security policy is comprehensive and detailed, most organizations choose to break the security policy down into smaller "subpolicies" that can be more easily referred to. The term *security policy* then becomes an umbrella term for all of the subpolicies included within it.

There are a large number of security subpolicies. Some of these are listed in Table 6-2.

Access Control

As its name implies, **access control** is granting or denying approval to use specific resources; it is *controlling access*. Although access control is sometimes thought of as physical, such as hardware locks, mantraps, and fencing, it is more properly the *mechanism* used in an information system to allow or restrict access to data or devices. Enforcing access control through technology is one means of providing security. In addition, procedural access control is also used for limiting access to help secure systems and data.

Name of Security Policy Subpolicy	Description
Acceptable encryption policy	Defines requirements for using cryptography
Anti-virus policy	Establishes guidelines for effectively reducing the threat of computer viruses on the organization's network and computers
Audit vulnerability scanning policy	Outlines the requirements and provides the authority for an information security team to conduct audits and risk assessments, investigate incidents, to ensure conformance to security policies, or to monitor user activity
Automatically forwarded e-mail policy	Prescribes that no e-mail will be automatically forwarded to an external destination without prior approval from the appropriate manager or director
Database credentials coding policy	Defines requirements for storing and retrieving database usernames and passwords
E-mail policy	Creates standards for using corporate e-mail
E-mail retention policy	Helps employees determine what information sent or received by e-mail should be retained and for how long
Information sensitivity policy	Establishes criteria for classifying and securing the organization's information in a manner appropriate to its level of security
Server security policy	Creates standards for minimal security configuration for servers
VPN security policy	Establishes requirements for Remote Access Virtual Private Network (VPN) connections to the organization's network
Wireless communication policy	Defines standards for wireless systems used to connect to the organization's networks

Table 6-2 **Security policy subpolicies**
© Cengage Learning 2014

Technology Access Control There are several technologies that can be used for implementing access control. These include group policy and account restrictions.

Group Policy In an organization with hundreds of computers, how can access control be implemented? One solution for organizations using Microsoft Windows is to use **Group Policy**. This is a Microsoft Windows feature that provides centralized management and configuration of computers and remote users using the Microsoft directory service Active Directory (AD). Group Policy is usually used in enterprise environments to enforce access control by restricting user actions that may pose a security risk, such as changing access to certain folders or downloading executable files. Group Policy can also control a user's script for logging on and off the system, folder redirection, Internet Explorer Web browser settings, and Windows Registry settings (the *registry* is a database that stores settings and options for the operating system).

Group Policies are analyzed and applied for computers when they start up and for users when they log on. Every 1 to 2 hours, the system looks for changes in the Group Policy and reapplies them as necessary, although this time period to look for changes can be modified.

Account Restrictions Another means of enforcing access control is to place restrictions on user accounts. For example, *time of day* restrictions can be used to limit when a user can log on to a system. When setting these restrictions, an administrator would typically access a *logon hours* setting, select all available times, and then indicate *logon denied*, effectively denying all access at all times. The administrator would then select the time blocks the user is permitted to log on and indicate *logon permitted* for those times.

Time of day restrictions in a Windows environment can be set through a Group Policy.

Account Expiration *Orphaned accounts* are user accounts that remain active after an employee has left an organization, while a *dormant account* is one that has not been accessed for a lengthy period of time. These types of accounts can be a security risk. For example, an employee who left under unfavorable circumstances may be tempted to "get even" with the organization by stealing or erasing sensitive information through their account. Dormant accounts that are left unchecked can provide an avenue for an attacker to exploit without the fear of the actual user or a system administrator noticing.

Locating and terminating orphaned and dormant accounts is a problem for many organizations. One study revealed that 42 percent of businesses do not know how many orphaned accounts exist within their organization, and 30 percent of respondents said they have no procedure in place to locate orphaned accounts. The study also said that 27 percent of respondents estimated they currently had over 20 orphaned accounts, 12 percent said it takes longer than one month to terminate an account, and 15 percent said that former employees had accessed their orphaned account at least once.[1]

To assist with controlling orphaned and dormant accounts, **account expiration** can be used. Account expiration is the process of setting a user's account to expire. Account expiration is not the same as password expiration. Account expiration indicates when an account is no longer active; password expiration sets the time when a user must create a new password in order to access his account. Account expiration can be explicit, in that the account expires on a set date, or it can be based on a specific number of days of inactivity.

Procedural Access Control In addition to technology, there are procedures that can be used in order to limit access control. These procedures include separation of duties, job rotation, mandatory vacations, and the principle of least privilege.

Separation of Duties News headlines such as "County Official Charged with Embezzlement" appear all too frequently. Often this fraud results from a single user being trusted with a set of responsibilities that place the person in complete control of the process. For example, one person may be given total control over the collection, distribution, and reconciliation of money. If no other person is involved, it may be too tempting for that person to steal, knowing that nobody else is watching and that there is a good chance the fraud will go undetected. To counteract this possibility, most organizations require that more than one person be involved with functions that relate to handling money, because it would require a conspiracy of all the individuals in order for fraud to occur.

Likewise, a foundational principle of computer access control is not to give one person total control. Known as **separation of duties**, this practice requires that if the fraudulent application of a process could potentially result in a breach of security, then the process should be divided between two or more individuals. It is recommended that these responsibilities be divided so that the system is not vulnerable to the actions performed by a single person.

Job Rotation Another way to prevent one individual from having too much control is to use **job rotation**. Instead of one person having sole responsibility for a function, individuals are periodically moved from one job responsibility to another. Employees can rotate either within their home department or across positions in other departments. The best rotation procedure involves multiple employees rotating across many positions for different lengths of time to gain exposure to different roles and functions.

Job rotation has several advantages:

- It limits the amount of time that individuals are in a position to manipulate security configurations.

- It helps to expose any potential avenues for fraud by having multiple individuals with different perspectives learn about the job and uncover vulnerabilities that someone else may have overlooked.

- Besides enhancing security, job rotation can also reduce "burnout," increase employee satisfaction, provide a higher level of employee motivation, enhance and improve skills and competencies leading to promotional advancement, and provide an increased appreciation for peers and decreased animosity between departments.

 Job rotation may not be practical for all organizations, and often is limited to less specialized positions.

Mandatory Vacations In many fraud schemes, the perpetrator must be present every day in order to continue the fraud or keep it from being exposed. Many organizations require **mandatory vacations** for all employees to counteract this. For sensitive positions within an organization, an audit of the employees' activities is usually scheduled while they are away on vacation.

Least Privilege Consider the rooms in a large office building, each of which has a door with a lock. Different classifications of employees could be provided different keys to open doors based on their jobs. For example, a typical office worker would not be given a key that opens every door in the building. There simply is no need for this classification of worker to have access to the contents of every room. If that key were lost or stolen, the thief could easily enter any office at any time to remove its contents. Instead, a typical office worker is only provided a key that opens the door to their office because that is all that is needed for the worker to do his job. A member of the building's security staff, on the other hand, would have a key that could open any office because his job function requires it.

Limiting access to rooms in a building is a model of the information technology security principle of **least privilege**. Least privilege in access control means that only the minimum amount of privileges necessary to perform a job or function should be allocated. This helps reduce the attack surface by eliminating unnecessary privileges that could provide an avenue for an attacker.

Least privilege should apply to both users as well as to processes running on a computer system. For processes, it is important that they be designed so that they run at the minimum security level needed in order to correctly function. Users also should be given only those privileges for which they need to perform their required tasks.

One of the reasons why home computers are so frequently and easily compromised is that they use an account with administrative privileges. A more secure option is to use a lower privileged account and then invoke administrative privileges when necessary.

Crisis Preparedness

Whereas a kitchen fire or successful infection by malware could have a serious impact on a user's home computer, the impact of an act of nature or a successful attack on an organization could be devastating. As the organization works to replace the damaged equipment or clean a network of malware, impatient customers may quickly turn to competitors in order to fulfill their needs. Every minute that an organization is "down" can result in lost revenue today and the potential for lost customers tomorrow. It is essential that organizations have plans and procedures in place in order to both prevent crises as well as recover from them. Crisis preparedness involves protecting against fires, using computer forensics, in creating and maintaining a disaster recovery plan.

Protecting against Fires

Damage inflicted as a result of a fire is a constant threat to persons as well as property. In order for a fire to occur, four entities must be present at the same time:

- A type of *fuel* or combustible material
- Sufficient *oxygen* to sustain the combustion
- Enough *heat* to raise the material to its ignition temperature
- A chemical *reaction* that is the fire itself

The first three factors form a fire triangle, which is illustrated in Figure 6-9. To extinguish a fire, any one of these elements must be removed.

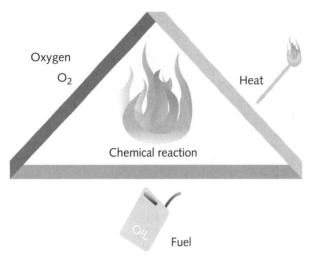

Figure 6-9 Fire triangle
© Cengage Learning 2014

Fires are divided into five categories. Table 6-3 lists the types of fires, their typical fuel source, how they can be extinguished, and the types of handheld fire extinguishers that should be used.

Class of Fire	Type of Fire	Combustible Materials	Methods to Extinguish	Type of Fire Extinguisher Needed
Class A	Common combustibles	Wood, paper, textiles, and other ordinary combustibles	Water, water-based chemical, foam, or multi-purpose dry chemical	Class A or Class ABC extinguisher
Class B	Combustible liquids	Flammable liquids, oils, solvents, paint, and grease, for example	Foam, dry chemical, or carbon dioxide to put out the fire by smothering it or cutting off the oxygen	Class BC or Class ABC extinguisher
Class C	Electrical	Live or energized electric wires or equipment	Foam, dry chemical, or carbon dioxide to put out the fire by smothering it or cutting off the oxygen	Class BC or Class ABC extinguisher
Class D	Combustible metals	Magnesium, titanium, and potassium, for example	Dry powder or other special sodium extinguishing agents	Class D extinguisher
Class K	Cooking oils	Vegetable oils, animal oils, or fats in cooking appliances	Special extinguisher converts oils to noncombustible soaps	Wet chemical extinguisher

Table 6-3 Fire types
© Cengage Learning 2014

Class K fires are actually a subset of Class B. In Europe and Australia, Class K is known as Class F.

In a server closet or room that contains computer equipment, using a handheld fire extinguisher is not recommended because the chemical contents can damage electrical equipment. Instead, stationary fire suppression systems are integrated into the building's infrastructure and release fire suppressant in the room. These systems can be classified as *water sprinkler systems*, which spray the area with pressurized water; *dry chemical systems*, which disperse a fine, dry powder over the fire; and *clean agent systems*, which do not harm people, documents, or electrical equipment in the room.

Computer Forensics

Forensics, also known as *forensic science*, is the application of science to questions that are of interest to the legal profession. Forensics is not limited to analyzing evidence from a murder scene; it can also be applied to technology. As computers are the foundation for communicating and recording information, a new area, known as **computer forensics**, which uses digital technology to search for evidence of a crime, can attempt to retrieve information from digital devices—even if it has been altered or erased—that can be used in the pursuit of the attacker or criminal.

Digital evidence can be retrieved from computers, cell phones, pagers, pads, digital cameras, and any device that has memory or storage.

The importance of computer forensics is due in part to the following:

- *Amount of digital evidence*. According to the Federal Bureau of Investigation (FBI) almost 85 percent of crimes committed today leave behind digital evidence that can be retrieved through computer forensics.[2]

- *Increased scrutiny by the legal profession*. No longer do attorneys and judges freely accept computer evidence. Retrieving, transporting, and storing digital evidence is now held to the same standards as physical evidence.

- *Higher level of computer skill by criminals*. As criminals become increasingly sophisticated in their knowledge of computers and techniques such as encryption, it often requires a computer forensics expert to retrieve the evidence.

When an employee discovers or views an illegal or unauthorized incident taking place at the office, that employee must follow the proper procedures for notifying the appropriate personnel. Organizations usually instruct their employees that the computer forensics response team must be contacted immediately. This team serves as first responders whenever digital evidence needs to be preserved.

In many instances, that same employee must also take the appropriate steps to secure the crime scene so that computer forensics can then be used by professionals to recover any digital evidence. It is important that action be taken immediately. Waiting even a few minutes can result in the digital evidence being contaminated by other users or may give the person time to destroy the evidence. When an event occurs, those employees in the immediate vicinity should secure the scene by performing *damage control*, which is the effort to minimize any loss of evidence. These steps include:

- Report the incident to security or the police
- Confront any suspects (if the situation allows)
- Neutralize the suspected perpetrator from harming others (if necessary)
- Secure physical security features
- Quarantine electronic equipment
- Contact the response team

TIP If the forensics response team is external to the organization, it is important that they accurately track their hours and expenses from the start of the investigation. This information can be entered into evidence in a court to prove that the response team was present from the beginning.

Disaster Recovery

MINIMIZE LOSSES *Business continuity* can be defined as the ability of an organization to maintain its operations and services in the face of a disruptive event. This event could be as basic as an electrical outage or as catastrophic as a Category 5 hurricane. *Business continuity planning and testing* is the process of identifying exposure to threats, creating preventive and recovery procedures, and then testing them to determine if they are sufficient. In short, business continuity planning and testing is designed to ensure that an organization can continue to function (*continuity of operations*) in the event of a natural (flood, hurricane, earthquake, etc.) or man-made (plane crash, terrorist attack, computer virus infection, etc.) disaster.

NOTE Business continuity may also include succession planning, or determining in advance who will be authorized to take over in the event of the incapacitation or death of key employees.

A subset of business continuity planning and testing is **disaster recovery**, also known as *IT contingency planning*. Whereas business continuity looks at the needs of the business as a whole in recovering from a catastrophe, disaster recovery focuses upon protecting and restoring the information technology functions and services that support the business. Generally, disaster recovery focuses on restoring computing and technology resources to their former state.

Disaster recovery involves creating a disaster recovery plan. These plans typically include procedures to address redundancy and fault tolerance as well as data backups.

Disaster Recovery Plan A **disaster recovery plan (DRP)** is a written document that details the process for restoring IT resources following an event that causes a significant disruption in service. Comprehensive in its scope, a DRP is intended to be a detailed document that is updated regularly.

All disaster recovery plans are different, but most address the common features included in the following typical outline:

Unit 1: Purpose and Scope. The reason for the plan and what it encompasses is clearly outlined. Those incidences that require the plan to be enacted should also be listed.

Unit 2: Recovery Team. The team that is responsible for the direction of the disaster recovery plan is clearly defined. It is important that each member know his or her role in the plan and be adequately trained. This part of the plan is continually reviewed as employees leave the organization, home telephone or cell phone numbers change, or new members are added to the team.

Unit 3: Preparing for a Disaster. A DRP lists the entities that could impact an organization and also the procedures and safeguards that should constantly be in force to reduce the risk of the disaster.

Unit 4: Emergency Procedures. The Emergency Procedures unit answers the question, "What should happen when a disaster occurs?"

Unit 5: Restoration Procedures. After the initial response has put in place the procedures that allow the organization to continue functioning, this unit addresses how to fully recover from the disaster and return to normal business operations.

Disaster exercises are becoming increasingly common in testing different types of DRPs. U.S. federal aviation regulations require all commercial U.S. airports to conduct a full-scale exercise at least once every three years. These are designed to assess the capability of an international airport's emergency management system by testing emergency responders and aid providers in a real-time, stress-filled environment in which personnel and equipment are actually mobilized and deployed.

Redundancy and Fault Tolerance One of the primary ways to ensure business continuity is to remove any *single point of failure*, which is a component or entity in a system which, if it no longer functions, will disable the entire system. Eliminating these points will result in *high availability*, or a system that can function for an extended period of time with little downtime. This availability is often expressed as a percentage of uptime in a year. Table 6-4 lists these percentages and the corresponding downtimes.

Percentage	Name	Weekly Downtime	Monthly Downtime	Yearly Downtime
90%	One Nine	16.8 hours	72 hours	36.5 days
99%	Two Nines	1.68 hours	7.20 hours	3.65 days
99.9%	Three Nines	10.1 minutes	43.2 minutes	8.76 hours
99.99%	Four Nines	1.01 minutes	4.32 minutes	52.56 minutes
99.999%	Five Nines	6.05 seconds	25.9 seconds	5.26 minutes
99.9999%	Six Nines	0.605 seconds	2.59 seconds	31.5 seconds

Table 6-4 Percentages and downtimes
© Cengage Learning 2014

One way to address a single point of failure is to incorporate redundancy and fault tolerance, which involves building excess capacity in order to protect against failures. Redundancy planning can involve redundancy for power and sites.

Power Maintaining electrical power is also essential when planning for redundancy. An **uninterruptible power supply** (**UPS**) is a device that maintains power to equipment in the event of an interruption in the primary electrical power source. A UPS is seen in Figure 6-10.

Figure 6-10 UPS
© vetkit/www.Shutterstock.com

There are two primary types of UPSs. An *offline UPS* is considered the least expensive and simplest solution. During normal operation the equipment being protected is served by the standard primary power source. The offline UPS battery charger is also connected to the primary power source in order to charge its battery. If power is interrupted, the UPS will quickly (usually within a few milliseconds) begin supplying power to the equipment. When the primary power is restored, the UPS automatically switches back into standby mode.

An *online UPS* is always running off its battery, while the main power runs the battery charger. An advantage of an online UPS is that it is not affected by dips or sags in voltage. An online UPS can clean the electrical power before it reaches the server to ensure that a correct and constant level of power is delivered to the server. The UPS can also serve as a surge protector, which keeps intense spikes of electrical current, common during thunderstorms, from reaching systems.

A UPS is more than just a large battery. UPS systems can also communicate with the network operating system on a server to ensure that an orderly shutdown occurs. Specifically, if the power goes down, a UPS can complete the following tasks:

- Send a message to the network administrator's computer, or page or telephone the network manager, to indicate that the power has failed

- Notify all users that they must finish their work immediately and log off
- Prevent any new users from logging on
- Disconnect users and shut down the server

Because a UPS can only supply power for a limited amount of time, some organizations turn to using a *backup generator* to create power. Backup generators can be powered by diesel, natural gas, or propane gas to generate electricity. Unlike portable residential backup generators, commercial backup generators are permanently installed as part of the building's power infrastructure. They also include automatic transfer switches that can detect in less than one second the loss of a building's primary power and switch to the backup generator.

Sites Just as redundancy can be planned for servers, storage, networks, and power, it can also be planned for the entire site itself. A major disaster, such as a flood or hurricane, can inflict such extensive damage to a building that it may require the organization to temporarily move to another location. Many organizations maintain redundant sites in case this occurs. There are three basic types of redundant sites that are used: hot sites, cold sites, and warm sites.

- *Hot site.* A **hot site** is generally run by a commercial disaster recovery service and allows a business to continue computer and network operations to maintain business continuity. A hot site is essentially a duplicate of the production site and has all the equipment needed for an organization to continue running, including office space and furniture, telephone jacks, computer equipment, and a live telecommunications link. Data backups of information can be quickly moved to the hot site, and in some instances the production site automatically synchronizes all of its data with the hot site so that all data is immediately accessible. If the organization's data-processing center becomes inoperable, it can move all data-processing operations to a hot site, typically within an hour.

- *Cold site.* A **cold site** provides office space, but the customer must provide and install all the equipment needed to continue operations. In addition, there are no backups of data immediately available at this site. A cold site is less expensive but takes longer to get an enterprise in full operation after a disaster.

- *Warm site.* A **warm site** has all of the equipment installed but does not have active Internet or telecommunications facilities, and does not have current backups of data. This is much less expensive than constantly maintaining those connections as with a hot site; however, the amount of time needed to turn on the connections and install the backups can be as much as half a day or more.

NOTE

Businesses usually have an annual contract with a company that offers hot and cold site services with a monthly service charge. Some services also offer data backup services so that all company data is available regardless of whether a hot site or cold site is used.

Data Backups Another essential element in any DRP is data backups. In an organization data backups are routinely performed by the IT department, although in some settings the employee is responsible for performing backups on data stored on their local computer.

One new feature of data backups that are performed at the organizational level is a technology known as **continuous data protection (CDP)**. As its name implies, CDP performs continuous data backups that can be restored immediately. CDP maintains a historical record of all the changes made to data by constantly monitoring all writes to the hard drive.

Some CDP products even let users restore their own documents. A user who accidentally deletes a file can search the CDP system by entering the document's name and then view the results through an interface that looks like a Web search engine. Clicking the desired file will then restore it. For security purposes, users may only search for documents for which they have permissions.

Chapter Summary

- Securing devices so that unauthorized users are prohibited from gaining physical access is an important step in security. Hardware locks for doors are important to protect equipment. The standard keyed entry lock is the most common type of door lock for keeping out intruders, but it provides minimal security. For rooms that require enhanced security, a lever coupled with a deadbolt lock, which extends a solid metal bar into the door frame for extra security, is often used. Because of the difficulties in managing keys for hundreds or thousands of users, an alternative to a key lock is a more sophisticated door access system using a cipher lock. Another option, instead of using a key or entering a code to open a door, is to use a proximity reader that detects an object (sometimes called a physical token) the user carries for identification. A mantrap is designed to separate a nonsecure area from a secured area by controlling two interlocking doors to a small room. Monitoring activity with a video camera can also provide a degree of security. Using video cameras to transmit a signal to a specific and limited set of receivers is called closed circuit television (CCTV). Securing a restricted area by erecting a barrier (fencing) can be an effective method for maintaining security.

- Passwords are commonly used to restrict access to computer systems but have weaknesses. Another type of authentication credential is based on the approved user having a specific item in his possession. A token is typically a small device (usually one that can be affixed to a keychain) with a window display that generates a code from the algorithm once every 30 to 60 seconds. There are several different types of cards that can be used as authentication credentials. A smart card contains an integrated circuit chip that can hold information, which can then be used as part of the authentication process.

- A security policy is a written document that states how an organization plans to protect the company's information technology assets. A standard is a collection of requirements specific to the system or procedure that must be met by everyone, while a guideline is a collection of suggestions that should be implemented. A policy is a document that outlines specific requirements or rules that must be met, and is the correct means to be used for establishing security. An effective security policy must carefully balance two key elements: trust and control. A security policy attempts to provide a balance between no trust and too much trust. The appropriate level of control is determined by the security needs and the culture of the organization. Because a security policy is comprehensive and detailed, most organizations choose to break the security policy down into smaller subpolicies.

- Access control is granting or denying approval to use specific resources. There are several technologies that can be used for implementing access control. Group Policy is a Microsoft Windows feature that provides centralized management and the configuration of computers that use Active Directory. Time of day restrictions limit when a user can log into a system. Account expiration specifies when a user's account expires.

- In addition to technology, there are procedures that can be used in order to limit access control. These include separation of duties (dividing a process between two or more individuals), job rotation (periodically moving workers from one job responsibility to another), mandatory vacations (requiring that employees take periodic vacations), and using the principle of least privilege (giving users only the minimal amount of privileges necessary in order to perform their job functions).

- Damage inflicted as a result of a fire is a constant threat to persons as well as property. Fires are divided into five categories. In a server closet or room that contains computer equipment, using a handheld fire extinguisher is not recommended because the chemicals can damage electrical equipment. Instead, stationary fire suppression systems are integrated into the building's infrastructure and release the suppressant in the room. These systems can be classified as water sprinkler systems, which spray the area with pressurized water; dry chemical systems, which disperse a fine, dry powder over the fire; and clean agent systems, which do not harm people, documents, or electrical equipment in the room.

- Forensic science is the application of science to questions that are of interest to the legal profession. Computer forensics attempts to retrieve information that can be used in the pursuit of computer crime. When an employee discovers or views an illegal or unauthorized incident taking place at the office, that employee must follow the proper procedures for notifying the appropriate personnel. In many instances that same employee must also take the appropriate steps to secure the crime scene so that computer forensics may then be used by professionals to recover any digital evidence. Employees in the immediate vicinity should secure the scene by perform damage control, which is the effort to minimize any loss of evidence.

- A subset of business continuity planning and testing is disaster recovery, also known as IT contingency planning. Whereas business continuity looks at the needs of the business as a whole in recovering from a catastrophe, disaster recovery focuses upon protecting and restoring the information technology functions and services that support the business. Disaster recovery usually focuses on restoring computing and technology resources. A disaster recovery plan (DRP) is a written document that details the process for restoring IT resources following an event that causes a significant disruption in service.

- One of the primary ways to ensure business continuity is to remove any single point of failure so that if it no longer functions will not disable the entire system. Maintaining electrical power is also essential when planning for redundancy. An uninterruptible power supply (UPS) is a device that maintains power to equipment in the event of an interruption in the primary electrical power source. Just as redundancy can be planned for servers, storage, networks, and power, it can also be planned for the entire site itself. A major disaster such as a flood or hurricane can inflict such extensive damage to a building that it may require the organization to temporarily move to another location. Many organizations maintain redundant sites in case this occurs. Another essential element in any DRP is data backups.

Key Terms

access control   The mechanism used in an information system to allow or restrict access to data or devices.

account expiration   The process of setting a user's account to expire.

cipher lock   Combination locks that use buttons that must be pushed in the proper sequence to open the door.

closed circuit television (CCTV)   Using video cameras to transmit a signal to a specific and limited set of receivers used for surveillance in areas that require security monitoring.

cold site   A remote site that provides office space; the customer must provide and install all the equipment needed to continue operations.

computer forensics   The use of digital technology to search for evidence of computer crime.

continuous data protection (CDP)   A data backup technology that performs continuous data backups that can be restored immediately.

deadbolt lock   A door lock that extends a solid metal bar into the door frame for extra security.

disaster recovery   The procedures and processes for restoring an organization's IT operations following a disaster.

disaster recovery plan (DRP)   A written document that details the process for restoring IT resources following an event that causes a significant disruption in service.

fencing   Securing a restricted area by erecting a barrier.

Group Policy   A Microsoft Windows feature that provides centralized management and configuration of computers and remote users.

hot site   A duplicate of the production site and has all the equipment needed for an organization to continue running, including office space and furniture, telephone jacks, computer equipment, and a live telecommunications link.

job rotation   The act of moving individuals from one job responsibility to another.

least privilege   Providing only the minimum amount of privileges necessary to perform a job or function.

mandatory vacations   Requiring that all employees take vacations.

mantrap   A device that monitors and controls two interlocking doors to a small room (a vestibule), designed to separate secure and nonsecure areas.

multifactor authentication   Using more than one type of authentication credential.

proximity reader   A device that detects an emitted signal from a badge in order to identify the owner of the badge.

security policy   A written document that states how an organization plans to protect the company's information technology assets.

separation of duties   The practice of requiring that processes should be divided between two or more individuals.

single-factor authentication   Using one type of authentication credentials.

smart card   A card that contains an integrated circuit chip that can hold information used as part of the authentication process.

token   A small device that can be affixed to a keychain with a window display that shows a code to be used for authentication.

uninterruptible power supply (UPS)   is a device that maintains power to equipment in the event of an interruption in the primary electrical power source.

warm site   A remote site that contains computer equipment but does not have active Internet or telecommunication facilities, and does not have backups of data.

Review Questions

1. The residential lock most often used for keeping out intruders is the _____.
    a. privacy lock
    b. passage lock
    c. keyed entry lock
    d. encrypted key lock

2. A lock that extends a solid metal bar into the door frame for extra security is the _____.
    a. deadman's lock
    b. full bar lock
    c. deadbolt lock
    d. triple bar lock

3. A mantrap _____.
    a. is illegal in the U.S.
    b. monitors and controls two interlocking doors to a room
    c. is a special keyed lock
    d. requires the use of a cipher lock

4. Which of the following cannot be used along with fencing as a security perimeter?
    a. Vapor barrier
    b. Rotating spikes
    c. Roller barrier
    d. Anti-climb paint

5. A token code is valid _____.

    a. for as long as it appears on the device

    b. for up to 1 hour

    c. only for the user who possesses the device

    d. if it is longer than 8 characters

6. A token system that requires the user to enter the code along with a PIN is called a _____.

    a. single-factor authentication system

    b. dual-prong verification system

    c. multifactor authentication system

    d. token-passing authentication system

7. Which of the following is not a characteristic of a policy?

    a. Policies communicate a unanimous agreement of judgment.

    b. Policies may be helpful in the event that it is necessary to prosecute violators.

    c. Policies identify what tools and procedures are needed.

    d. Policies define appropriate user behavior.

8. Which of the following is not an approach to trust?

    a. Trust no one at any time.

    b. Trust everyone all of the time.

    c. Trust authorized individuals only.

    d. Trust some people some of the time.

9. What is a collection of suggestions that should be implemented?

    a. Policy

    b. Guideline

    c. Standard

    d. Code

10. Each of the following is a category of fire suppression systems except _____.

    a. a clean agent system

    b. a dry chemical system

    c. a wet chemical system

    d. a water sprinkler system

11. Each of the following is required for a fire to occur except _____.

    a. a spark to start the process

    b. a type of fuel or combustible material

    c. sufficient oxygen to sustain the combustion

    d. a chemical reaction that is the fire itself

12. An electrical fire in a computer data center would be classified as what type of fire?

    a. Class A

    b. Class B

    c. Class C

    d. Class D

13. A(n) _____ is always running off its battery while the main power runs the battery charger.

    a. offline UPS

    b. backup UPS

    c. online UPS

    d. secure UPS

14. A _____ is essentially a duplicate of the production site and has all the equipment needed for an organization to continue running.

    a. cold site

    b. warm site

    c. hot site

    d. replicated site

15. A UPS can perform each of the following except _____.

    a. prevent certain applications from launching that will consume too much power

    b. disconnect users and shut down the server

    c. prevent any new users from logging on

    d. notify all users that they must finish their work immediately and log off

16. Each of the following is a good practice for key management except _____.

    a. change locks immediately upon loss or theft of keys

    b. keep track of keys issued, with their number and identification, for both master keys and duplicate keys

    c. replace all locks every three months

    d. issue keys only to authorized persons

17. What is the disadvantage of a cipher lock?

    a. It is slow.

    b. It can be vulnerable to shoulder surfing.

    c. Cipher locks keep a record of when the door was opened and by which code.

    d. They have less intelligence than a regular combination lock.

18. Which technology would be used with radio frequency identification (RFID) tags?

    a. Proximity reader

    b. Deadbolt lock

    c. Cipher lock

    d. Video lock

19. Dynamic passwords generated by tokens that change frequently are called _____.

    a. one-time passwords

    b. token authentication elements (TAE)

    c. static passwords

    d. revolving passwords

20. _____ in access control means that only the minimum amount of privileges necessary to perform a job or function should be allocated.

    a. Administrator privilege

    b. Need to know

    c. Dynamic control

    d. Least privilege

Hands-On Projects

Project 6-1: Setting Windows 7 Local Security Policy—Part 1

A Group Policy is a Microsoft Windows feature that provides centralized management and configuration of computers and remote users using the Microsoft directory services. It is usually used in enterprise environments to enforce access control by restricting user actions that may pose a security risk. A Local Group Policy has fewer options than a Group Policy, and generally a Local Group Policy is used to configure settings for a local computer that is not part of Active Directory. In this project, you will view and change local security policy settings.

You will need to be an administrator to open the Local Group Policy Editor. The Local Group Policy Editor is only available in the Windows 7 Professional, Ultimate, and Enterprise editions; it is not available on Windows 7 Starter, Home Basic, and Home Premium editions.

1. Click **Start**.

2. Type **local security policy** into the Search box, and then click **Local Security Policy**. The Local Security Policy window is displayed, as shown in Figure 6-11.

3. First create a policy regarding passwords. Expand **Account Policies** in the left pane, and then select **Password Policy**.

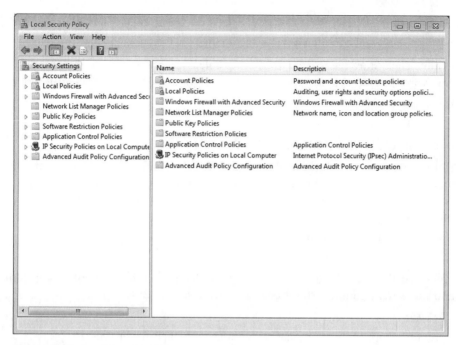

Figure 6-11 Local Security Policy
Source: Microsoft Windows 7

4. Double-click **Enforce password history** in the right pane. This setting defines how many previously used passwords Windows 7 will record. This prevents users from "re-cycling" old passwords.

5. Change **passwords remembered** to **4**.

6. Click **OK**.

7. Double-click **Maximum password age** in the right pane. The default value is 42, meaning that a user must change his password after 42 days.

8. Change **days** to **30**.

9. Click **OK**.

10. Double-click **Minimum password length** in the right pane. The default value is a length of 8 characters.

11. Change **characters** to **10**.

12. Click **OK**.

13. Double-click **Password must meet complexity requirements** in the right pane. This setting forces a password to include at least two opposite case letters, a number, and a special character (such as a punctuation mark).

14. Click **Enable**.

15. Click **OK**.

16. Remain in the Local Security Policy for the next project.

Project 6-2: Setting Windows 7 Local Security Policy—Part 2

In this project, you will continue to view and change local security policy settings.

1. Double-click **Store passwords using reversible encryption** in the right pane. Because passwords should be stored in an encrypted format this setting should not be enabled.

2. If necessary, click **Disabled**.

3. Click **OK**.

4. In the left pane, click **Account Lockout Policy**.

5. Double-click **Account lockout threshold** in the right pane. This is the number of times that a user can enter an incorrect password before Windows will lock the account from being accessed (this prevents an attacker from attempting to guess the password with unlimited attempts).

6. Change **invalid login attempts** to 5.

7. Click **OK**.

8. Note that the Local Security Policy suggests changes to the **Account lockout duration** and the **Reset account lockout counter after** values to 30 minutes.

9. Click **OK**.

10. Expand **Local Policies** in the left pane, and then click **Audit Policy**.

11. Double-click **Audit account logon events**.

12. Check both **Success** and **Failure**.

13. Click **OK**.

14. Right-click **Security Settings** in the left pane.

15. Click **Reload** to have these policies applied.

16. Close all windows.

Project 6-3: Block a USB Flash Drive

Malware can easily be spread from one computer to another by infected USB flash drives. This is a problem particularly for businesses when employees bring infected flash drives from home. Many businesses configure their computers to block USB flash drives. One of the methods for blocking a USB drive is to use third-party software that can control USB device permissions. In this project, you will download and install a software-based USB write blocker to prevent data from being written to a USB device.

1. Open your Web browser and enter the URL **www.irongeek.com/i.php?page=security/thumbscrew-software-usb-write-blocker**

The location of content on the Internet such as this program may change without warning. If you are no longer able to access the program through the above URL, then use a search engine to search for "Irongeek Thumbscrew".

2. Click **Download Thumbscrew**.

3. When the File Download dialog box appears follow the instructions to save this file in a location such as your desktop or a folder designated by your instructor. When the file

finishes downloading extract the files in a location such as your desktop or a folder designated by your instructor. Navigate to that location. double-click on **thumbscrew.exe,** and follow the default installation procedures.

4. After installation, notice that a new icon appears in the system tray in the lower-right corner of the screen.

5. Insert a USB flash drive into the computer.

6. Navigate to a document on the computer.

7. Right-click on the document and then select **Send to**.

8. Click the appropriate **Removable Disk** icon of the USB flash drive to copy the file to the flash drive.

9. Now make the USB flash drive write protected so it cannot be written to. Click on the icon in the system tray.

10. Click **Make USB read only.** Notice that a red circle now appears over the icon to indicate that the flash drive is write protected.

11. Navigate to a document on the computer.

12. Right-click on the document and then select **Send to**.

13. Click the appropriate **Removable Disk** icon of the USB flash drive to copy the file to the flash drive. What happens?

14. Close all windows.

Project 6-4: Detect and Install Software Updates Using Secunia Personal Software Inspector (PSI)

Although large vendors such as Microsoft and Apple have an established infra-structure to alert users about patches and to install them, few other vendors have such a mechanism. This makes it necessary to regularly visit all the Web sites of all the installed software on a system to stay current on all software updates. To make the process more manageable, online software scanners were created that can compare all applications on a computer with a list of known patches from the different software vendors and then alert the user to any applications that are not properly patched or automatically install the patches when one is detected as missing. In this project, you will use the Secunia Personal Software Inspector (PSI) to determine if your computer is missing any security updates.

The current version of PSI contains several advanced features. It support applications from over 3,000 different software vendors and also encapsulates all of the vendor patches for your computer into one proprietary installer. This installer suppresses any required dialogs so everything can be patched silently without any user intervention. You can even create rules, such as telling PSI to ignore patching a specific application. PSI is available in five different languages, and it is free for personal use.

1. Open your Web browser and enter the URL **secunia.com/vulnerability_ scanning/personal/.**

NOTE The location of content on the Internet such as this program may change without warning. If you are no longer able to access the program through the above URL, then use a search engine and search for "Secunia Personal Software Inspector".

2. Click **PSI 3.0 Walkthrough,** which is a YouTube video about PSI. Click your browser's **Back** button when finished.

3. Click **Download.**

4. If necessary click **Save** and save the program to the desired location on your local computer.

5. When the download completes, click **Run** to install the application.

6. Select the appropriate language and click **OK.**

7. Click **Next** on the Welcome screen, then click **I accept the terms of the License Agreement.** Click **Next.**

8. Check the box **Install updates automatically** if necessary. Click **Next.**

9. Click **Finish.**

10. When asked **Would you like to launch Secunia PSI now?,** click **Yes.** Depending upon the computer, it may take several minutes to load the program and its modules.

11. If you are asked to **Join our community!** click **No thanks, don't show this again.**

12. If necessary click **Scan now.**

13. When the scan is finished, the results will appear like those in Figure 6-12.

Figure 6-12 Secunia PSI
Source: Secunia Personal Software Inspector

14. Applications that can be automatically updated will start the download and installation automatically. On any applications that need manual updates click **Click to update** and select the appropriate application.

15. Close all windows.

The Secunia PSI application will continually run in the background checking for updates. If you do not want this functionality on the computer, you can uninstall the application.

Case Projects

Case Project 6-1: Security Policy Review

Locate the security policy for your school or organization. Based on what you now know about security, do you think it is sufficient? Does it adequately address security for the organization? Is it up to date and timely? What changes would you suggest? Write a one-page paper on your findings.

Case Project 6-2: Best Practices for Access Control

Search the Internet for one instance of a security breach that occurred for each of the four best practices of access control (separation of duties, job rotation, mandatory vacations, and least privilege). Write a short summary of that breach. Then, rank these four best practices from most effective to least effect. Give an explanation of your rankings.

Case Project 6-3: Personal Disaster Recovery Plan

Create a one-page document of a personal disaster recovery procedure for your home computer. Be sure to include what needs to be protected and why. Also include information about where your data backups are stored and how they can be retrieved. Does your DRP show that what you are doing to protect your assets is sufficient? Should any changes be made?

Case Project 6-4: Business Continuity Plan

Select four risks that your school or organization may face, and develop a brief business continuity plan. Use the steps outlined earlier in the chapter. Share your plan with others, or if possible, test your plan. What did you learn? Modify your plan accordingly.

Case Project 6-5: Home UPS

UPS devices are becoming more commonplace in homes as well as in organizations. Use the Internet to research home UPS devices. Identify five different models, and create a table listing their features and costs. Which would you recommend and why?

Case Project 6-6: Information Security Community Site Activity

The Information Security Community Site is a Course Technology/Cengage Learning information security course enrichment site. It contains a wide variety of tools, information, discussion boards, and other features to assist learners. Go to **community.cengage.com/infosec**. Click **Log In (for full access)** at the top of the page and enter your sign in name and password that you created in Chapter 1. Visit the Discussions page by going to the **STUDENTS** tab and selecting the **DISCUSSION BOARDS** link from the dropdown menu, where you can read the following case study and submit your answers.

How restrictive are the security policies at your school? What are you not allowed to do that you feel that you should be able to do? Or, should your school provide unhindered access to all material because you paid tuition for this privilege? Whom would you complain to in order to give the policy change? What about that at work? Why would an employer want to restrict where their employees can go on the Internet or what they can do? Couldn't free access provide more opportunities for employees to discover the latest trends and thus help the business? Record your responses on the Community Site discussion board.

Case Project 6-7: North Ridge Computer Consultants

North Ridge Computer Consultants (NRCC) is a local information technology company that specializes in security. In order to encourage students to enter the field of information security, NRCC often hires student interns to assist them with projects.

Brentwood Orthopedic Alliance (BOA) is a regional sports medicine provider with clinics in several different locations in the area. Recently, a retail store located in the same hall as one of the BOA Clinics was destroyed by a fire that was started by a lightning strike. The directors of BOA decided that now would be an excellent time to review their disaster recovery plan. They have hired NRCC to assist them.

Create a PowerPoint presentation of at least eight slides that describes what a disaster recovery plan is and now it is used. Be sure to emphasize the advantages of a DRP.

References

1. Boatman, Kim, "Downsizing Dilemma: Dealing with Orphaned Accounts," *Inc. Technology*, retrieved Apr. 16, 2011, http://technology.inc.com/security/articles/200902/accounts.html.

2. "Digital Forensics," *D.63*, Jan. 26, 2011, retrieved May 4, 2011, http://www.directive63.com/digital-forensics.

Glossary

access control The mechanism used in an information system to allow or restrict access to data or devices.

access point (AP) A more sophisticated device used in an office setting instead of a wireless broadband router.

account expiration The process of setting a user's account to expire.

ActiveX A set of rules for how applications under the Microsoft Windows operating system should share information.

ActiveX control A specific way of implementing ActiveX.

ad hoc network A direct peer-to-peer network that connects a wireless device directly to another wireless device.

administrator account The highest level of user account and provides the most control over a computer.

adware A software program that delivers advertising content in a manner that is unexpected and unwanted by the user.

algorithm Procedures based on a mathematical formula used to encrypt and decrypt data.

antivirus (AV) Software that can examine a computer for any infections as well as monitor computer activity and scan new documents that might contain a virus.

arbitrary code execution An attack that allows an attacker to gain control of the victim's computer to execute the attacker's commands, turning it into his own remote computer.

asset An item that that has value.

attachments Documents that are connected to an e-mail message, such as word processing documents, spreadsheets, or pictures.

auto-lock A mobile device setting that locks down the device when it has not been used for a set period of time.

availability Security actions that ensures that data is accessible to authorized users.

backdoor Software code that gives access to a program or a service that circumvents normal security protections.

blacklist A list of senders from which the user does not want to receive any e-mail.

bluejacking An attack that sends unsolicited messages to Bluetooth-enabled devices.

bluesnarfing An attack that accesses unauthorized information from a wireless device through a Bluetooth connection.

Bluetooth A short-range wireless technology designed for interconnecting computers, peripherals, handheld devices, and cell phones.

botnet A logical computer network of zombies under the control of an attacker.

bot herder An attacker who controls a botnet.

browser A program for displaying Web pages.

brute force attack A password attack in which every possible combination of letters, numbers, and characters is used to match passwords.

buffer overflow An attack that substitutes the "return address" pointer and points to another area in the computer's memory area that contains malware code

cable lock A device that can be inserted into the security slot of a portable device to protect it from theft.

California Database Security Breach Act The first state database security law that covers any state agency, person, or company that does business in California.

cipher lock Combination locks that use buttons that must be pushed in the proper sequence to open the door.

ciphertext Text that is scrambled so that it cannot be read by an unauthorized party.

closed circuit television (CCTV) Using video cameras to transmit a signal to a specific and limited set of receivers used for surveillance in areas that require security monitoring.

cold site A remote site that provides office space; the customer must provide and install all the equipment needed to continue operations.

computer forensics The use of digital technology to search for evidence of computer crime.

computer virus (virus) Malicious computer code that reproduces itself on a single computer.

confidentiality Security actions that ensure that only authorized parties can view information and prevents disclosure to others.

continuous data protection (CDP) A data backup technology that performs continuous data backups that can be restored immediately.

cookie A file created by a Web server and stored on the local computer that contains user's preferences.

cryptography The science of transforming information into a secure form so that unauthorized persons cannot access it.

cybercrime Targeted attacks against financial networks, unauthorized access to information, and the theft of personal information.

cybercriminals A generic term used to describe individuals who launch attacks against other users and their computers; also describes a loose-knit network of attackers, identity thieves, and financial fraudsters.

cyberterrorism A premeditated and politically motivated attack that results in violence.

cyberterrorists Online attackers whose motivation is ideology, or attacking for the sake of their principles or beliefs.

data backups Copying files from a computer's hard drive onto other digital media that is stored in a secure location.

deadbolt lock A door lock that extends a solid metal bar into the door frame for extra security.

decryption Changing encrypted text back into its original format that can be read.

dictionary attack A password attack that compares common dictionary words against those in a stolen password file.

digital certificate A technology that can associate a user's identity to a public key and that is digitally signed by a trusted third party.

disaster recovery The procedures and processes for restoring an organization's IT operations following a disaster.

disaster recovery plan (DRP) A written document that details the process for restoring IT resources following an event that causes a significant disruption in service.

drive-by download An attack that results from a user visiting a specially crafted malicious Web page.

dumpster diving Digging through trash receptacles to find information that can be useful in an attack.

embedded hyperlinks Links contained within the body of the message as a shortcut to a Web site.

encryption Changing the original text into a scrambled message that cannot be read by unauthorized users.

evil twin An AP or another computer that is set up by an attacker designed to mimic the authorized Wi-Fi device.

exploiting The act of taking advantage of a vulnerability.

Fair and Accurate Credit Transactions Act (FACTA) of 2003 A U.S. law that contains rules regarding consumer privacy.

feature phone A traditional cellular telephone that includes a limited number of features.

fencing Securing a restricted area by erecting a barrier.

first-party cookie A cookie that is created from the Web site that a user is currently viewing.

Flash cookie A cookie named after the Adobe Flash player.

Gramm-Leach-Bliley Act (GLBA) A law that requires banks and financial institutions to alert customers of their policies and practices in disclosing customer information.

Group Policy A Microsoft Windows feature that provides centralized management and configuration of computers and remote users.

guest account An account that is intended for users who need temporary use of a computer.

hactivists Attackers who attack Web sites as a form of protest, usually in retaliation for a prior event.

Health Insurance Portability and Accountability Act (HIPAA) A law designed to guard protected health information and implement policies and procedures to safeguard it.

hoax A false warning.

hot site A duplicate of the production site that has all the equipment needed for an organization to continue running, including office space and furniture, telephone jacks, computer equipment, and a live telecommunications link.

hyperlinks Links that allow users to jump from one area on the Web to another with a click of the mouse button.

Hypertext Markup Language (HTML) A language that allows Web authors to combine text, graphic images, audio, and video into a single document.

Hypertext Transfer Protocol (HTTP) A subset of a larger set of standards for Internet transmission.

identity theft Stealing another person's personal information, such as a Social Security number, and then using the information to impersonate the victim, generally for financial gain.

image spam Spam that uses graphical images of text in order to circumvent text-based filters.

IMAP (Internet Mail Access Protocol) An advanced e-mail protocol.

IMAP4 The version of IMAP current at the time of writing.

impersonation Creating a fictitious character and then playing out the role of that person to influence a victim.

information security The tasks of securing information that is in a digital format.

integrity Security actions that ensure that information is correct and no unauthorized person or malicious software has altered that data.

Internet A worldwide set of interconnected computers, servers, and networks.

Internet service provider (ISP) A business from which users purchase Internet access.

Institute of Electrical and Electronics Engineers (IEEE) The most widely known and influential organization in the field of computer networking and wireless communications.

jailbreaking Removing the built-in limitations and protections of a mobile device.

Java A complete programming language that can be used to create stand-alone applications.

Java applet A smaller Java application that is a separate program.

JavaScript A type of mobile code embedded within HTML documents that is downloaded and executed in the user's Web browser.

job rotation The act of moving individuals from one job responsibility to another.

key A mathematical value entered into an algorithm in cryptography.

key file A separate unique file used in password management applications that can be carried on a USB flash drive or other similar device.

keylogger Hardware or software that captures and stores each keystroke that a user types on the computer's keyboard.

least privilege Providing only the minimum amount of privileges necessary to perform a job or function.

macro A series of instructions that can be grouped together as a single command and are often used to automate a complex set of tasks or a repeated series of tasks.

macro virus A computer virus that is written in a script known as a macro.

mandatory vacations Requiring that employees take vacations.

mantrap A device that monitors and controls two interlocking doors to a small room (a vestibule), designed to separate secure and nonsecure areas.

Media Access Control (MAC) address A unique hardware number that is "burned in" to each wireless network interface card adapter.

mobile code Special computer code that is downloaded and executed in the Web browser.

mobile malware Malware that is specifically directed at tablets and smartphones.

multifactor authentication Using more than one type of authentication credential.

password A secret combination of letters, numbers, and/or symbols that serves to authenticate a user by what he or she knows.

password management application A program that lets a user create and store multiple strong passwords in a single user database file that is protected by one strong master password.

patch A general software security update intended to cover vulnerabilities that have been discovered.

personal firewall Software that runs as a program on a computer designed to prevent malware from spreading into the computer.

pharming Automatically redirecting a user to a fake Web site.

phishing Sending an e-mail or displaying a Web announcement that falsely claims to be from a legitimate enterprise in an attempt to trick the user into surrendering private information.

plug-in A software component added to a Web browser that adds new functionality.

POP3 The version of the Post Office Protocol current at the time of writing.

pop-up blocker A Web browser setting that limits or blocks most pop-ups.

port number An identifier that indicates the program or service that is being requested.

Post Office Protocol (POP) The protocol for e-mail that handles incoming mail.

private key One key of public key cryptography that must be kept secret.

private key cryptography (symmetric cryptography) Cryptography that uses same single key to encrypt and decrypt sensitive information.

program virus A computer virus that infects program executable files.

Protected View A Microsoft Office function that automatically opens selected documents in a read-only mode and disables editing functions.

protocol A set of standards.

proximity reader A device that detects an emitted signal from a badge in order to identify the owner of the badge.

public key cryptography (asymmetric cryptography) Cryptography that uses two mathematically related keys instead of only one.

public key One key of public key cryptography that is known to everyone and can be freely distributed.

reading pane An e-mail client feature that allows the user to read an e-mail message without actually opening it.

remote code execution (RCE) Another name for arbitrary code execution.

remote wipe A cellular phone app that can erase the contents of the device if it is lost or stolen

risk The likelihood that a threat agent will exploit the vulnerability.

rootkit A set of software tools used by an attacker to hide the actions or presence of other types of malicious software.

sandbox A software technology that surrounds a program and keeps it away from private data and other resources on a local computer.

Sarbanes-Oxley Act (Sarbox) A law designed to enforce internal controls on electronic financial reporting systems.

scareware Software that displays a fictitious warning to the user in the attempt to frighten the user into an action.

script kiddies Individuals who want to break into computers to create damage yet lack the advanced knowledge of computers and networks needed to do so.

secure desktop A mode in which the entire screen is temporarily dimmed to prevent an attacker from manipulating any UAC (User Account Control) messages that appear on the screen.

security policy A written document that states how an organization plans to protect the company's information technology assets.

separation of duties The practice of requiring that processes should be divided between two or more individuals.

service pack An operating system update that is a cumulative package of security patches or updates plus other features.

Service Set Identifier (SSID) The network name identifier in a Wi-Fi network.

short message service (SMS) A service that provides the ability to send and receive text messages.

shoulder surfing Viewing information that is entered by another person.

signature file File that contains known patterns or sequences of bytes (strings) found in viruses; used by antivirus software to identify malware.

signed Java applet A Java applet that has information that indicates the program is from a known source and has not been altered.

Simple Mail Transfer Protocol (SMTP) The protocol for e-mail that handles outgoing mail.

single-factor authentication Using one type of authentication credentials.

smart card A card that contains an integrated circuit chip that can hold information used as part of the authentication process.

smartphone A cellular phone that has an operating system that allows it to run third-party applications.

spam Unsolicited e-mail.

spam filters Software that inspects e-mail messages to identify and stop spam.

spear phishing A phishing attack that targets only specific users.

spy A person who has been hired to break into a computer and steal information.

spyware A general term used to describe software that spies on users by gathering information without consent, thus violating their privacy.

standard account An account that is designed for everyday computing activities.

social engineering A means of gathering information for an attack by relying on the weaknesses of individuals.

social networking Grouping individuals and organizations into clusters based on an affiliation.

strong password A long and complex password.

tablet computer Portable computing device with a screen size that ranges from 5 to 10 inches (127 to 254 millimeters), designed for user convenience.

tailgating Following an authorized person into a restricted area.

third-party cookie A cookie that is created by a third party.

threat A type of action that has the potential to cause harm.

threat agent A person or element that has the power to carry out a threat.

token A small device that can be affixed to a keychain with a window display that shows a code to be used for authentication.

Transmission Control Protocol/Internet Protocol (TCP/IP) The standards for Internet transmissions.

Trojan An executable program advertised as performing one activity but actually does something else (or it may perform both the advertised and malicious activities).

uninterruptible power supply (UPS) A device that maintains power to equipment in the event of an interruption in the primary electrical power source.

unsigned Java applet A Java applet that does not come from a trusted source.

user account An account that indicates the privilege level of a user.

User Account Control (UAC) A Windows security function that provides information to users and obtains their approval before a program can make a change to the computer's settings.

username A unique name used for identification.

virtual private network (VPN) A technology that uses an unsecured public network, such as the Internet, as if it were a secure private network.

vishing A phishing attack in which the attacker calls the victim on the telephone.

vulnerability A flaw or weakness that allows a threat agent to bypass security.

war driving Searching for wireless signals from an automobile or on foot using a portable computing device.

warm site A remote site that contains computer equipment but does not have active Internet or telecommunication facilities, and does not have backups of data.

weak passwords A password that can easily be broken and compromises security.

whaling A phishing attack that targets wealthy individuals, who typically would have larger sums of money in a bank account that an attacker could access.

whitelist A list of senders from which the user will accept e-mail.

whole disk encryption Cryptography that can be applied to entire disks.

Wi-Fi (wireless fidelity) A wireless data network that is designed to provide high-speed data connections for mobile devices.

Wi-Fi Protected Access 2 (WPA2) Personal A security setting that provides the optimum level of wireless security.

Wi-Fi Protected Setup (WPS) A simplified and optional method for configuring WPA2 Personal wireless security.

wireless broadband router A device used for a home-based Wi-Fi network that combines several networking technologies.

wireless client network interface card adapter A device that allows a mobile device to send and receive wireless signals.

wireless local area network (WLAN) The technical name for a Wi-Fi network.

World Wide Web (WWW) A network composed of Internet server computers on networks that provide online information in a specific format.

worm A malicious program designed to take advantage of a vulnerability in an application or an operating system in order to enter a computer.

zombie An infected "robot" (bot) computer that is under the remote control of an attacker.

Index